Coinage in Medieval Scotland (1100–1600)

The Second Oxford Symposium on Coinage and Monetary History

edited by

D. M. Metcalf

British Archaeological Reports 45

1977

British Archaeological Reports

122, Banbury Road, Oxford OX2 7BP, England

Details of all issues of British Archaeological Reports will be sent free of charge and without any obligation to purchase, on request from the above address.

B.A.R. 45, 1977: "Coinage in Medieval Scotland (1100-1600)".
© The individual authors, 1977.
Price £4.00 post free throughout the world. Payments made in currency other than sterling must be calculated at the current rate of exchange and an extra 10% added to cover the cost of bank charges.
ISBN 0 86054 002 2

Cheques and postal orders should be made payable to "British Archaeological Reports" and sent to the above address.

For a list of other B.A.R. publications, please see the last page.

Printed in Great Britain

PREFACE

The second Oxford Symposium on Coinage and Monetary History, which took the uses of money in medieval Scotland as its theme, was held partly in the Coin Room of the Ashmolean Museum and partly in Wolfson College. Two dozen invited guests met for supper on the Friday evening, and on Saturday and Sunday attended eight lectures on invited topics. The general idea, as it had been the year before when a similar gathering was arranged to discuss English monetary affairs in the period 1279-1344, was to bring together numismatists, archaeologists, and historians, and to invite them, from the standpoint of their different disciplines, to pool their insights into the evidence that coinage offers for monetary history. There is plenty of preliminary work that the three disciplines can legitimately undertake on their own — in the case of archaeology literally, one may say, the spade-work. But it is never the wrong time to try to learn from each other. The most serious failure arising from limited cooperation is that students have been deflected from the central topics, and from the questions of most general interest, by their feeling unable to tackle them single-handed. Many numismatists have in the past verged towards antiquarianism; and historians have sometimes felt nervous about exposing their numismatic inexperience in the face of what they imagined to be an impenetrable craft mystery. (Actually, numismatic research follows procedures which are particularly straightforward).

We met, then, to discuss not the coins themselves, but the evidence that coinage can provide about monetary affairs. The sort of information that may constitute evidence for that purpose usually has little to do with the designs and inscriptions on the coins, and even less with their artistic quality. It tends more towards interpreting government decisions, for example, about the work of the mints or about monetary reform, and towards describing and explaining gradual changes in the size and overall composition of the currency.

How many coins are there in Scotland at the present day? No statistics are available, and certainly none which would help to show the regional distribution of coinage in different parts of Scotland (except for the odd survey of the age-structure of the currency). An informed guess, based on the holdings of silver coin by the banks, would be some £40 millions, or a total of approximately 800-900 million coins: an astonishing 150 each for every man, woman, and child. Each person's share has a face value of between £7 and £8. This is very much the same rate of provision as in England and Wales, and the overall figure is quite accurately known. In the period directly following decimalization the U.K. total was about 7,000 million, and has since then crept up to 9,000 million or more. But the estimate for Scotland's share could well be in error by plus or minus 10 per cent, and there is apparently no way of checking it. We can judge the number of coins in Scotland in the thirteenth century almost as reliably, although hampered by exactly the same problem of guessing how much of a common currency was circulating north of the Border.

A comparable estimate — but still only an estimate — was made at the time of the recoinage of 1707. The value of the silver money which circulated in Scotland before the Union, and which, immediately after it, was brought into the Bank of Scotland in order to be recoined, amounted to £411,118. This sum was made up of Scottish hammered coin (£142,180), Scottish milled coin (£96,857), English milled coin (£40,000), and foreign silver coin (£132,081). The gold coin in circulation at the same date was not easy to estimate, but the total currency in 1707, Adam Smith suggested, cannot have been less than a million sterling. It was thus only about a fortieth of the present metallic currency (though not at constant prices); moreover the modern total of course does not include the paper money and bank deposits which are nowadays the staple.

"There is at this day a village in Scotland where it is not uncommon, I am told, for a workman to carry nails instead of money to the baker's shop or the alehouse". Smith, who gave us this vignette, had many informed observations to make about monetary affairs in Scotland, and about the effect that changes in the circulating medium had had upon the country's economic history. His book, The Wealth of Nations, published just two hundred years ago, offers a careful theoretical analysis of the economic benefits of a properly regulated paper currency, with facts drawn from the Scottish experience in his lifetime. In the third quarter of the eighteenth century, he tells us, new banking companies were set up in almost every considerable town and even in some country villages. Business was almost entirely carried on, at the time when he was writing, by means of the paper of these different banking companies. Silver very seldom appeared except in the change of a twenty shilling bank note, and gold still seldomer. From the time when the Bank of Scotland and the Royal Bank were established (in 1695 and 1727) until Smith's day, the trade and industry of Scotland increased very considerably — even, it was said, as much as four-fold. He was careful to point out that monetary expansion was unlikely to have been the sole cause of such a striking expansion in the nation's wealth.

There is virtually no first-hand information, whether anecdotal or otherwise, about Scottish monetary affairs in the middle ages. Ideas about the state of the currency and its possible influence on the national economy are recorded in only the most token fashion, in statutes and in the archives of royal government. And it is illusory to imagine that anyone can accurately observe economic facts other than purposefully; the monetary and economic analysis behind the medieval records (such as they are) was short on theory, and perfunctory as to its statistical basis.

The student today is entitled, therefore, to come to the subject with an open mind. In the absence of first-hand information he must rely on the methods of enquiry of the historian, and — especially for the earlier middle ages, from which the documentary record is slender — on the methods of the archaeologist. And in exploring an age in which, unlike our own, coinage and money were almost one and the same, he will need to make use of the systematic knowledge that has been built up about the coins themselves.

Scotland has been well served by numismatists. Burns was ahead of his time, and the handsome volumes that he and Cochran-Patrick have given us are still the starting-point for a working library. From the first half of the

twentieth century there are many articles of record by Macdonald and others.
In recent decades the British Numismatic Society has been the main forum,
and the exceptionally high standards of careful scholarship which the Society
has devoted to English medieval coins have extended also to the Scottish series.
The leading exponent of our knowledge at the present day is Mr. Ian Stewart,
whose handbook, The Scottish Coinage, is widely consulted. The standard
work on Scottish medieval coins, however, is his more recent and more detailed
monograph, "Scottish mints", published in the Albert Baldwin memorial volume
Mints, Dies and Currency. A full bibliography can be compiled without too
much difficulty from the notes in that volume and this, from the publications
of the International Numismatic Congresses, and from the bibliographical
periodical Numismatic Literature.

The major collections of Scottish coins have not as yet been systematically
published. The finest is that of the National Museum of Antiquities of Edinburgh. There are others in the British Museum, the Hunterian Museum, the
Ashmolean Museum, and elsewhere. These are rivalled by at least one private collection. One hopes that all may eventually be catalogued in the Sylloge
of Coins of the British Isles. Meanwhile, a large number of coins in aggre-
gate have been illustrated in auction sale catalogues, among which the Lockett
collection catalogues are useful for their illustrations of sterlings.

D. M. M.

CONTENTS

ABBREVIATIONS

APS   The Acts of the Parliaments of Scotland

BAR   British Archaeological Reports

BNJ   British Numismatic Journal

CP   R. W. Cochran-Patrick, Records of the Coinage of Scotland.
2 vols. Edinburgh, 1876.

Dumfriesshire Trans:.   Transactions of the Dumfriesshire and Galloway
Natural History and Antiquarian Society.

ER   The Exchequer Rolls of Scotland (Edinburgh, 1878-1903)

NC   Numismatic Chronicle

NCirc   Numismatic Circular

PSAS   Proceedings of the Society of Antiquaries of Scotland

RMS   Registrum magni sigilli regum Scotorum

RPCS   The Register of the Privy Council of Scotland

RSS   Registrum secreti sigilli regum Scotorum (Edinburgh, 1908-66)

SCBI   Sylloge of Coins of the British Isles

SRO   Scottish Record Office

TA   The Accounts of the Lord High Treasurer of Scotland.
(Edinburgh, 1877-1970).

THE EVIDENCE OF SCOTTISH COIN HOARDS FOR
MONETARY HISTORY, 1100-1600

D. M. Metcalf

In English medieval studies, economic history has been a flourishing dis-
cipline for half a century, and a lively debate has been made possible by the
abundance of surviving financial accounts and other commercial and fiscal
records. Scottish economic history is not quite so fortunately endowed with
facts to examine, particularly for the twelfth and thirteenth centuries, for
which we may blame Edward I.[1] Its perspectives and outlines, which are the
immediate context for Scottish medieval monetary history, are necessarily
rather general, and cannot often be tested quantitatively.

Monetary affairs rarely obtrude into the foreground of Scottish medieval
history, where the dominant themes are altogether more dramatic and personal.
In the background, however, generally passed over almost in silence by the
historical sources (as is the unceasing, careful round of animal and crop husbandry which sustained life), there is a money economy. We can be confident
that this is so, and that the use of coinage was linked, from the earliest date
from which documentary sources survive, if not indeed from the late eleventh
century, with the burghs, with markets and local trade in bread, oats, ale,
meat, fish, salt, fuel, cloth and leather goods, with the southward shipping
trade in wool and hides and in victuals, and with tolls and aids.[2]

Money nowadays means paper: five-pound notes; cheques; computerized
credit transfers; and sophisticated government intervention in the money markets as a major instrument of policy. In the middle ages, money meant coinage,
and very little else, as commercial credit was relatively undeveloped, and such
credit as existed at a local level could stretch the money supply only in the
sense that it increased the velocity of circulation.[3] Equally, coinage meant
gold and silver coins of a good intrinsic value, for although Scotland was early
in the European community to use low-grade silver-copper alloy for coins,
the budgetary significance of their token valuation was small. The Scottish
currency thus consisted essentially of a certain number of intrinsically valuable coins, unevenly distributed regionally, and unevenly distributed among
the social classes. The precise embodiment of the country's money supply in
the form of these small metal discs, scattered in private ownership and con-
tinually changing hands, imposed various limitations - for example on political
choice and on the opportunities of economic development. The same characteristics of coinage, namely its untraceability and the fact that it was closely
analogous to private property, imposed continuity on the currency. For the
mints to put coins into circulation was like turning sheep out onto the moor:
letting them loose is easy enough, but rounding them up again is more troublesome. Thus the currency, which was physically dispersed throughout Scotland,
had a degree of inertia for technical reasons and was not subject to the same

short-term fluctuations as mint-output often was. We may envisage it as a continuum, in space and time. As such, it underlay the country's money economy. Indeed, it did more. It was the necessary physical form of money, and the pattern of its distribution largely defined and sometimes limited the extent of the money economy.

When we have the opportunity to study a hoard of coins accidentally brought to light in modern times, we are able to take a sounding in that continuum. The hoard gives us a glimpse of the currency at a particular moment in time and a particular place. It may or may not be a fair sample, and in order to discount any particularities, one does better to examine a whole series of hoards in the chronological order of their concealment, and so to chart the statistical contours of the currency. As with the sea bed, there is a presumption of gradual change, but sudden changes can occur, and if an insufficient number of separate soundings have been taken, the chart may unfortunately omit features. There is no way in which we can recover a detailed factual description of the Scottish currency as it developed through the middle ages except by starting from the evidence of the hoards. They show us not only what kinds of coin were entering the currency, but also how long they remained in use: that is to say, they illustrate the changing age-structure of the currency,-a concept which is quite similar to that of the age-structure of a population. In certain proportionately few of the hoards come from the larger burghs where monetary circulation was presumably as its most intense. The evidence of the hoards nevertheless enjoys a primacy.

An account based on hoard-evidence alone would be incomplete in ways that are of central interest to the monetary historian. In particular, one cannot derive any exact idea from the hoards as such about the size of the currency - there may have been three to five million sterlings in circulation in Scotland in the mid-twelfth century, and probably 30 to 50 millions by the later thirteenth century [4] - and this information should obviously influence historical judgements on the extent of the monetary sector of the economy. For the English coins which for centuries were the major element in the Scottish currency, we have excellent documentary information about the quantities struck. For the Scottish issues, estimates have to be based on the counting of dies and die-duplicates, and on comparisons with the English evidence, and on the careful assessment of the quirks of survival. Ian Stewart presents this important information below. Again, one cannot tell much from hoards about the velocity of circulation, which economists see as a component in the total size of the money supply. Also, one needs to know something about the intrinsic and the official value of coins of different varieties in relation to one another. But the hoards define the currency of a region, and they are the factual starting-point.

When Francis Bacon, in his writings on the philosophy of science, discussed the art of discovery, he spoke about aids to the senses, such as the microscope and the telescope, which enable us to see objects not clearly visible to the naked eye, and he went on by analogy to develop the idea of aids to the memory - for example methods of recording and describing detail which allow us to grasp or visualize complex information. For numismatists, and indeed for monetary historians, an assemblage of all the hoards from a region is just such an instrument of study, an excellent example of which is Michael Dolley's critical survey of the Edwardian hoards from Scotland and elsewhere.[5] A find-assemblage marshals the primary evidence for monetary circulation, and it reveals the statistical patterns and trends in the composition of the currency. A listing of Scottish medieval hoards is the basis of this paper. From the period c. 1100-1600 we know of about 260 hoards. Their distribution is shown on two maps (Fig. 1, 2), the first covering the period c. 1100-c. 1360 but reflecting chiefly the fourteenth century, and the second continuing from c. 1360-c. 1600. Throughout the middle ages, the hoards are very largely confined to the Lowland zone, in sharp contrast with the preceding Viking-age hoards of Anglo-Saxon and other coins, most of which are from the Highlands and Islands, and were presumably not concealed in the context of a local money economy. One is entitled to ask whether, in the middle ages, there was any significant use of coinage beyond the Great Glen, but, as always with negative evidence, it is as well to err on the side of caution in drawing conclusions, and the more so as there are exceptions to the rule, in particular the early and very interesting Dun Lagaidh hoard found during excavations beside Loch Broom in 1968.[6] Nevertheless, if the consensus is that the later historical distinction between Highlands and Lowlands had hardly developed before the mid-fourteenth century, the hoards offer us a sharp reminder of difference in one respect at least. In the east and south of Scotland there are hoards from almost every district. A significant proportion of them have been found within a few miles of the coast, but the strongest impression, for the period 1100-1360, is of numerous hoards from the open countryside, found by chance during ploughing or draining of the land. Sometimes the coins were concealed in a cow's horn or hoof,[7] sometimes in a cloth or leather purse or a pirlie pig,[8] sometimes in a bronze tripod cooking-vessel or water-jug,[9] and often in an earthenware pot or jug. Hoards have been found in remote and uncultivated places, by shepherds, for example, at Langhope, and in Glenetive and Glen Afton:[10] other finds have come from high up on hillsides, as in Strathdon, and Glenbrerarchan.[11] Anyone who was concealing coinage would, obviously, prefer to be unobserved, and hoarding in what was so far as we can tell open countryside is the dominant feature of the distribution, but there are secondary patterns, of hoards from the burghs,[12] from churchyards or burial-grounds,[13] from the vicinity of castles or mottes,[14] and occasionally from stone-quarries and from monastic sites.[15] This balance does not necessarily bear a close relationship to the local whereabouts of the currency in circulation: obviously, for example, castles and monasteries enjoyed a relative security and continuity of communal life which would favour the recovery of money set aside. A special explanation has been put forward for the thick cluster of hoards from Nithsdale and the coast of Dumfriesshire, many of which are likely to have been concealed because of the fighting in the 1330's. Similarly, many of the east-coast hoards, from Perthshire northwards to Aberdeen, should probably be explained in military terms.[16] If one tries to discount all the hoards from the 1320s or 1330s, the residual pattern is quite neutral, and does not draw attention to any particular region of Scotland. It harmonizes quite well with the geographical distribution of burghs.[17] The distribution-map for 1360-1600 is not very different from the earlier one, although there is a greater concentration of hoards in the burghs, and within a radius of a few miles of the larger burghs, and a greater emphasis on the central lowlands. This may reflect the inadequacy of the currency, and perhaps also a growth in urban population.

The original publication of the 260 hoards has been sadly uneven. Many were described inexpertly, and in only a sentence or two, since when the coins have been dispersed or melted down. Such hoards cannot now be dated exactly, and it is impossible to bring the numismatic detail of their composition into the sharp focus which permits percentage comparisons with other hoards, and which so often suggests interesting and unexpected lines of enquiry. Their topographical value remains; and they help to confirm the general composition of the currency at different periods. Arguments about the clustering of hoards in particular districts certainly need to take all the available evidence into account. The hoards published in an entirely satisfactory manner number at most 50, and the only consolation is that chance discoveries are still putting new hoards into our hands from time to time, and that they now stand a better chance of receiving expert scrutiny and detailed publication than was once the case. The hoards are uneven, also, in their chronological spread. For the period from 1100-1250, from which we should most welcome their evidence since documentary information is so restricted, there are unfortunately very few, and those few are mostly lost to us without proper record. By contrast there are (as already mentioned) numerous hoards from the first half of the fourteenth century, concealed because of the military campaigns of the 1330s. Warfare and instability meant that many of those who concealed their money for safety never returned to recover it. Crawford has pointed out, in another context,[18] that the regions from which hoards have been reported may not coincide exactly with the areas of conflict: soldiers, for example, may bury their cash at home on the farm, before going away to fight, and to be killed, elsewhere. With that thought in mind, it might be worth enquiring, about the places where fourteenth-century hoards have been found, who were the tenants-in-chief.

The hoards show that until the late fourteenth century the Scottish coinage and the currency of Scotland were by no means one and the same thing. As much as 95% of the hoard material consists of English coins. The circulation of foreign coinage is quite anomalous in medieval England, and indeed was widely discouraged by strong governments everywhere throughout medieval Europe. Normally, we may say, the rulers of each state insisted so far as they were able on close control of the national currency and the strict exclusion of foreign coins from circulation. Any that entered the country by trade were required to be exchanged. The Scottish kings during much of the middle ages found it advantageous or expedient that they should break the general rule, and give their sanction to the use of English money. Likewise, Scots coins were permitted to circulate in England, and although naturally they rarely made up more than three or four per cent of the hoards because of the disparity between the total size of the two coinages, they did circulate freely in southern as well as northern England. There are modern analogies, although they may be partly misleading. The circulation of English coins in Ireland, for example, is perhaps no more than a hangover from the period before 1921, but still the Irish exchange-rate is tied to the English, and other significant aspects of Irish financial and fiscal policy are in effect determined at Westminster or on the London Stock Exchange. Similarly the Scottish medieval coinage was until the later fourteenth century tied to the English and only then began to diverge. The weight-standards and alloy of the coins were, with some temporary deviations, the same; the denominations - sterlings,

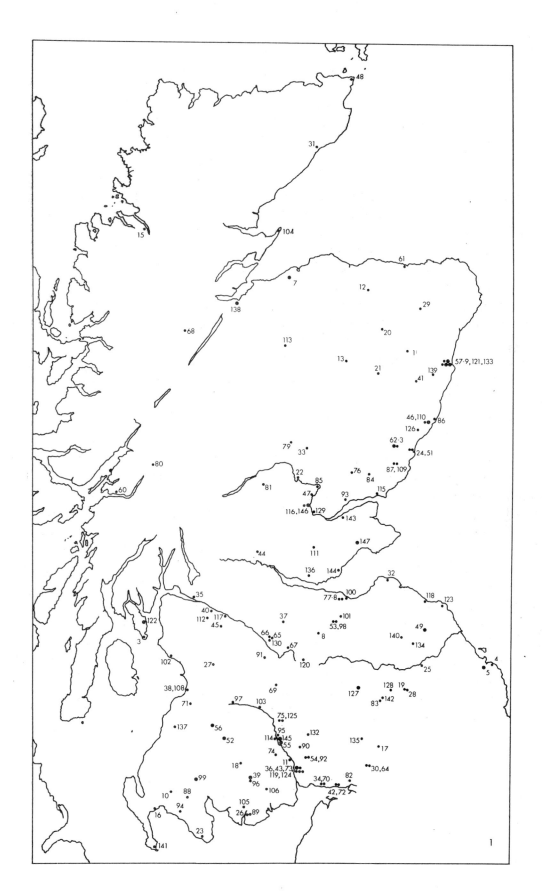

halfpennies, groats – were the same; the designs of the coins were closely derivative, even the artistic style is astonishingly similar; and when at intervals the English coin design was changed, the Scots followed suit. Once launched upon this course, there would be powerful reasons for keeping to it, but it was not as inevitable as it may appear after the event.

In October 1367, Scotland devalued. The groat, although it was still of " as good and pure metal as the money now made in the Kingdom of England" weighed less, and had an intrinsic value of only about five-sixths the corresponding English coin. In England it was soon ordered to pass at threepence, that is, at a heavy discount of between 13 and 14 per cent on its metallic value. The old system had been brought to an end a few years earlier, when Edward III prohibited the currency of coins of David II in England under severe penalties, on the ground that they were inferior in weight and alloy to the stated and traditional standard – i.e. they were bad money in terms of Gresham's Law. Edward's letter of 1355/6 to the Sheriff of Northumberland implies that it was simply by immemorial custom that Scots money had been permitted to circulate in England. The embargo is said to have been lifted in 1358, but was later reimposed and in effect withdrawn in 1374 by the introduction of a different exchange-rate.[19] Thus 1356/1374 is a turning point in Scottish monetary history. The currency followed a rapid series of reductions in intrinsic value and corresponding devaluations against the English denominations, as the pound has done against the dollar in recent years. The circulation of English coins in Scotland gradually declined in importance. At the middle of the fifteenth century there was a three-fold difference in the nominal value of the currencies, that is to say, the Scottish groat, while it was of almost the same weight as an English groat of four pence, had become a coin of twelve pence. At the Union of the Crowns, in 1603, the difference was twelve-fold.

In our own time, we have witnessed a three-fold decline in the real value of the currency since the early 1960s. A similar degree of inflation spread over about a century – as happened in medieval Scotland – no longer has the power to shock us. Our currency, however, is entirely fiduciary (if fiduciary is the word), whereas the problems of managing a gold and silver currency of correct intrinsic value in a period of fairly rapid change were rather greater. If our understanding of the way those problems were handled in the middle ages had to be derived only from the coins themselves and from the hoards, it would be imperfect indeed, since the coins bear no indication of their original valuation and of course none of any re-tariffing. Fortunately, the detailed comments and instructions contained in Acts of Parliament, Proclamations, the Exchequer Rolls, and other official documents surviving from 1357 onwards[20] inform us of the main outlines of monetary policy, and provide insights into the reasoning behind the government decisions. From the period before David II's return to Scotland there is very little monetary documentation, and it is just as well, therefore, that monetary mechanisms, uninfluenced at that time by bimetallism or by rapid depreciation, were relatively stable and simple.

Thus, the interpretation of the hoard-evidence, and its particular difficulties, will vary from century to century, with the weight of interest attaching to the earlier middle ages. Let us attempt to characterize the problems in successive periods.

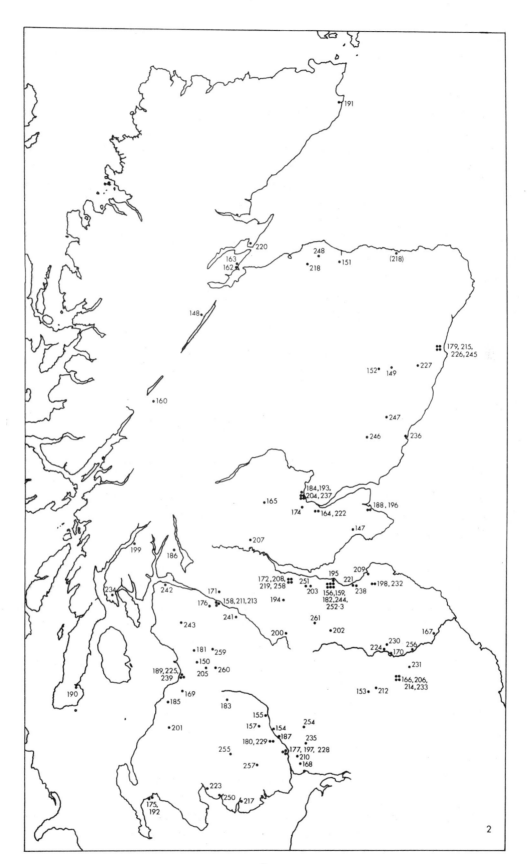

I. From the beginnings of the national coinage to c. 1174. Although there are several finds from the 1030s,[21] there is as yet no numismatic evidence that English sterlings circulated in Scotland in the hundred years before David's first issues of coinage. These cannot possibly have begun until after 1135, as they are a close imitation of the early coins of Stephen. Apart from two stray Norwegian pennies of the late eleventh century from Shetland[22] and from North Uist,[23] a single Arabic gold dinar found in Aberdeenshire is all that the numismatist can offer.[24] Negative evidence is of course inconclusive, and we have ample reason to believe that there was a developed money economy before c. 1136. The idea that David virtually introduced the use of coinage into the Scotland of his day, as part of a package of political ideas and developments imported from the south, should therefore be firmly resisted, and the central question is rather to what extent the successful growth of the money economy was linked with the prosperity of the burghs. A general deficiency of coinage in England may have influenced David's original decision to strike his own sterlings. He was using money in Scotland even before he became king. He gave Glasgow cathedral, probably c.1114, a money income of 100s. a year deriving from estates near Northampton, and a similar grant was made at about the same time to the monks of Selkirk. In 1124 x 1128 the church at Dunfermline was given 100s. a year deriving from England. The canons of Jedburgh in their turn, a few years later, received a temporary grant of money revenues to set them up, and were in due course required to surrender it, like the churches already mentioned, in exchange for endowments in land.[25] It will be noticed that this evidence for the use of coinage before c. 1136 is not confined to the Borders, but extends beyond the Forth, and to Glasgow. The most illuminating of the early documentary sources is David's foundation-charter to Holyrood Abbey, which points to a burghal currency, connected primarily with foreign trade by sea, down the east coast. In that charter, not later than the mid-1140s, the king makes provision for the support of the canons, in the first instance by income in kind from lands and rents and rights and tithes, and the free taking of timber, and oil from stranded whales, and much else, and then goes on to give them also, apparently, a cash income: " forty shillings from my burgh of Edinburgh yearly; and a rent of a hundred shillings yearly for the clothing of the canons, from my cain of Perth, and this from the first ships that come to Perth for the sake of trade; and if it happens that they do not come, I grant to the aforesaid Church, from my rent of Edinburgh forty shillings, and from Stirling twenty shillings, and from Perth forty shillings." Further, the canons are freed from tolls and customs " on all things that they buy and sell".[26] Here at a date very close to 1136, when David began to strike coinage (and then only on a small scale), is clear evidence of a money economy, and of established patterns of trading, in Edinburgh, Perth, and Stirling and also at a more local level, which can hardly have been of very recent or rapid growth. So much for the negative evidence of hoards! And so much for the negative evidence of archaeological site finds or other stray finds from, for example, Perth and Edinburgh.

An existing money economy is thus the background to David's decision to copy Stephen's coinage so closely in all particulars. But there are virtually no pre-1174 hoards from Scottish territory. The large Outchester hoard of 1817, from the 1170s, may reflect the local currency before 1157 when

Northumberland was under Scottish rule. Similarly the Bute hoard of 1863, although from Norse territory, presumably derives directly from the Scottish currency. The only hoard from Scotland proper consists of a mere half-dozen coins and is of unknown provenance, and yet is of the highest interest, as it shows David minting at Perth and at Aberdeen, whereas hitherto the evidence has been that his issues were confined to the Borders and to Edinburgh.[27] At Carlisle and Newcastle, it might have been argued, no great political significance need be read into David's decision to strike coins: bullion continued to be brought to the existing mints, and it was a necessary and not very difficult decision to name the new ruling authority on the obverse of the coins. But if mints were opened as far north as Perth and Aberdeen, the full development of the Scottish national coinage was apparently envisaged at a very early date. The implications of the decision are of some political interest.

As there are so few hoards from the early period, it is worth mentioning the stray finds, which are almost equally scarce. There are three if not four of the rare coins of Earl Henry, namely one from Brough-under-Stainmore, one obtained at Morpeth, another found nearby at Blyth, and the fourth found c. 1820 "at the mouth of the River Tyne."[28] A coin in the name of David was reported from Lochmaben;[29] and a broken coin was found at a silver mine near Alston (the presumed source of some at least of the silver minted at Carlisle and Newcastle).[30] The pattern is peripheral to what one must suppose were the main centres of circulation of coinage, namely the burghs on the east coast. It is with some hesitation that one points to the apparently high ratio of Scottish to English coins everywhere except in the Outchester hoard. Even there, there were about 150 Scottish coins to 700 English cross-and-crosslets sterlings - an issue which was itself by no means copious, having been struck from a total of perhaps 1,350 dies. Probably the earliest national currency was more self-contained in its circulation than it became in the thirteenth and fourteenth centuries.

II. **From c. 1174 to 1296.** In the twelfth and thirteenth centuries the English currency was completely replaced, with a change of design, at intervals of a generation or more. The same practice of renewal was followed by the Scottish mints, the English "Short cross" type being adopted (according to the Melrose Chronicle) in 1195, the "Long cross" type in 1250, and the Edwardian type in 1280. During each recoinage there was an initial phase of intensive mint activity, contrasting with intermediate periods during which the geographical pattern of minting, and the reasons for minting, were generally quite different, depending more upon the country's net balance of foreign trade.[31] Provincial mints were called into activity to implement a recoinage; at other times mints at the frontier or at points where merchants usually entered the country, namely Canterbury and London, accounted for most of the minting activity. Questions of interest for monetary history are to what extent before 1280 the Scottish provincial mints had the same reasons for activity as the English mints, and to what extent the border mints of Roxburgh and especially Berwick, functioned as "point of entry" mints when obviously no attempt was made to exclude English coin from circulation. Merchants are hardly likely to have taken their money to the exchanges as a voluntary activity: was it only continental silver, arriving by sea, that was required to be recoined?[32]

On this important point, some working ideas still need to be formulated. In many ways the Scottish mints seem to be analogous to the English mints other than London and Canterbury, and their coins circulated in both countries just like those of the English provincial mints. A useful view of the pattern of Scottish mint activity will be essentially quantitative. It will have to be obtained from a statistical analysis of some large thirteenth-century hoards (of which remarkably few have yet been published in detail). In order to bring the numismatic evidence into any sort of exact coordination with trends in economic history, it is necessary to date the successive minor varieties of the coin types as precisely as possible: the "Short cross" type, for example, ran for seventy years, but the coins, and the hoards, are susceptible of being dated very much more closely. The total numbers of coins struck in each subvariety at each Scottish mint may eventually reveal geographical shifts in the pattern of minting in the monetarily crucial decades around the middle of the thirteenth century, and it should then be possible to contrast this pattern with that for the regional composition of the currency - the freedom with which it circulated from one part of Scotland to another, and the rate at which issues wasted away through wear and tear, reminting, export, hoarding, and various other unaccountable losses. This programme for the future may help to explain why detailed hoard reports are the straw without which we cannot make bricks, and to emphasize the pitiful lack of information about the currency (as such) of twelfth and thirteenth-century Scotland. Thus, for example, William the Lion's crescent-pellet coinage, struck apparently from c. 1174, provides a terminus post quem for two or three hoards, but they were so sketchily recorded as to be almost useless. The best one can say is that a very large find from the churchyard at Dyke, near Inverness, in 1780, is notable for its northerly provenance. It might be from the time of William's expedition of 1187, when he led an army to Inverness and consolidated his control of Moray.[33] Both at Dyke and at Baddinsgill in Peeblesshire, William's coins apparently accounted for all the Scottish portion of the hoard, earlier issues being absent. Either they had dwindled away and gradually disappeared from use or, as seems more likely, an attempt may already have been made to recall earlier issues and to renew the currency (as had happened in England in 1158). A small hoard found on the Isle of Man before 1769, and with a more extended age-structure, need not be taken as evidence to the contrary, as Man lay outside the sphere of a regulated Scottish currency.

Scottish coins from the second quarter of the thirteenth century onwards are plentiful today, but to a surprising extent the hoards that have brought them to light are not from Scotland, where the finds appear to consist entirely or almost entirely of English coins. The paradox is more apparent than real. If we should expect Scottish issues to be only, say, 5% as numerous as English, then the absence of any Scottish sterlings in a hoard of up to 50 or 60 coins would would hardly be statistically significant. This applies to the finds from Tom a' Bhuraich, Dun Hiadin, Newcastleton, and Balmaclellan. It is because one needs to explore small percentages that the evidence of very large hoards is so valuable. Thus, the Eccles hoard from Lancashire, concealed c. 1230, contained 96 Scottish among nearly 6,000 English sterlings - a mere 1.6%. The Colchester hoard of 1902, concealed c. 1237, contained 168 among nearly 11,000, and the Colchester hoard of 1969, dating from c. 1256, contained 489 among about 11,000. The enormous Brussels hoard of 1908, concealed c. 1264, contained about 2,200 Scottish coins along with 80,000 English. To say that most of the Scottish coins available to us today were in use outside Scotland at the moment when they were hoarded is not necessarily the same as to say that most of the Scottish coinage circulated outside Scotland, although this was almost certainly the case. Let us look at the arithmetic, taking some very simple figures as an example. Suppose that the hoards tell us that 6% of the Scottish currency consisted of Scottish coins, and that 4% of the English currency consisted of Scottish coins. We can estimate the volume of the English coinage, which is, let us say, between 200 and 300 million coins existing in the third quarter of the thirteenth century, and (from Stewart's researches presented below) we have a good idea of the volume of the Scottish coinage at the same date, let us say comparably between 10 and 15 million coins in existence. It is difficult to be more precise because of the heavy wastage rates which quickly reduced the total original output of the mints. At first glance one might imagine that one could calculate some statistics for the size of the Scottish currency from these several pieces of information. Unfortunately, it is arithmetically impossible to do so, as we simply do not know what proportion of the grand total of coins were circulating in Scotland. This really is an impasse, since the size of the currency and not the size of the Scottish issues is, of course, the information which is of primary interest for Scottish monetary history, as a pointer to the extent of the monetary penetration of the economy, as an index of long-term trends in economic history, and for purposes of comparison with the contemporary situation in England. Common sense suggests that between 10 and 20% of the total may have been in Scotland, that would be between 20 and 60 million pence, but so far as I can see there is not a shred of direct evidence for the ratio in which the two countries shared their common currency, and it is extraordinarily difficult to devise any statistical procedure to estimate the Scottish currency, as the usual methods based on die-duplication are inapplicable. The best that can be said - and this serves to underline the important contribution made by Stewart's calculations - is that the recoinage of 1250 onwards, which was implemented by a network of some 16 mints throughout Scotland, and which may have recycled a high proportion of the coin, both English and Scottish, then available in Scotland, points us towards a probable minimum total of 12-19 million pence, and the Alexandrian recoinage of 1280 similarly to a figure of 35-50 million pence. This is, of course, before there is any question of English military intervention affecting the Scottish currency.

III. From 1296 to the introduction of groats and gold coinage. There are far more coin hoards of the Edwardian period from Scotland than there are from England, even though England was the wealthier country.[34] The great increase over the number of thirteenth-century hoards from Scotland need not in any way imply that there was more money about: the opposite was probably true. On a general view, there can be little doubt that many of the Scottish hoards were concealed and were not recovered because of the insecurity and warfare of the times. A cluster of hoards in Perthshire and Angus, and another in Dumfriesshire, have been associated with the arrival of Edward Balliol and the "Disinherited" in 1332 and with the various military campaigns of 1332-8. Several hoards from Aberdeen have been associated with the sacking of the town by Sir Thomas Roscelyn in 1336. One cannot, of course, be sure of the

circumstances attaching to any one particular hoard (and Aberdeen, for example, was damaged by fire in 1326), but where there are so many from a
short period, it is reasonable to explain most of them in terms of warfare.
Within the context of this general explanation, a more detailed analysis still
seems desirable. Why, for example, should there be so many hoards from
Nithsdale, whereas there are hardly any from Annandale? Might they reflect
changes in the political allegiance of the district; or a tenurial structure of
small fiefs held directly from the Crown; or the proximity of castles and strong
strong-points;[35] or cattle droving, [36] or simply the use of the valley as a
main routeway? A convincing interpretation remains very elusive. The large
size of some of the hoards - over 9,000 coins at Montrave, for example, and
over 12,000 in the Aberdeen Upperkirkgate find - may reflect military expenditure either directly or at one or two removes. The Brechin hoard of 1785 and
those from Dumfries, 1849 and from Croalchapel (alias Closeburn) also were
reportedly very large. Although the numbers of coins seem vast, the sums of
money they represent, e.g. £40 and £50, are not particularly large by comparison
with many recorded transactions of the time. A farmer, perhaps, sold some
cattle or horses to the army; or a landowner sold some timber for building
works. (Note also various hoards from quarries.) In other parts of Europe one
can point to hoards which demonstrate that the presence of an army injected
an excess money supply into a region, and that some of the coinage stagnated
there for decades, insufficient use being found for it. [37] There seems to be a
contrast between the proportion of large hoards from Scotland, and the corresponding proportion from southern England, in spite of the greater prosperity
of the south, and it is this general contrast in the size of the hoards which
encourages one to wonder whether warfare may have affected the patterns of
availability of coinage as well as the patterns of hoarding and non-recovery.

Any such influence would seem to have been on only a small scale, since
there is no clear evidence that the age-structure of the currency was different
in Scotland and England. If excess money had stagnated in Scotland, one would
expect it to have suffered less wastage than in England, and one would see that
reflected in the relative proportions of coins of a particular vintage in hoards.[38]
There is, as ever, a shortage of large, carefully-published hoards on which to
base comparisons, but those that are available point to an identical age-structure
in Scotland and in the south of England, and thus, apparently, to a very rapid
circulation of coinage between north and south. [39]

To put the matter in perspective one may say that even if hoards of a
special character can be recognised in fourteenth-century Scotland, and it is by
no means beyond dispute that they can, these are merely eddies in the rock pools,
compared with the flow of the tide which washed so much English money into
Scotland in the thirteenth century, and inexorably sucked it back out again in the
fourteenth as England's stock of bullion ebbed away. It is difficult to envisage
the exact monetary and economic mechanisms by which millions of coins
emanating from the London and Canterbury mints were rapidly transferred from
region to region in response to market conditions. Even the simplest model
seems to call for a sensitive money market, in addition to a lively commerce.

Among the Edwardian hoards sufficiently well recorded to be dateable, there
is an early group from c. 1300. Several of these contain an exceptionally large

proportion of continental sterlings, or even are composed entirely of continental coins, which may, in a brief episode, have been thriftily carried to Scotland when they had been called down or demonetized in England. The Mellendean hoard seems, however, to be two or three years earlier than the others in this groups,[40] which may include the Perth find of 1812.

There are a few hoards consisting ostensibly only of coins of Alexander III, and one wonders whether official payments were ever made solely in Scots coin. Two such finds are from Aberdeenshire, and thus among the more remote provenances.[41] But they are by no means well-attested, and should probably be discounted unless similar, but more reliable, information comes to light.

The larger Edwardian hoards provide splendid opportunities for numerical analysis, and they demonstrate an impressive homogeneity in the currency throughout Britain, the mechanics of which have never been convincingly explained. The Boyton hoard from Wiltshire, for example, shows no significant differences from the Aberdeen hoard, although the percentage of Scottish coins was actually slightly higher in Wiltshire. In the table below, it will be seen that even the Irish and Continental proportions match closely. The size of the Scots coinage relative to the English, at around 2-3%, is less than it had been in the preceding Short-cross and Long-cross periods, or in the years immediately following the recoinage of 1280. Some of the apparent discrepancies, such as the 4.4% Scottish element at Bootham, or the 3.0% at Montrave, are not true variations, for they obviously arise from the age-structure of the hoards. If one compares the Alexandrian coins with the earlier Edward classes, I-V only, the proportions are more consistent. There is a technical difficulty here, to distinguish between hoards of anomalous age-structure, such as savings-hoards, and hoards offering genuine evidence of differences in the age-structure of the currency. The Renfrew "double" hoard, for example, may be untypical, but comparison with other early Edwardian hoards found in central Scotland in the future will be the only method of proof.

In the present state of our knowledge, these statistics are a cardinal point of reference in interpreting the evidence of Scottish hoards for monetary history. They are cardinal because they prove that in spite of all the caveats one must enter in seeking to interpret the hoards - the uncertainties of negative evidence, the bias of the evidence - there was in the fourteenth century a remarkable consistency in the composition of the currency, which seems to imply a vigour of monetary circulation, a thoroughness of mixing, which one would not otherwise have ventured to assume. Coinage obviously circulated with great swiftness, and was carried from end to end of the land. Even the issues of the various Scottish mints seem hardly to be localized within Scotland.[42] Another testimony to the effectiveness of monetary circulation is that, in all the Edwardian hoards, the survival of coins struck before the reforms of 1279-80 is minimal.[43] It is because the currency tended to so surprising a degree to become homogenous that one can look for differences and contrasts in the hoards as evidence for trends or chronological patterns in monetary history. At some future date, it may be possible to extend the Edwardian statistical analyses in order to trace the development of the currency in other periods on the basis of far richer information deriving from large hoards as

Date	Hoard	Scottish	Berwick	English	Irish	Continental	Other
c. 1290	Coventry 1937	6.2	–	86.8	2.8	4.2	–
c. 1290	Broughton	10.00	–	85.2	3.3	1.5	–
c. 1295/1300	Mellendean	7.3	–	79.0	2.1	11.6	–
c. 1300	Canonbie	3.8	6.4	88.5	1.3	–	–
c. 1300	Renfrew (first section)	22.9	0.4	69.3	7.4	–	–
After c. 1310	Middridge, Durham	9.1	0.6	85.1	3.8	0.8	0.6
After c. 1311	Whittonstall, Northumberland	3.5	6.0	88.9	1.1	0.4	0.1
1318-25	Blackhills	2.0	3.4	92.4	1.4	0.5	0.3
c. 1325-30	Boyton, Wilts.	2.3	1.6	93.4	1.3	1.4	–
c. 1325-30	Bootham, Yorks.	4.4	1.0	91.5	1.8	1.3	–
c. 1331-35	Loch Doon	2.4	2.1	91.0	1.6	1.4	1.5
1336?	Aberdeen	1.1	1.8	95.0	0.7	0.9	0.5
1363-70	Montrave	3.0	1.7	87.8	1.4	3.0	3.1

yet unknown. For the foreseeable future, however, we are severely limited in the information available, except for the second quarter of the fourteenth century.

IV. The later middle ages

Although the sterlings issued in the first quarter of the fourteenth century continued to supply the currency without much supplementation until the 1360s, and are therefore prominent in hoards such as Montrave and Croalchapel, the currency was dwindling as it drained out of the country. From as early as 1331 a tax of twelve pence in the pound was imposed on the export of money, and the rate was subsequently increased to half a mark.[44] Other measures may have been intended, at least as part of their purpose, to block the drain. Scottish mint output under Robert II seems to have remained at relatively quite a high level, which was not the case in England under Richard II, and English complaints that the Scots by their subtlety were attracting good English money to make into their own worse money may have had some substance. The weight-reduction in 1367 may for a time have made it profitable to holders of English coin in Scotland to take it to the mints as bullion. There are several hoards of groats from the later fourteenth century, which show that English money had almost disappeared from use by the 1380s. They make very clear the meaning of the phase, "the usual money of Scotland", which begins to appear in documents at about that time.

English money made a partial come-back in the currency of Scotland from time to time in the next two hundred years, in particular around the third quarter of the fifteenth century. Hoards indicate that sometimes as much as half the silver was English.

The use of gold coinage in Scotland from the middle of the fourteenth century reminds us that the currency was still automatically under the pressure of English monetary influence, and had to react to it - either for or against - even when in their outward form the two national coinages had diverged. Edward III committed England to bimetallism, rather late in the day by European standards, and Scotland seems to have accepted the noble promptly following its introduction. The new coin, at 6s. 8d., was worth vastly more than the silver penny which had for so long been the highest denomination. The importance of gold from a monetary point of view is that the coins, being of high value, made a significant addition to the total size or book value of the currency. Historians have tended to minimize the role of gold coinage in a country's internal economy, but Lloyd has recently argued that the price-rises of the 1350s, when silver was scarce, are linked with the effective addition which the Edwardian nobles made to the size of the money supply.[45] The use of hoards as evidence for the composition of the Scottish currency becomes more complicated, since gold and silver tended to be hoarded on their own, and there are thus two strands of information which need to be traced out seperately, and then combined.

David II struck c. 1357 a small number of gold nobles modelled in every detail on those of Edward III; but their monetary significance was minimal. Perhaps one should consider whether they are reliable negative evidence. English nobles were the standard gold coinage of Scotland from the mid-fourteenth century: a hoard of them is known from Raehills, in Dumfriesshire. A Scottish gold coinage was firmly established in the time of Robert III, (1390-1406) and we have one hoard, found at Glasgow in 1837, which shows Robert's lions mingled in roughly equal numbers with nobles of Edward III and Richard II, "mostly from different dies and in fine preservation". The Crieff hoard apparently consisted only of Robert's coins; but at Dryburgh Abbey, along with Scottish gold of Robert and James, Edwardian nobles were again present. A hoard from Cadder Castle seems to have been purely Scottish in content, with 118 demies or lions and 23 other gold coins of James I and II, and in the Lochar Moss hoard, and also in the late-fifteenth century hoard of Glen Afton, all the gold was similarly Scottish, of James I and II.

From the middle of the fifteenth century, while gold seems to have been reasonably plentiful, silver was obviously still in short supply. In the absence of Scots half-groats, the light-weight groats of James I and II circulated as halves, along with worn old English coins, particularly half-groats of Edward III, clipped down in order to make them approximate to the current Scottish weight standard. Alloyed groats and placks were introduced to fill this gap in the denominational system, and the placks eventually came to be the most plentiful coin found in hoards. Billon, a copper-based alloy sometimes containing very little silver, was an established coinage-metal in France and the Low Countries, but was never used in medieval England - perhaps to that country's economic disadvantage. The billon placks authorized by James V in 1533 contained only two-twelfths silver. Even lower in the denominational system there were pennies, of which the purchasing power in real terms was quite modest. The early billon pennies, of James II and III, have been studied very fully from the Glenluce and Rhoneston hoards.[46] The supposedly ecclesiastical issues of St. Andrews,[47] known particularly from the Crossraguel Abbey find, seem even to have been of pure copper or brass. The existence of such coins is not in itself a sign of monetary decline: on the contrary, a plentiful petty currency is of great economic usefulness. Inflation, also, is not necessarily an evil. If kept within limits, it may be in a country's best interest, and no more contrary to natural justice than the alternatives. But when one sees billon being hoarded, misgivings are aroused. Throughout medieval Europe, wherever several coin-denominations were in use side by side, it was normal to hoard the larger denominations, and rigorously to exclude the smaller coins from hoards. There are exceptions, of course. Sometimes money was concealed in great haste. There are mixed hoards, of gold and silver, or silver and billon; and there are hoards comprising such small sums of money that they are necessarily of low-value coins. But as a rule, hoards are put together from the best and most valuable coins available. When in sixteenth-century Scotland we see numerous hoards consisting of little but billon - particularly, it seems, in the larger burghs - there is a strong implication that, for most people, good silver coinage was not obtainable.

The later fifteenth and sixteenth centuries witnessed many different issues of Scottish coinage, which were a matter of detailed concern at the time, and which have attracted equally detailed numismatic study and interpretation. This should not be allowed to obscure the main point, which is that most of the coinages were on a relatively small, or even a very small scale, and that billon dominates the hoards to a surprising extent. There are, however, hints of a regional difference in the character of the hoards. Good-quality silver, and gold of various kinds, seems to have been rather more freely available for hoarding in northerly or westerly districts, particularly in Ayrshire and at Glasgow. This may have been the corollary of a less active monetary circulation, a national currency that was in some ways inadequate tending to " retreat" to the burghs.[48]

The relative poverty of Scotland that was highlighted by the contrast between the court circles of Edinburgh and London in 1603 should not be allowed to colour unduly our ideas about the economic history of the middle ages. The gap was probably wider at the time of the Union of the Crowns than it had been for centuries - certainly wider than it was before 1296. And there is some reason to think that in the later middle ages coinage for technical reasons was in itself an instrument which increased inequality between nations. When the money supply was inadequate, what little there was tended in those centuries to be drawn away from the poorer regions, and the resultant shortages of cash hampered their economic development. The gap between rich and poor tended to widen for that reason, and there was no internationally or regionally redistributive taxation such as exists at the present day, for example, within the European Economic Community. Any technical hindrance to economic progress in Scotland, arising from the limited control that could be exercised over the currency, was of course compounded in the fourteenth and fifteenth centuries by frequent political misfortune, and by other damaging conditions, such as bloody quarrels and a general lack of solidarity, which were of Scotland's own devising.

NOTES

1. He was responsible for removing the state papers from Edinburgh Castle.

2. A. A. M. Duncan, Scotland: the Making of the Kingdom, 1975, chapters 18 and 19.

3. Loans and credits among neighbours and residents in a mainly peasant society in medieval Cumbria (offering some analogies at least with the Scottish situation) are discussed by G. P. Jones in Trans. Cumberland and Westmorland Antiq. and Arch. Soc. NS LXXV (1975), 275-92. If actual cash was lent, the lender was deprived of its use, and the money supply was therefore increased only in terms of velocity of circulation, i.e. the lender might not have had occasion to use the cash. Deferred payment amounts to the same thing in terms of this economic analysis. When letters of credit become negotiable instruments, one enters a different era.

4. Estimates are, in the present state of the available information, inevitably influenced by personal judgment. They follow on from the (more-securely based) figures for the size of the English coinage, which also increased phenomenally during the thirteenth century. For the procedures by which the size of the Scottish currency may be estimated, see further below at pp. 65f.

5. R.H.M. Dolley, " The Irish mints of Edward I in the light of the coin hoards from Ireland and Great Britain", Proceedings of the Royal Irish Academy LXVI C, no. 3 (1968), 235-97. The development and practice of this method of studying a find-assemblage is associated particularly with the German school of medieval Münz- und Geldgeschichte.   It is a very necessary technique in central Europe, where the currency was fragmented and mixed.

6. No. 15 in the Inventory below.

7. See nos. 75, 95, 166, 168, and 242; no. 67 was concealed in a cow's hoof.

8. Nos. 23, 43 and 64 in purses; no. 82 in a small wooden box; no 137 in a bronze weight-box; nos. 201, 204, 217, and perhaps 188 in pirlie-pigs.

9. Nos. 57, 68, 127, 145, 147, and 162.

10. Nos . 80, 127, and 183.

11. Nos. 13 and 79. Also no. 20.

12. In particular from Aberdeen, Dumfries, Perth, Glasgow, and Edinburgh, but also Haddington, Hawick, Jedburgh, Linlithgow, Renfrew, and Montrose. Note, in the index, the finds under "Castlehill" and "High Street" - find-spots that are within the built-up area today were not necessarily so at the date of concealment.

13. Nos. 1, 7, 60, 62, 68, 115, 149, 151, 152, 161, etc.

14. Nos. 21, 49, 106, 137, 171, and 176. Cf. nos. 85, 94, and 184 found actually within castles.

15. From quarries, note nos. 29 and 47. From religious houses (cf. churchyards), sometimes in a niche in the wall, perhaps the following, although the circumstances of concealment are conjectural: nos. 3, 11, 128, 148, 158, 165, 170, 177, 248.

16. This is discussed further below.

17. See An Historical Atlas of Scotland, c. 400-c.1600, ed. P. McNeill and R. Nicholson, (Conference of Scottish Medievalists), 1975, pp. 133-4 for distribution-maps of the burghs.

18. M.H. Crawford, " Coin hoards and the pattern of violence in the late Republic", Papers of the British School at Rome XXXVII (1969), 76-81, See also J.P.C. Kent, " Interpreting coin-finds", Coins and the Archaeologist (British Archaeological Reports, Vol. IV), 1974, 184-98.

19. R. Nicholson, Scotland, The Later Middle Ages, 1974, 175-6, 268; H.J. Dakers, " The first issue of David II", BNJ XXIII (1938-41), 51-8. David is said to have petitioned Edward in 1358 that the money of the two countries should again be interchangeable - Exchequer Rolls, II p.xcvii.

20. R.W. Cochran-Patrick, <u>Records of the Coinage of Scotland</u>, 1876.

21. For hoards from the period <u>c</u>. 795-1105, see the list in R.H.M. Dollwy, <u>The Hiberno-Norse Coins in the British Museum</u> '(<u>SCBI</u> vol. VIII,) 1966, 47-54. This should be supplemented from the more detailed notes in R.B.K. Stevenson, <u>SCBI Edinburgh</u>, I, pp. xvii-xxiii. Note two coins of Edward Confessor of unknown provenance, p. xxii, and two Hiberno-Norse pennies of the late eleventh century, possibly of Scottish provenance, nos. 751-2.

22. M. Dolley, 'A Viking-age coin of Norway discovered in Shetland', <u>PSAS</u> C (1967-8), 193-5. The coin is dated to a little before <u>c</u>. 1080, and is apparently from the Jarlshof site at Sumburgh.

23. M. Dolley and K. Skaare, "To penninger fra Harold Hardråde funnet på Vesterhavsøyene," <u>Nordisk Numismatisk Unions Medlemsblad</u> VIII, 221-7; I. Crawford and R. Swtisur, "Sandscaping and C14: the Udal, N. Uist", <u>Antiquity</u> LI (1977) 124ff. The coin, although minted <u>c</u>. 1055-65, may have been lost in 1098 when Magnus Barefoot raided the Western Isles.

24. No. 1 in the inventory below: this gold coin, although a single find, may well have been a deliberate concealment, and has accordingly been included as a "hoard" of minimum size.

25. G.W.S. Barrow, <u>The Kingdom of the Scots</u>, 1973, pp. 180-3. Cf. also the arrangements at Dunfermline Abbey, <u>ibid</u>., pp. 194-5; and a payment of 10 marks of silver a year, as a temporary substitute for half a knight's fee, "from my chamber" - <u>ibid</u>., p. 281.

26. G. Donaldson, <u>Scottish Historical Documents</u>, 1970, 20-3.

27. I am indebted to Mr. Stewart for allowing me to mention this hoard in advance of its detailed publication.

28. Lockett sale, part V (Glendining, 18 June 1957, lot 16, Carlisle mint; Burns, p. 36 (fig. 23) and p. 38; <u>SCBI Oxford</u> 291; the third coin, for information about which I am indebted to Mr. H.E. Pagan, was in the J.T. Brockett sale <u>c</u>.1823, and read EDICI CON. It was described as having been recently found at the mouth of the river Tyne. There is some doubt whether it might not be the Oxford specimen. The possibility should also be considered of a hoard, perhaps at Blyth, from which the Blyth and Morpeth specimens might have come.

29. I.H. Stewart, "A twelfth-century Scottish sterling from Annandale", <u>Dumfriesshire Trans</u>. 3rd ser. XLIX (1972), 116-17.

30. Burns, p. 31.

31. A detailed survey of the reasons for activity at the various Scottish mints will be found in I. Stewart, "Scottish mints" <u>Mints, Dies and Currency</u> (ed. R.A.G. Carson), 1971, 165-289, particularly pp. 166-78. Stewart perhaps emphasized the political reasons at the expense of the economic and commercial, whereas the two co-existed, and explanations in different terms need not exclude each other. On the contrast between re-coinages and intermediate activity, see the arguments as developed in

relation to England in D.M. Metcalf, "Geographical patterns of minting in medieval England", Seaby's Coin and Medal Bulletin 1977, 314-17.

32. The changing of money at Berwick is mentioned in 1329, but this is probably not directly relevant to the period before 1296. See Exchequer Rolls, I, 216.

33. D.P. Kirby, "Moray in the twelfth century", in An Historical Atlas of Scotland, pp. 48-9.

34. On the basis of Dolley's listing, there are from the period c.1280-c. 1350 some 68 hoards from Scotland and a further 15 from north-eastern England, as against 16 from the rest of England; but the disparity is greater than these figures imply, as the total from Scotland can now be seen to be 114.

35. The expansion of the Douglas family in fourteenth-century Nithsdale is sketched in Royal Commission on Ancient and Historical Monuments, Dumfriesshire (1920), pp. xxiv-xxix; R.C. Reid, "Edward de Balliol", Dumfriesshire Trans., 3rd ser., XXXV (1956-57), 38-63; A.B. Webster, "The English occupation of Dumfriesshire in the fourteenth century", ibid., 64-80, draws attention to the destructive campaign of the autumn of 1337; G. Stell, "Mottes", in An Historical Atlas of Scotland, pp. 28-9.

36. Should one take note of the hoards concealed in cow's horns, e.g. from Durisdeer, Morton, and Lochar Moss?

37. D.M. Metcalf, "Coinage and coin finds associated with a military presence in the medieval Balkans", Kovanje i kovnice antickog i srednjovekovnog novca, Belgrade, 1976, pp. 89-97.

38. To appreciate the dramatic extent of wastage, one may study the diagram at p. 94 in N.J. Mayhew, "Imitative sterlings in the Aberdeen and Montraive hoards", Numismatic Chronicle 1976, 85-97.

39. The statistics are well set out in P. Woodhead, I.H. Stewart, and G.L. V. Tatler, "The Loch Doon treasure trove, 1966", BNJ XXXVIII (1969) 31-49.

40. Argued by Mayhew, below pp. 88f.

41. Cockmuir hill, and Coull castle. See nos. 20-23 in the inventory below.

42. Again, regrettably, we lack "Long-cross" hoards from which to speak about mints of the 1250 recoinage. The 1280 Scottish coins were not mint-signed, but it is believed that the number of "points" of the mullets and stars on the reverse was used as a system of privy-marking. It has been guessed that 24 points indicates Berwick, 26 Perth, 25 Roxburgh, 20 and 23 Edinburgh and Aberdeen, and that 28, 27, 22, and 21 points signify certain minor mints (Stewart, "Scottish mints", pp. 220-1). Some statistics are tabulated by Woodhead et al., BNJ 1969, p. 38, where it can be seen that the 23-point coins are perhaps over-represented in the Loch Doon hoard, but that the percentages are otherwise quite consistent, even when the actual totals are small. One might now add the

Aberdeen hoard to the table (Mayhew, BNJ 1975), with 24 points, 77%; 26 points, 18%; 25 points, 5%: no sign of influence of the local mint.

43. In the Loch Doon hoard there were 7 Short-cross and 1 Long-cross sterlings, amounting to 0.5% of the hoard. Coins of "Henry III" are mentioned in two or three other large hoards where they may have made up an equally small proportion - Inverness, concealed after c.1350; Redgorton 1834, concealed after 1300; and Langhope, concealed after 1318; also at Kirkcudbright 1851, from c.1300.

44. Exchequer Rolls II, xxxviii, note 4.

45. T.H. Lloyd, " Overseas trade and the English money supply in the fourteenth century" , Edwardian Monetary Affairs (1279-1344), A Symposium held in Oxford, August 1976, (ed. N. J. Mayhew) (BAR XXXVI), 1977, 96-124, at p. 111. This conclusion is supported and developed further in a forthcoming paper by M. Mate.

46. B.H.I.H. Stewart, " The Glenluce and Rhoneston hoards of fifteenth-century coins" PSAS XCIII (1959-60), 238-44.

47. The question of their attribution has been re-opened in I. Stewart, " Scottish mints" , in Mints, Dies and Currency (ed. R.A.G. Carson), 1971, 165-289, at p. 242.

48. There may be a slight bias in the evidence, in that finds of billion from the countryside, being of little present-day commercial value, have tended not to be reported to the authorities.

ACKNOWLEDGEMENTS

I am indebted to my colleague Mr. Mayhew for the benefit of numerous discussions about work in progress. Mrs. Murray, Mr. Stevenson, and Mr. Stewart all generously placed unpublished papers at my disposal, and were kind enough to read an earlier draft of the article. They saved me from various errors, and offered a number of valued suggestions for improvements to the text.

AN ANNOTATED BIBLIOGRAPHY
OF SCOTTISH COIN HOARDS, c.1100-1600

There are records of the discovery of coin hoards in Scotland from the late fifteenth century onwards. Details of ex gratia payments to the finders are given in the Accounts of the Treasurer and in the Register of the Privy Seal. These accounts unfortunately include no information about the coins themselves, and thus are of largely antiquarian interest. They are discussed in J. Murray, "Hoards in Scotland under James IV", Numismatic Circular LXXVII (1969), 199. See also Register of the Privy Seal VII, 23, no. 145, for a late-sixteenth century hoard from Haddington.

The Statistical Account of Scotland (1791-9) produced a crop of hoard-reports which, although brief and sometimes obviously inaccurate, are not without value. More were added in the New Statistical Account. I am greatly indebted to Mr. R. B. K. Stevenson who kindly invited me to consult the MS notes of Mr. R. Kerr taken from the Statistical Accounts, and also his own annotated card-index of finds not in Thompson's Inventory. I have checked the Statistical Accounts and added one or two further hoards from that source. Lindsay too published brief notices of eighteenth-century Scottish hoards, deriving extensively from a manuscript by Wright, with additions by W. Ferguson.

From the 1860s or thereabouts, more technically adequate hoard-reports began to be published. Increasingly, hoards have been published with sufficient detail to permit their re-evaluation from time to time as research has progressed.

The bibliographical information gathered here is intended to guide the reader to the most up-to-date or reliable account or summary of each hoard, and to any comments published elsewhere on its interpretation, and to draw attention to any addenda to the standard references. Those hoards of which part of the contents have been adequately published are marked with an asterisk, and those that have been fully published are marked with two asterisks. A few hoards which are of particular note, for their size and for the care and reliability with which they have been studied, are given three asterisks. Brief notes have been added on some of the more interesting points, and on hoards of which the publication is relatively inaccessible.

An attempt has been made to list the hoards in the approximate order of their date of deposit, although there is considerable overlap, as many ill-recorded finds cannot be dated to within half a century. The list is intended to include all hoards from within the modern boundaries of Scotland (and therefore some early hoards from areas then under Norse or Manx control), and also from areas of northern England which formed part of the Scottish kingdom or were under Scottish control at the date of concealment. In marginal cases, Border hoards have been included rather than excluded.

ABBREVIATIONS

B	E. Burns, <u>The Coinage of Scotland,</u> 3 vols., 1887.
BD	I. D. Brown and M. Dolley, <u>A Bibliography of Coin Hoards of Great Britain and Ireland, 1500-1967</u>, 1971. I. D. Brown, "First addendum to the Bibliography of Coin Hoards of Great Britain and Ireland, 1500-1967", <u>Numismatic Circular</u> LXXXI (1973), 147-51.
BNJ	British Numismatic Journal.
CH	Coin Hoards.
D	R. H. M. Dolley, "The Irish mints of Edward I in the light of the coin-hoards from Ireland and Great Britain", <u>Proceedings of the Royal Irish Academy</u> LXVI C, no. 3 (1968), 235-97.
L	J. Lindsay, <u>A View of the Coinage of Scotland,</u> Cork, 1845. <u>A Supplement to the Coinage of Scotland,</u> Cork, 1859. <u>A Second Supplement to the Coinage of Scotland,</u> Cork, 1868.
M	D. M. Metcalf, "Some finds of medieval coins from Scotland and the north of England", <u>BNJ</u> XXX (1960-1), 88-123.
NC	Numismatic Chronicle.
NSAS	The New Statistical Account of Scotland, 15 vols., Edinburgh and London, 1845. (Where more than one shire is included in a volume, each is separately paginated.)
PSAS	Proceedings of the Society of Antiquaries of Scotland.
SAS	J. Sinclair, <u>The Statistical Account of Scotland, Drawn up from the Communications of the Ministers of the Different Parishes,</u> 21 vols., Edinburgh, 1791-9.
SS	W. A. Seaby and B. H. I. H. Stewart, "A fourteenth century hoard of Scottish groats from Balleny townland, Co. Down", <u>BNJ</u> XXXIII (1964) 94-106.
T	J. D. A. Thompson, <u>Inventory of British Coin Hoards, A.D. 600-1500</u>, 1956. D. M. Wilson, "Some archaeological additions and corrections to J. D. A. Thompson, <u>Inventory of British Coin Hoards,</u>" Medieval Archaeology II (1958), 169-71; J. D. A. Thompson, "Some additions and corrections to J. D. A. Thompson, <u>Inventory of British Coin Hoards:</u> a recension", <u>ibid</u>., III (1959), 280-2.
W	J. Williams, "Coin finds and hoards from Dumfriesshire and Galloway", <u>Numismatic Circular</u> LXXVIII (1970), 288-9, 331-3, 388-9, 442-4, 491-3.

1. *MONYMUSK (Churchyard), Aberdeenshire, 1823   after 1097

    M.120 NSAS XII, 464. (An Arabic gold dinar of
    Yusuf bin Tashfin, minted at Marrakesh [Morocco],
    491 H./A.D. 1097. Weight, 62 gr. Monymusk =
    Eglismenythok: see Barrow, The Kingdom of the
    Scots, p. 63, and map at p. 62. On the House of
    Culdees at Monymusk, see Easson, Medieval Re-
    ligious Houses, s.v.

2. *STEWART PARCEL   early 1150s

    To be published by Ian Stewart. (Includes David I
    coins of Perth and Aberdeen.)

    WESTRUTHER

    See below, no. 140. (Unlikely to be David I.)

3. *BUTE, ISLE OF, 1863   1150s

    T.63. (In a wall near the chapel of St. Blane.)

4. BAMBURGH (Castle), Northumbria, 1844   c.1160?

    L., p. 270. B, p. 19. T. 31. (Stewart is of the
    opinion that it is merely a parcel from Outchester,
    no. 5 below.)

5. OUTCHESTER, Northumbria, 1817   1170s

    T. 299 and refs. cited there. (Found a few miles from
    Bamburgh. Said to have contained about 150 Scottish
    coins along with some 700 English coins of the Cross-
    and-crosslets issue (1158-80). There are unproven-
    anced specimens probably from the hoard in various
    collections. The terminus post quem is fixed by a
    coin of Class E of the Cross-and-crosslets coinage
    (c. 1170), and the concealment may have been at the
    time of the rising of the Young King, 1173-4).

6. *MAN, ISLE OF, before 1769   c.1180

    Stewart in BNJ XXXIII (1964), 48-56.

7. DYKE (Churchyard), Elgin, 1780   1180s?

    T. 150. T. 273. M, p. 122, nos. 150 and 273.
    SAS XX, 224-5. Dolley in BNJ XXIX (1958-59), at
    p. 299 voices a suspicion that the English element in
    the hoard was Short-cross rather than Cross-and-
    crosslets. His proposed dating of c. 1240 should
    evidently be rejected, however, on the basis of the
    Scottish coins. (The find consisted "chiefly of
    William's coins with crescents on the reverse",

although another writer states that "a very considerable number" of English coins of Henry II were mixed with those of William. The hoard was removed clandestinely by the finder, who allegedly grew prosperous on the proceeds, the main part of the hoard being sold as bullion for £46 and, no doubt, melted down. The coins of William were not at first recognized as being Scottish. Some were dispersed by itinerant pedlars. The <u>Statistical Account</u> records that there were some coins of Striveling (Stirling) reading RE VILLAM: these are unknown at the present day, and are probably misread coins of the moneyer Raul Derling.)

8. BADDINSGILL, Peeblesshire, 1834

1180 x 1250

    T. 304. (The hoard has recently come to light again, after being in family possession for many years. It has been acquired by Mr. Ian Stewart, who hopes to publish a detailed account of it.)

9. LEWINSHOPE Farm, Selkirkshire, 1865

1180 x 1250

    T. 232. (Short-cross sterlings.)

10. GLENCHAMBER Moss, New Luce, Wigtownshire, 1859

1180 x 1250

    T. 285. (4 miles E of New Luce.)

11. HOLYWOOD (Churchyard), Dumfriesshire, 1904

1205 x 1250

    W., p. 333 (Four short-cross sterlings found "in graves" — ? a hoard — from the site of Holywood or Dercongal Abbey: Easson, s.v.)

12. KEITH (Coldhome farm), Banffshire, 1881

1205 x 1250

    CH II, 449. <u>BNJ</u> XXX, 95. <u>PSAS</u> 1881-2, <u>431</u>-43. (Coldhome or Cauldhame farm is $1\frac{1}{2}$ miles SW of Keith. The hoard was found just east of of Douglas-brae old lime quarry, and near the old cliff of the River Isla.)

13. TOM A'BHURAICH, (GARCHORY), Strathdon, Aberdeenshire, 1822

<u>c</u>.1210 x 1250

    T. 361. T. 169. Dolley in <u>PSAS</u> XCV (1962), 241 ff. (Confused records, ably interpreted by Dolley, of a hoard that is important as evidence for the northerly availability of halfpence and farthings. Found $3\frac{1}{2}$ miles above the Doune of Invernochty, on the hillside opposite Garchory.)

14. *DUN HIADIN, Isle of Tiree, 1787   After c.1240

Dolley in BNJ XXIX (1958-59), 318-19. (Concealed in a pottery container two to three feet
below the surface, in the immediate vicinity of
Dun Hiadin. Forty coins from the hoard are in
the British Museum: the terminus post quem is
given by Class VIIc.)

15. **DUN LAGAIDH, Lochbroom, Ross and Cromarty, 1968   After 1242

CH II, 451. Glasgow Arch. J. III (1974), 78-81.
E. W. MacKie, Excavations on Loch Broom...
Second Interim Report, Glasgow, 1968. (Excavated in a small castle, made out of a converted
round drystone dun. Fourteen pennies and 8 halves,
including a halfpenny in the name of William the
Lion. Cf. no. 13.)

16. GLENLUCE Sands, Wigtownshire, before 1880   1247 x 1280

PSAS XV (1880-1), 275. (A long-cross sterling
with 3 cut halves.)

17. **NEWCASTLETON, Roxburghshire, 1937   1253 or later

T. 283 (A small, scattered hoard but apparently
fairly complete. Dated by class Vc.)

18. *HAZELRIGG, Balmaclellan, Dumfriesshire, c. 1924   c.1270
Dumfriesshire Trans. XXVI (1947-48), 100-13. (A
group of 64 English and 4 Scottish coins from the
hoard are listed in detail, and run up to class Vh.
One continental sterling of John I (1261-94), Duke
of Brabant, Ch. viii, 4.)

19. JEDBURGH (the Castlehill), Roxburghshire, before 1831   XII/XIII

M.21. (Ten sterlings of Henry, and two others.)

20. COCKMUIR hill, Kennethmont parish, Aberdeenshire,
before 1845   1250 x 1350

NSAS XII, 585. ("A bag of small silver coins, with
Alexander I engraved on one side" [Alexander III?],
found in trenching the hill.)

21. COULL castle, Aberdeenshire, before 1792   1250 x 1350

SAS III, 201. (Several coins of Alexander III.)

22. DUNKELD, Perthshire, 1860   1250 x 1350

M. 12. (Three coins of Alexander III.)

23. *GLASSERTON, Wigtownshire, 1886   After 1280

   W, p. 491 and p. 492 (Sorby parish). (A leather
   purse containing two farthings of Alexander III
   and a spindle whorl of steatite.)

24. MONTROSE (High Street), Angus, 1859   <u>c</u>.1296?

   Nineteen silver Edwardian coins, with spoon, etc.
   — MS note in NMA, Edinburgh. Cf. <u>PSAS</u> IV
   (1860-2), 397.

25. ***MELLENDEAN farm, near Sprouston, Kelso,
Roxburghire, 1911   <u>c</u>.1295 x <u>c</u>.1302

   G. Macdonald in <u>NC</u> 1913, 57ff. D. 38 and
   pp. 266-7. <u>PSAS</u> 1911-12, 90, 200, 374; <u>ibid</u>.,
   1913-14, 17; 1951-2, 211 f. <u>PSAntiq</u>. New-
   <u>castle</u> 1911-12, 139; <u>ibid</u>., 1925-6, 138.
   (There were 103 continental sterlings in a
   hoard of some 890 coins.)

26. **KIRKCUDBRIGHT (near), 1850 or earlier <u>c</u>.1296 x <u>c</u>.1302

   E. Hawkins in <u>NC</u> 1850-1, 86-94. D. 35 and
   pp. 265-6. W. p. 443. (There were 92 coins,
   found on the property of the Earl of Selkirk,
   in the neighbourhood of Kirkcudbright —
   Dolley's listing of the find-spot as Kirkcudbright Burgh is unsupported — but it is difficult
   to reconstruct the total from Hawkins's account.
   Apparently all but 7 of the coins were continental,
   the others being of Henry III (1), Edward I (4),
   Alexander III (1), and a barbarous imitation of an
   Irish penny. The foreign coins may have been
   exported from England to Scotland when they were
   called down to a halfpenny and subsequently proscribed in England, from Christmas 1299 onwards.
   It seems likely that the concealment of this and
   similar hoards in Scotland, for which the coins give
   a <u>terminus post quem</u> of 1296, was in 1300 or
   later. Although no documentary evidence survives,
   the continental sterlings were presumably proscribed
   in Scotland also, as there is no sign that they persist
   in later hoards.)

27. ***GALSTON (Auchenbart), Ayrshire, 1922 1296 x <u>c</u>.1302

   G. Macdonald in <u>NC</u> 1923, 60ff. T. 168. D. 111
   and p. 249. (There were 228 sterlings, of which
   221 were foreign and 7 were of Edward I, including a contemporary forgery, in an earthenware
   jug. The original total is believed to have been
   240 to 250, See the note above, under Kirkcudbright.)

28. **CLEUCHHEAD farm, near Jedburgh, Roxburgh-shire, 1897   1296 x c.1302

    A. B. Richardson in PSAS XXXII (1898), 295ff.
    D. 99 and pp. 265-6. (The hoard consisted of
    138 continental sterlings. See above, under
    Kirkcudbright. Found in Hill End Field, not
    far from "Old Roman Road" [Dere Street?].)

29. **FYVIE, Aberdeenshire, before 1898   c.1300?

    Dolley in NC 1961, 169-70. D. 92. The date
    of deposit is discussed by Mayhew, p. 86f
    below.(Continental sterlings, found in an aban-
    doned quarry.)

30. *CANONBIE (Woodhead), Dumfriesshire, 1863 (1861?)   1298 x c.1302

    D. 14 and p. 259. W., p. 289. PSAS LVIII
    (1923-4), 160-84. (Included brooches, 2 gold
    rings, and beads. On Canonbie priory, see
    Easson, s.v.)

31. **BRAEMORE (Caithness?), before 1900   1301 x 1320

    Stewart in NC 1973, 138-9. (Presumed on general
    grounds not to be from the Braemore near Loch
    Broom; but cf. now Dun Lagaidh.)

32. NORTH BERWICK, East Lothian, 1882   1302 x c.1330

    D. 50 and p. 271.

33. KIRKMICHAEL, Perthshire, 1867   1303 x c.1330

    D. 96 (Concealment c. 1332-6? — Mayhew 1975).

34. NETHERFIELD (Cummertrees parish),
Dumfriesshire, 1860   1305 x c.1320

    D. 45 and pp. 268-9. W, p. 331.

35. DUMBARTON (Castle Rock), 1975   1307 x 1330
    CH II, 455.

36. DUMFRIES, 1849   c.1310 x 1330?

    D. 110. W., p. 331. ("About £80 worth".)

37. *FAULDHOUSE, West Lothian, 1913   1311 x c.1320

    D. 29 and p. 263. M., p. 122. PSAS 1913-14, 17.

38. *AYR, 1874   1318 x c.1320

    D. 4 and p. 257. Stewart in NC 1973, 142-4.
    (Included brooches.)

39. **BLACKHILLS farm, Parton, Kirkcudbright-shire, 1911   1318 x c.1335

> G. Macdonald in NC 1913, 57ff. D. 8 and
> p. 258. CH II,456. Mayhew, in BNJ XLV,
> 1975, 35, queries whether the hoard may not
> have been concealed c. 1332-5. (More than
> 2,000 coins, found in a wooden bowl, "about
> 400 yards from the Urr Water and 700 yards
> from Corsock Tower", i.e. about a mile S. of
> Corsock Village, at NG 760750 approx. Cf.
> the Nether Corsock hoard, no. 96 below, which
> was found about a mile further south.)

40. ***RENFREW (Bell Street), 1963   1320 x 1322

> P. Woodhead and I. Stewart, "The Renfrew treasure
> trove, 1963", BNJ XXXV (1966), 128-47. D.57
> and p. 273. A. S. Robertson, "The Renfrew (1963)
> coin hoard", Glasgow Archaeological Journal I (1969),
> 72-4. (An unusual double hoard, comprising a
> savings hoard put away in late 1299 or 1300, plus
> a cash element added twenty years later, with an
> exceptionally high proportion of halfpennies and
> farthings.)

41. CRATHES, Aberdeenshire, 1863   1320 x c.1336

> Publication forthcoming by Mayhew, who suggests
> (BNJ XLV, 1975, 35) 1333-6 as a possible date of
> concealment.

42. DORNOCK, Dumfriesshire, 1871   1320 x c.1335?

> D. 25 and p. 262. W., p. 331. Mayhew, in BNJ
> XLV, 1975, 35, queries whether the hoard may
> not have been concealed c.1332-5. (Found in a
> horn "on a farm in the parish". Cf. what is ap-
> parently another, larger hoard from Dornock,
> no. 72 below, but which might be the same.)

43. DUMFRIES, 1878   c.1324 x 1335?

> D. 27 and pp. 262-3. PSAS LVIII (1923-4), 160-
> 84. W. p. 331. Mayhew, in BNJ XLV, 1975,
> 35 queries whether the hoard may not have been
> concealed c.1332-5. (In a purse in the wall of
> an old house. With silver jewellery, including
> a cross, a chain, a brooch, a small bow handle,
> etc. A coin of class XVc in Edinburgh.)

44. **DUNBLANE, Perthshire, 1937   c.1322 x 1336

> D. 28 and p. 263. Mayhew, in BNJ XLV, 1975, 35
> suggests 1333-6 as a possible date of concealment.
> See the note on Carsphairn, no. 52 below.

45. GIFFNOCH, Renfrewshire, 1879   1320 x 1335?

> D. 30, and pp. 263-4 (Included brooches).

46. KINGHORNIE (Inverbervie farm), Kincardineshire, 1893   c.1320 x 1336?

> D. 103 and pp. 278-9. ("Curiously enough,
> this jar ... was lying over the site of a chapel
> erected by David II, in 1342, in gratitude for
> his escape from shipwreck". Concealment
> c.1332-6? — Mayhew, 1975: but cf. another
> hoard ploughed up on the same farm, no. 110
> below, for which a date of deposit in the 1290s is
> very likely. On a [later?] religious house at
> Inverbervie, see Easson, s.v.)

47. STANLEY, Perthshire, 1834   1318 x c.1340

> D. 98. M., p. 122. (In an old quarry. Con-
> cealment c.1332-6? — Mayhew 1975.)

48. *DUNCANSBY HEAD, Ladykirk, Caithness, 1969   After c.1318

> Stewart in NC 1973, 134-44.

49. DUNS Castle, Berwickshire, 1811   1318 x 1350

> T. 145. (2,361 coins in a pewter jug and wooden
> cup, in a meadow in front of the castle.)

50. UNKNOWN SCOTTISH PROVENANCE, 1783   1318 x 1350

> D. 58 and pp. 273-4.

51. **MONTROSE (Castle Street), Angus, 1973   1322 x 1370

> CH I, 373. Mayhew, in BNJ XLV, 1975, 35
> suggests 1333-6 as a possible date of concealment.

52. **CARSPHAIRN (Craigengillan farm), Kirkcudbrightshire, 1913   1324 x c.1335

> G. Macdonald in PSAS 1914, 398-402. D. 15
> and p. 259. W., p. 442. The hoard was made
> a crux for the reattribution of unsigned coins of
> Thomas de Bourlemont, bishop of Toul, to Ferri
> IV of Lorraine, and also for the reattribution of

Anglo-Gascon coins of Edward III to Edward II.
See G. C. Brooke in <u>NC</u> 1914, 382-3. While both
reattributions are quite probably correct, the
argument from the Carsphairn hoard does not stand
up. Nor does the Dunblane hoard, no. 44 above,
offer unequivocal evidence, <u>pace</u> Dolley in <u>NCirc</u>
1962, 80. Cf. also no. 54. (Over 2,000 coins
found in an earthenware jug in a marshy hollow on
Goat Craig Hill. Mayhew, in <u>BNJ</u> XLV, 1975, 34f.,
notes the proximity of the find-spot to that of the
Loch Doon hoard, and queries whether the hoard
may not belong to a group concealed <u>c</u>. 1332-5.)

53. *PENICUIK (Fallhills Wood, Mt. Lothian),   c.1324 x 1340
Midlothian, 1898

    Dolley in <u>BNJ</u> XXVII (1953), 215-18. D.52
    and pp. 271-2. (Dated by class XVc.)

54. **LOCHMABEN, Dumfriesshire, 1904   1329 x c.1335

    G. Macdonald in <u>NC</u> 1905, 63ff. D.37 and
    p. 266. W., p. 388. Mayhew, in <u>BNJ</u> XLV,
    1975, p. 34, n.2 and p. 35, records the presence
    of class XVd in the hoard. The coin attributed
    to Thomas de Bourlemont is probably of Ferri
    IV of Lorraine: cf. the note under no. 52 above.
    (Found in an earthenware jug, in a park near
    the town.)

55. **BERSCAR, Closeburn parish, Dumfriesshire, 1900   1331 x c.1335

    D. 11 and p. 258. W. p. 289. Mayhew, in
    <u>BNJ</u> XLV, 1975, pp. 34, n.2 and 35, notes that
    there were several coins of class XVd in the
    hoard, including a York coin which gives a
    <u>terminus post quem</u>. Republished using the Fox
    classification in Stewart, <u>BNJ</u> XLVII, 1977.

56. ***LOCH DOON, Ayrshire, 1966   1331 x c.1335

    D. 36 and p. 266. P. Woodhead, I. H. Stewart,
    and G. L. V. Tatler, "The Loch Doon treasure
    trove, 1966", <u>BNJ</u> XXXVIII (1969), 31-49. A
    cyclostyled list of the weights of the coins has been
    circulated separately. (1,887 coins, dated by a
    class XVd penny of York. Found on the east shore
    of the loch, below Muckle Eriff hill, at NS 483004.
    Perhaps associated with the arrival of Edward
    Balliol and the "Disinherited" in Scotland in 1332, or
    with the military campaigns of 1332-35. The authors
    give a valuable comparative statistical analysis of
    hoards of the period.)

57. ***ABERDEEN (Upperkirkgate), 1886   1331 x 1336

>   D. 1 and pp. 254-5. N. J. Mayhew, "The
>   Aberdeen Upperkirkgate hoard of 1886", BNJ
>   XLIV (1975), 33-50. For the imitative
>   sterlings, see Mayhew, in NC 7.XVI (1976),
>   85-97. (Over 12,000 coins in a bronze tripod
>   cooking pot. Terminus post quem given by an
>   Edwardian coin of class XVd, and a (signed)
>   continental sterling of bishop Bourlemont of
>   Toul (1330-53). Cf. Carsphairn, no. 52. Con-
>   cealment possibly when Roscelyn sacked the
>   town in 1336.)

58. ABERDEEN (St. Nicholas Street), 14 November 1807   1280 x 1360

>   T. 1-2. ("Union Street"). Medieval Archaeology
>   II (1958), 169; ibid., III (1959), 280. D. 85.
>   J. C. Williams in Numismatic Circular LXXXIII
>   (1975), 478. An "immense number" of coins in a
>   large wooden vessel, found about 10 feet below
>   street level, in digging foundations for some new
>   buildings in the line of the intended opening [of St.
>   Nicholas Street] into Union Street. Dispersed
>   without any detailed information about the coins
>   ('Edward I and Alexander III"): concealment pos-
>   sibly in 1326 or 1336. Cf. no. 121 below.

59. ABERDEEN 1867   1280 x 1360

>   D. 86 (Concealment 1326 or 1336?)

60. BAILE MHAODAIN burial ground, Ardchattan, Argyll, 1829   1280 x 1360

>   NSAS VII, 500. Coins of London, Canterbury, and
>   perhaps Exeter. (NM 971 354. There was a
>   house of Valliscaulian monks at Ardchattan, founded
>   in 1230 or 1231: see Easson, s.v.)

61. BANFF, not long before 1836   1280 x 1360

>   D. 87. NSAS XIII, 31. (On the site of a new house
>   on the high shore, at the foot of the Castlehill.
>   Edwards (11 seen), Alexander III (1).)

62. BRECHIN, (Churchyard), Angus, 1785   1280 x 1360

>   D. 88 M., p. 121. (A very large quantity. With
>   silver spoons. Concealment c. 1332-6? —
>   Mayhew 1975.)

63. BRECHIN, Angus, 1891

> D. 89. PSAS LVIII (1923-4), 160-84. (Found "in a garden." Included silver spoons and brooches. Concealment c. 1332-6? — Mayhew 1975.)

64. CANONBIE, Dumfriesshire, 1811

> W., p. 289. NSAS IV, 490. ("In some marshy ground near the place where the Rowan Burn falls into the Liddle. They were contained in an old purse".)

65. CARLUKE (St. Oswald's Chapel), Lanarkshire, before 1793

> SAS VIII, 136-7. Coins of (?) Alexander III, etc., found in the SE of the parish, near a field called Friar's Croft.

66. CARLUKE (Chapel Yard), Lanarkshire, before 1793

> SAS VIII, 136-7. Coins of (?) Alexander III, etc., found on the W. corner of the parish.

67. CARSTAIRS, Lanarkshire, 1838

> NSAS VI, 554. On the side of a reclaimed moss, 36 Edwardian sterlings, neatly packed into a cow's hoof.

68. CORRIMONY (Churchyard), Inverness-shire, 1870

> D. 90. (At the head of Glen-Urquhart. One of the very few hoards recorded from west of the Great Glen. The coins were carefully packed edgeways in a copper pot, and almost all those examined were of the Lincoln mint. This last seems highly implausible.)

69. CRAWFORDJOHN, Lanarkshire, before 1836

> NSAS VI, 503. An Edwardian hoard including coins of Dublin and Waterford.

70. CUMMERTREES (Hurkledale farm), Dumfriesshire, 1833

> D. 21 and p. 261. W. p. 331. Found on a piece of moss recently brought under cultivation.

71. DALRYMPLE, Ayrshire, 1835

> NSAS V, 279. (Four silver coins "of Edward I and III" found in a ploughed field near the village.)

72. DORNOCK, Dumfriesshire before 1889

> W, p. 331. (At Stapleton Tower near Woodhall.
> Cf. no. 42 above — same hoard?.)

73. DUMFRIES, undated

> W, p. 332, no. 6. Mayhew in BNJ XLV (1975),
> 35. ("£80 worth".)

74. DUNSCORE, Dumfriesshire, undated

> W, p. 332.

75. DURISDEER, Dumfriesshire, 1815/20

> W, pp. 332-3. (Over 1,000 coins in a horn. Found
> at Inglestone.) (Listed by Williams under Sanquhar,
> p. 388, in all probability the Durisdeer hoard.)

76. EASSIE, Angus, before 1795

> SAS XVI, 219. NSAS II, 476. ("Several of
> Edward I, on a large circular mound about a
> mile from the old church of Eassie.")

77. EDINBURGH (South Bridge), 23 June 1787

> SAS VI, 584. The Scots Magazine XLIX, July
> 1787, p. 358, gives the following fuller account:
> 'The workmen employed in digging the foundation
> of one of the houses on the east side of the South
> Bridge, Edinburgh, found deposited in a cavity,
> which appeared to have been made for the purpose,
> a vast quantity of silver coin... EDWAR. ANGL.
> DNS HYB', etc.

78. EDINBURGH (Niddry's Wynd), before 1787

> AS III, 65. (Nine Edwardian sterlings = 77?)

79. GLENBRERARCHAN, Moulin parish, Perthshire,
before 1835

> NSAS X, 467-8 and 650. D. 97 s.v. Monlin.
> "On Stronchane farm, at the head of Glen-
> briarchan, well up towards the ridge of a lofty
> hill, nearly two dozen sterlings of the Edwards
> and Alexander III."

80. GLENETIVE (Inbhirfhaolain farm), Ardchattan parish,
Argyllshire, 1830

> NSAS VII, 501. An Edwardian hoard, found near

the river by a shepherd sheltering from a storm
close to a large upright stone often used for such
purposes.

81. GLEN QUAICH, Kenmore, Perthshire, before 1845

NSAS X, 467-8. Edwardian sterlings, found in
a field near the head of Loch Freuchie.

82. GRETNA, Dumfriesshire, before 1791

D. 113. SAS I, 528. (25 Edwardian sterlings
and 4 somewhat smaller [halfpence?] in a small
wooden box in a moss near the Hirst. Also in
NSAS IV, s.v. Graitney.)

83. HAWICK (Hislop), Roxburghshire, before 1845.

NSAS III, 394. Many coins, found in a piece of
moss ground: one was of Alexander III.

84. INVERARITY, Angus, before 1797

SAS XIX, 560. Seven hundred Edwardian sterlings
and 4 of Alexander III. Cf. the Longforgan hoard,
no. 93, which was believed to have been identical
in its composition. If reliable the low proportion
of Alexandrian coins suggests a date well into the
fourteenth century.

85. KINCLAVEN CASTLE, Perthshire, 1803

D. 93. M. 23. (Concealment c. 1332-6? —Mayhew
1975. Found in the ruins of the castle.)

86. KINNEFF Church, Kincardineshire, c. 1788

D. 105. SAS VI, 209. (About $1\frac{1}{2}$ pounds of
sterlings of the Edwards and Alexander III,
including a few halfpennies, in an earthen pot.
Concealment possibly in 1336, when the English
occupied the castle?).

87. KINNELL, Angus, 1790

D. 94. SAS II, 494. NSAS XI, 398. Between
Hatton and Hatton-mill, in the face of the bank
above the river Lunan (in the S of the parish),
under a stone (SAS II), [?] in an earthenware pot
(NSAS XI). Silver pennies. Cf. Kinnell, no. 109.

88. KIRCOWAN (Glassnock Farm), Wigtownshire, before 1836

D. 115. (Cf. Penninghame?.)

89. KIRKCUDBRIGHT parish (Loch Fergus farm), before 1845   1280 x 1360

       W, p. 443. NSAS IV, 24. (One mile to the east, near the road leading down into Kirkcudbright.)

90. KIRKMICHAEL, Dumfriesshire, 1821   1280 x 1360

       W, p. 388. NSAS IV, 71. (Half-way between Nether-Garrell and Courance.)

91. LESMAHAGOW, Lanarkshire, c. 1815   1280 x 1360

       D. 116. NSAS VI, 33. Found below a large stone.

92. LOCHMABEN, Dumfriesshire, before 1823   1280 x 1360

       W. p. 388. Cf. Archaeologia Scotica III (1831), 78n. (Paper on Lochmaben castle, read 1823), referring presumably to the same hoard. (In Whitehills Moss, about three-quarters of a mile from the town.)

93. LONGFORGAN, Perthshire, before 1797   1280 x 1360

       SAS XIX, 559-60. Near a barrow known as Market Knowe, an earthen pot containing 700 Edwardian sterlings and 4 of Alexander III. Cf. the Inverarity hoard, no. 84, from about 12 miles away: it was conjectured that two brothers might have divided a sum of money equally between them.

94. MOCHRUM (Castle Loch Mochrum), Wigtownshire   1280 x 1360

       W, p. 492. (Found during excavations at the castle site: stray finds or hoard? Deposit dated after 1309 by coin of John the Blind?)

95. MORTON parish (Thornhill), Dumfriesshire, 1866   1280 x 1360

       W, p. 388. (Found in a horn container.)

96. NETHER CORSOCK farm, Parton, Kirkcudbright, c. 1840   1280 x 1360

       D. 120. M. 40. Mayhew, in BNJ XLV, 1975, 35 suggests 1332-5 as a possible date of conceal-ment. (Found at NG 760 730 approx., some 2 miles S of Corsock and "three-quarters of a mile" S of the Blackhills farm hoard, no. 39.)

97. NEW CUMNOCK (Whitehill Farm), Ayrshire, c. 1830   1280 x 1360

       D. 118. Stewart, in NC 1973, 134-44.

98. PENICUIK (Eastfield farm), Midlothian, 1792

PSAS XXVIII (1893-94), 239. The small jug, which was "filled with coins of Alexander III, and Edward I and II", is illustrated in T., pl. IVb, where it is mistakenly assigned to the Penicuik 1898 hoard.

99. PENNINGHAME, Wigtownshire, 1835

D. 53 and p. 272. Mayhew, in BNJ XLV, 1975, 35 suggests 1332-5 as a possible date of concealment.

100. PORTOBELLO Links, Midlothian, 1852

D. 54 and p. 272. M., p. 122. (About 600 coins.)

101. ROSLIN (Harpers Hill Brae), Midlothian, before 1843

NSAS I, 352. (Three Edwardian sterlings, found "on the public road". A silver buckle of rough workmanship and a brooch, found at the same place, were perhaps associated.)

102. SALTCOATS, Ayrshire, before 1781

D.121. M. 45.

103. SANQUHAR, Dumfriesshire, 1892

W., p. 388. (In Crawick Water near its junction with the Nith, half a mile west of Sanquhar.)

104. TARBAT Churchyard, Ross and Cromarty, date?

PSAS XXVI (1891-2), 60. (Donation of a foreign sterling, (?) from a hoard.)

105. TWYNHOLM, Kirkcudbrightshire, 1842

D. 122. W, p. 491. Mayhew, in BNJ XLV, 1975, 35 suggests 1332-5 as a possible date of concealment.

106. URR (near Motte of Urr) 1950/1

W., p. 491.

107. WIGTOWNSHIRE, 1838

M. 54.

108. AYR, 1892

D. 108 (1862). PSAS 1891-2, 60. Ibid., 1923-4,

160-84. (Found in an earthenware jar; included brooches. Dated by coin of John Balliol.)

109. KINNELL, Angus, 1805   1292? x 1360

   D. 95. NSAS XI, 398. An earthenware pot of coins found in the same place as Kinnell, no. 87 (by the brother of the finder of the earlier hoard). One or other of the hoards contained a halfpenny of John Balliol. Mayhew, 1975, suggests concealment of both hoards c. 1332-6.

110. KINGHORNIE, (Inverbervie farm), Kincardineshire, 1902   1292 x 1360

   D. 104. M. 24. (Found on the same farm as Kinghornie, no. 46. The exceptionally high proportion of coins of John Balliol suggests a date of deposit in the 1290s; unless we are dealing with a savings hoard or "double" hoard.)

111. KINROSS (Coldon), 1820   1292 x 1360

   D. 34 and p. 265. NSAS IX, 11. Between 300 and 400 Edwardian sterlings, with some of John Balliol, found in a field in the south of the parish of Kinross. (Concealment c. 1332-6? — Mayhew, 1975.)

112. PAISLEY (near), Renfrewshire, 1791   1292 x 1360

   D. 119. L., p. 263. (515 Edwardian sterlings, 5 of Alexander III, 3 of John Balliol. The low proportion of Alexandrian coins suggests a date well into the fourteenth century.)

113. COULNAKYLE, Abernethy parish, Elgin, 1870   1296 x 1360

   D. 91. (Dated by coin of Berwick mint.)

114. KEIR MILL (Beuchan), Dumfriesshire, 1865   1296 x 1360

   D. 114. W., p. 333. Mayhew, in BNJ XLV (1975), 35, suggests 1332-5 as a possible date of concealment. (Beuchan is about 1 mile S of Keir Mill.)

115. *MONIFIETH (Churchyard), Angus, 1854   1300 x 1360

   D. 39 and p. 267. L. (S), p. 52. (Terminus post quem from coin of Hull mint. Mayhew, in BNJ XLV, 1975, 35 suggests 1332-6 as a possible date of concealment. On an earlier house of Culdees here, see Easson, s.v.)

116. REDGORTON (Thistle Bridge), Perthshire, 1834   1300 x 1360

> D. 56. NSAS X, 177. (About 1,500 silver coins, of Henry III and the Edwards, and including John Balliol. Dated by coins of the Hull mint. Found under a large stone, close beside the Thistle bridge.)

117. GLASGOW (South Bridge, at foot of Niddry's Wynd), 1787   1303 x 1360

> M., p. 122. D. 112. (Dated by coin of Gaucher de Châtillon. Possible confusion with Edinburgh? — cf. nos. 77, 244.)

118. COCKBURNSPATH (Blackburn farm), Berwickshire, 1856   c.1310 x 1360

> D. 17 and p. 260. (See Dolley in NCirc 1962, 80 for sterlings of Ligny.)

119. DUMFRIES, undated   c.1310 x 1360

> W, p. 332, no. 10 (excavated at the "Traveller's Rest".)

120. CROSSCRYNE, Biggar, Lanarkshire, before 1868   c.1317 x 1360

> D. 109. Stewart in NC 1973, 139-40 and earlier notes cited there. CH I, 371. (Dated by class XIV.)

121. ABERDEEN (Dyer's Hall), 17 November 1807   1318 x 1360

> Mayhew, in BNJ XLV (1975), 36. J. C. Williams, in Numismatic Circular LXXXIII (1975), 478. "Workmen, in digging near the site of Dyer's Hall, found an earthenware jar containing nearly 2,000 pieces of various reigns and value. They are for the most part silver pennies of Edward I, II, and III; some of Alexander III; and, it is said, some of Rupert I and II." (These may have been coins of Robert I). An Elizabethan sixpence (?) was probably intrusive. The site, between George's Street and Union Street, was close to that of the Aberdeen hoard of 14 November 1807. Date of concealment 1326 or 1336? Cf. no. 58 above.

122. ASCOG, Isle of Bute, 1813   1318 x 1360

> T. 64. Wilson, Guide to Bute, 1848. Ordnance Survey Name Book, 1869. J. Blain, History of Bute, 1880, p. 47. (An immense quantity—

Craig-Brown says 4,000 — of Edwardian sterlings, with some of Alexander and of Robert, and one or two of John Balliol; coins of Flanders, etc. Lindsay describes the find-spot as "by the seaside at the foot of Mount Stewart". OS records give Ascog Bank, Millbank (NS 106638), correctly following Blain.

123. COLDINGHAM (Cairncross), Berwickshire, 1853 1318 x 1360

  D. 100 (Dated probably after 1318 by coin of Robert Bruce.)

124. DUMFRIES, before 1793 1318 x 1360

  W., p. 332. (Near Queensberry Square. Dated by coin of Bruce? Several coins, along with 4 or 5 fibulae or brooches, in a leather bag within an earthenware pot.)

125. DURISDEER (Chapel), before 1876 1318 x 1360

  W., p. 333. (Found in a well.)

126. GARVOCK (Arthurhouse farm), Kincardineshire, c. 1830 1318 x 1360

  D. 102. NSAS II, 38. (Included Robert I. Concealment c. 1332-6? — Mayhew 1975.)

127. LANGHOPE, Kirkhope parish, Selkirkshire, 1880 1318 x 1360

  D. 106. PSAS LVIII (1923-4), 160-84. T. Craig-Brown, History of Selkirkshire, I, 364. (A bronze tripod vessel 10" deep, 7" wide at the mouth, 29" in circumference, full of coins. Over 4,000 sterlings of Edward I, II, and III, Henry III, Alexander III, John Balliol, Robert I, and continental copies, together with a silver ring, two silver brooches, etc., discussed in PSAS. Found "about a mile and a quarter up the Langhope burn, in a small gulley which branches off to the left. [NT 412197?] Opposite...are two vertical ridges of bare rock, which may have been the mark by which the depositor hoped to identify the place of burial". It was suggested that the concealment may have been in 1356 during "the burnt Candlemas" or during the subsequent disorderly retreat of the English army, on the grounds that "many of the English pennies were coined just before 1356", and none later. Although Edward III pennies were identifiable by 1880, it is not clear how reliable this information is.) Brooches in Edinburgh.

128. MINTO Church, Roxburghshire, 1831   1318 x 1360

> D. 107. NSAS III, 371. About 400 English coins,
> and one or two Scottish, of Alexander and Robert,
> concealed in a wall in the church.

129. PERTH (High Street), 1818 (1812)   1318 x 1360

> NSAS X, 73. Coins found when Parliament House
> was pulled down, "chiefly of Bruce, Balliol, and
> Alexander, all pennies except for a few [halfpennies]
> of Bruce". A confused reference to the hoard of
> 1812, on which see Addendum, p. 54.

130. BROWNLEE, Lanarkshire, 1770   After 1340

> T. 60. L., p. 260. (Found in a pot.)

131. *SCOTLAND, nineteenth century?   After 1344

> D. 59 and p. 274.

132. RAEHILLS, Johnstone parish, Dumfriesshire, 1864   After 1344

> W., p. 333. ("Edward III gold rose nobles".)

133. ABERDEEN (Footdee), 1827   After 1344

> T. 3. M., p. 122, under Wellington St., Footdee
> (The account cited by Thompson does not mention
> gold coins, but merely says that "the greater part
> of them were silver, larger than a shilling".)

134. GREENLAW (Black Dykes), Berwickshire, c. 1843   After 1344

> NSAS II, 43. ("A number of gold and silver
> coins of Edward III".)

135. ARKLETON, Dumfriesshire, 1883   1344 x c.1355

> D. 3 and pp. 255-57. W., p. 333. (Silver.)

136. **DUNFERMLINE, Fife, 1896   1344 x c.1355

> T. 142. (Silver. 265 coins in a bronze jug,
> which is now in the British Museum.)

137. DALQUHARRAN Castle, Dailly, Ayrshire, c. 1818   c.1350 x c.1360

> T. 114. Dolley in BNJ XXIX (1958-9), 421.
> (Dated by penny of David II. Contained in bronze
> weight-box now in Edinburgh — cf. Med. Arch.
> III, 1959, 281.)

138.　INVERNESS, 1824 or earlier　　　　　　　　c.1350 x 1370

More than 3,000 silver coins of Henry III, the
Edwards, Alexander, Robert; pennies of David
II; in a jar. Found near Greyfriars churchyard.
Barron, The Northern Highlands in the Nineteenth
Century, I, 249. (The name rests on a confusion with
with the Blackfriars — see Easson, s.v.)

139.　PETERCULTER, Aberdeenshire, before 1795　　After c.1350?

SAS XVI, 365. "Near a handful" of silver
pennies reading Davidus Rex."

140.　WESTRUTHER (Flass farm), Berwickshire,
before 1845　　　　　　　　　　　　　　After c.1350?

NSAS II, 72. ("A few coins, belonging to the
age of David I". More likely to be David II,
unless linked with the Bamburgh find of 1844
or the coins acquired in Berwick at about the
same date.)

141.　ST. MEDAN'S CAVE, near Portankill, Wigtownshire,
c. 1825　　　　　　　　　　　　　　　　After c.1350?

PSAS XX (1885-6), 86. Sterling hoard dated by
a coin of David?

142.　*COCKLAW Castle, Hawick, Roxburghshire, before 1878　　1351 x 1370

Stewart in NC 1973, 140-2. (Silver. Found about
a hundred yards from the site of the castle [NT
524 143], one mile east of Hawick.)

143.　FLISK (East Flisk farm), Fife, before 1845　　1351 x c.1360?

NSAS IX, 601. (Silver coins of Edward III
found on the farm, described as sixpences,
shillings, and half-crowns.)

144.　ABDEN ("Kinghorn"), Fife, 1864　　　　　　c.1355

D. 33, and p. 265. PSAS V (1862-4), 137-8.
(Found close to the old mansion-house of Abden,
perhaps the site of a hunting-seat of the early
Scottish kings. Abden is perhaps the location
of Ecclesmaline. See Barrow, The Kingdom
of the Scots, p. 43.)

145.　CROALCHAPEL, Closeburn, Dumfriesshire, 1844　　After 1357

L., pp. 269-70. T. 92-3. M., p. 122. (Groats of
Edward III and David II, pennies of Edward I, II and

III, Alexander III, etc. At least 10,000 coins. About 1 mile SE of Closeburn, (?) near Closeburn Castle.)

146. REDGORTON (Balmblair farm), Perthshire, 1789   After 1357

     SS xxviii.

147. ***MONTRAVE, Fife, 1877   After 1363

     Burns, vol. i, pp. 186-220. Tatler and Stewart in BNJ XXXI (1962), 80-7. SS xii. D. 41 and pp. 267-8. Mayhew in NC 1976, 85-97. (On the basis of this famous hoard, which contained over 9,000 coins, Burns evolved his classification of Edwardian sterlings. It has continued to be a focus of numismatic study. Tatler and Stewart re-assessed the English component in 1962, offering a concordance between the Burns and Fox schemes of classification. Seaby and Stewart, with Stevenson, have established a terminus post quem of 1363. Dolley has suggested that it may have been a double hoard, the main part of which was put together in the 1330s. Montrave is an important source for imitative sterlings, which have been studied by Mayhew.)

148. DRUMNADROCHIT (St. Ninian's Chapel), Inverness-shire, 1931   After 1371

     PSAS LXVI (1931-2), 138, but Mrs. J. Murray has kindly supplied the following fuller account: David II, 11 groats and 1 half-groat, of Edinburgh; Robert II, 12 Edinburgh groats and 9 Perth groats, one half-groat, Perth.

149. LUMPHANAN, Aberdeenshire, before 1750   After 1371

     The Scots Magazine XII, 1750, 253. (In digging a new entry to the church-yard of Lumphanan, workmen found an earthen pot full of silver coins, many very corroded. Those that were legible were of David [II] and Robert [II], from the mints of Edinburgh, Perth, and Aberdeen. Cf. SAS VI, 388n. and BD:SZ 22.)

150. CRAIGIE (Camsiscan farm), Ayrshire, 1893   c.1380 x c.1390

     T. 104. D.20 and p. 261. SS xxii.

151. DIPPLE (Old Kirk), Morayshire, 1868   1385 x 1390

     Stewart in BNJ XL (1971), 57-61.

152. BIRSE (Churchyard), Aberdeenshire, before 1842   After 1371

       SS xxviii. NSAS XII, 792.

153. BRANXHOLM, Roxburghshire, 1860   After 1371

       T. 53. PSAS LVIII (1923-4); 160-84. SS xx.
       (Included brooches.)

154. CLOSEBURN, Dumfriesshire, 1829?   After 1371

       M.7.

155. DRUMLANRIG, Nithsdale, Dumfriesshire, early
nineteenth century   After 1371

       SS xxiv.

156. EDINBURGH (Samson's Ribs, Holyrood), 1831   After 1371

       SS xxv.

157. TYNRON (Pingarie Craig), Dumfriesshire, 1836
or earlier   After 1371

       SS xxviii.

158. *GLASGOW Cathedral, 1837   1390s?

       T. 172. (Gold. Lindsay records donations from
       the hoard to ten institutions.)

159. EDINBURGH, 1846   c.1390 x 1406

       T. 153.

160. KILLICHONATE farm, Kilmonivaig parish, (near
Spean Bridge, Lochaber), Inverness-shire, c. 1831   After 1390

       SS xxvi.

161. ESHA NESS (Churchyard), Shetland, 1949   After 1396

       M. 14. (Two sterlings of Eric of Pomerania.)

162. **FORTROSE, Cromarty, 1880   c.1400 x 1406

       T. 165. NC[3] IV, 189-200. PSAS LIV (1919-
       20), 51 (forgeries). SS xxvii. PSAS 1947-8,
       322. (About 1,100 groats, used by Burns
       in classifying the issues of Robert III.)

163. FORTROSE (Rosemarkie parish), Cromarty, c. 1794   After c.1400?

       SS xxviii.

164. BALGONY Farm, Abernethy parish, Perthshire, 1822 c.1400 x 1406

      Stewart in BNJ XL (1971), 57-61. Probably the
      same as M. 42, "Perthshire". (A large hoard
      of groats and half-groats of Robert III, dated
      by light coins of the Dumbarton mint.)

165. CRIEFF Church, Perthshire, 1787   After c.1410

      T. 105. SAS IX, 598. (Light lions of Robert
      III, found in a niche of the wall, 6 feet above
      the floor of the church. There were over 40
      coins, much worn, and described as "the breadth
      of a George III guinea and precisely a quarter
      of it in weight".)

166. JEDBURGH (Swinnie), Roxburghshire, before 1845   After 1424

      NSAS III, 13. (Coins of James I, concealed in
      a horn. Cf. no. 231.)

167. MILNE GRADEN, Coldstream, Berwickshire, c. 1830   After 1424

      NSAS II, 207. ("Several old coins, chiefly Scotch,
      in the reigns of the James." The house is $3\frac{1}{2}$
      miles NE of Coldstream.)

168. LOCHAR MOSS, Dumfriesshire, 1765   After c.1430

      M. 30. (Gold and silver coins, in a cow's
      horn.)

169. DALRYMPLE (Churchyard), Ayrshire, c.1827?   After 1437

      NSAS V, 279. Half-groats or groats of James I
      [sc. James II]. The two coins described are fleur-
      de-lis groats. No half-groats of this type are known,
      although they were referred to in 1451. But such
      light groats could easily have been wrongly described
      as half-groats.

170. DRYBURGH Abbey, Berwickshire, 1820   After 1437?

      L., p. 267. T. 132. ("Several gold coins of
      Robert III, James II, and Edward III".)

171. CADDER Castle, Lanarkshire, 1815   After 1437?

      T. 65. M., p. 121. (Gold. 118 lions and
      23 other gold coins of James I and II. Dug up
      in front of Cadder House among the foundations
      of the old tower. In a vessel.)

172. LINLITHGOW, June 1789   After 1437?

    SAS XIV, 570-1. The Scots Magazine LI, 1789,
    299, describes the finding of two hoards on one
    occasion: '....they, in digging four feet below
    the surface of the sand, found several pieces,
    and, upon digging a little deeper, found an earthen
    vessel with a large quantity.' (About 20 gold
    coins, and about 480, or 'upwards of 300' silver
    coins, of the different James and Henry IV. De-
    posited during the reign of James IV or V?) Cf.
    no. 256 below.

173. HIGHLANDS OF SCOTLAND, 1784   After 1437?

    M. 19. (Groats and half-groats of James I
    and II.)

174. FORGANDENNY (Freeland), Perthshire, 1876   After 1437?

    T. 163. (21 English and 16 Scottish silver coins,
    found at Freeland.)

175. GLENLUCE SANDS, Wigtownshire, 1934   After 1460

    M. 15. (Six farthings.)

176. CROOKSTONE, Renfrewshire, 1797   After 1461?

    T. 107. (In the neighbourhood of the castle.)

177. DUMFRIES (St. Mary's Friary), before 1791   After 1461?

    Metcalf in NC 1958, 80-1. (" Near the site of
    the friary at Dumfries". See Easson, s.v.)

178. AYRSHIRE, 1782   After 1461

    T. 21 (English and Scottish silver.)

179. **ABERDEEN (Bridge of Don), 1937   After c.1468

    Allen in BNJ XXXIII (1931), 282-5. (The hoard
    consisted mostly of English groats 30-40 years
    old at the time of concealment, almost all
    clipped. Found in a small, handled pottery jug.)

180. DUNSCORE, Dumfriesshire, 1961   After 1470?

    W. 332.

181. KILMARNOCK, c. 1869   1470 x 1490

    Burns, ii, 114n.

182. EDINBURGH, near, 1852   c.1480

    L., Suppl., p. 52. B II, 156. (3 or 4 silver coins
    and 3 billon placks, all of James III.)

183. **GLEN AFTON (New Cumnock), Ayrshire, 1822   c.1480?

    T. 284. (Gold and silver. All the gold was
    Scottish. The date of deposit may be earlier,
    since the firm terminus post quem is given by
    the Edward IV heavy groat. The absence of
    Scottish groats is puzzling. Over Black Craigs
    is not the find-spot.)

184. PERTH, (Castle) 1803   After 1488

    M. 41. BD:SL3. (Scottish silver and billon,
    found in a bag, in an old wall in the castle gable.)

185. ***CROSSRAGUEL ABBEY, 1919   After 1488

    PSAS 1919-20, 20ff. Ibid., 1949-50, 109ff. M. 10.
    BD:SL2. (A large hoard or accumulation of petty
    currency from a drain, including the coinages de-
    bateably attributed to bishop Kennedy of St.
    Andrews.)

186. LUSS (St. Michael's Chapel, Glenluss), Argyllshire,
before 1869   After 1488?

    W. Fraser, Chiefs of Colquhoun, vol. II, 1869,
    p. 61. Two gold and one silver coin, identified
    as unicorns of James III and IV, the silver worn.
    Found in a corner of the wall.

187. **RHONESTON, Nithsdale, Dumfriesshire, 1961   c.1490

    B. H. I. H. Stewart and R. B. K. Stevenson, in
    BNJ XXXIV (1965), 109-17; I. H. Stewart, "The
    Glenluce and Rhoneston hoards of fifteenth-
    century coins", PSAS XCIII (1959-60), 238-44.
    (83 silver and billon coins).

188. ST. ANDREWS, (North Castle Street) Fife, 1792   After 1490

    SAS XIII, 215-16. PSAS XLVI (1911-12), 351-2.
    A pottery vessel, perhaps a pirlie pig, contain-
    ing 8 gold and 150 silver coins, the latter in
    very friable condition; there were supposedly
    coins of Robert I [II] and James I. SAS describes
    what must be a rider (or possibly a half-rider)
    of James III, and a unicorn of James IV or later,
    i.e. not with EXVRGAT on both sides. A MS note

in Edinburgh records that the find was made in
a garden on the east side of Castle Wynd [now
North Castle Street], and that there were more
than 200 English, Scottish, and French silver
coins, with the names of Henry, David, and James.

189. **AYR (Wheatsheaf Inn), 1863   After c.1490

     T. 20. (Scottish and English groats, etc.)

190. ***KILKERRAN, Kintyre, Argyllshire, 1892   After c.1490

     T.208. (66 silver coins and 1 billon coin.)

191. *WICK, Caithness, 1881   After c.1490

     T. 377. (Mostly Scottish, English, and foreign
gold.)

192. ***GLENLUCE SANDS, Wigtownshire, 1956   c.1495

     B. H. I. H. Stewart, "The Glenluce hoard, 1956",
BNJ XXIX, 362-81; E. M. and H. M. Jope, I. H.
Stewart, and J. D. A. Thompson, in Medieval
Archaeology III (1959), 259-79; I. H. Stewart,
"The Glenluce and Rhoneston hoards of fifteenth-
century coins", PSAS XCIII (1959-60), 238-44
(12 silver and 100 billon coins found by Professor
and Mrs. Jope concealed in a purse or bag beside
the site of a building with a hearth.)

193. ***PERTH, 1920   After 1496

     G. Macdonald in NC 1921, 294ff. and in PSAS
1921-2, 321-4. T. 309. BD:SL4. J. E. L.
Murray in BNJ XL, 72 dates the introduction
of the light groats of James IV to 1496. One
such (broken) coin establishes the terminus
post quem. For a criticism of the attribution
of some of the coins to James IV, see I.
Stewart, "The attribution of the thistle-head
and mullet groats", BNJ XXVII, 1953, 66;
Stewart, The Scottish Coinage, pp. 66f. 18 gold,
coins, of which 17 Scottish and a Burgundian
noble; 256 English and 355 Scottish silver coins,
including a large proportion of English half-
groats; 499 placks and half-placks of billon.)

194. *** WHITBURN (Cowhill farm), Linlithgowshire, 1921   After 1496

     PSAS 1921-2, 321-4. (One gold coin, 71 English
silver, 167 Scottish silver and 5 billon. Dated
by James IV light groats with QRA — see J. E. L.
Murray in BNJ XL, 72.

195. LEITH, Midlothian, c. 1850   c.1500 or later

    M. 29 ('Billon farthings', presumably James
    IV pennies.)

196. ST. ANDREWS (Kirkhill), Fife, 1860   c.1500 or later

    M. 44 (Four copper pennies.)

197. DUMFRIES, 1615   After 1500?

    DB:SL5.

198. HADDINGTON, East Lothian, 1813   After 1509

    L., p. 266 A.S. 1890, App., p. 6 (3 gold coins
    of Henry VIII.)

199. *** CREGGAN, Argyllshire, 1876   After 1513

    BD:SL1 (219, mostly placks of James IV and V;
    one counterfeit groat; 36 James IV pennies with
    crowns and fleur-de-lis on rev.)

200. CARNWATH, Lanarkshire, 1928   After 1513

    BD:SM9.

201. **BARR (Balligmorie Farm), Girvan, Ayrshire, 1955   c.1515 x 1520

    BD:SM1 (578 billon placks, pennies, etc. of
    James III, IV, and V, in a spherical pottery
    slot-bank or "pirlie-pig".)

202. EDDLESTON (Kingside farm), Peeblesshire, 1794   After 1513

    BD:SM7

203. CLIFTON (Kirkliston parish), West Lothian, 1830   After 1513

    BD:SM4 (A large hoard of silver. BD give the
    find-place as Edinburgh.)

204. PERTH, 1896   After 1513

    BD:SM2 (French, Spanish, and Portuguese gold,
    in a pirlie pig.)

205. MAUCHLINE (Netherplace House), Ayrshire   c.1520

    Joan E. L. Murray and Ian Stewart, in BNJ
    (forthcoming). (45 English groats and half-groats,
    Edward III to Henry VIII, including 2 of Tournai
    and one of London, i.m. castle. 49 Scottish
    silver, Robert II to James IV. 2 placks, 4 pennies,
    and 1 forgery, of James IV. 1 plack of James V.
    BNJ XLI, 199 and 201.)

206. JEDBURGH (Scoonie), Roxburghshire, 1833   After 1526?

> BD:SM5. Included 2 groats given to James V.
> If correctly identified (i.e. not James III, S.
> group II), this gives a terminus post quem of
> 1526.

207. **DUNBLANE, Perthshire, 1869   1526 x c.1539

> BD:SM3. (180 gold coins, comprising 83
> Scottish, 13 English, and 84 French and
> Burgundian. Terminus post quem from the
> James V crowns.)

208. *LINLITHGOW, West Lothian, 1963   c.1530

> BD:SM6. (A large hoard of billon. Terminus post
> quem from 3 James V groats.)

209. ABERLADY, East Lothian, 1972   c.1546

> CH I, 382. (A small hoard of billon.)

210. *COLLIN (Rigghead), Torthorwald parish, Dumfriesshire,
1963   After 1553

> BD:SN1 (5 French gold crowns, 29 groats, and
> 163 billon coins.)

211. *GLASGOW, 1795   1553 x 1567

> BD:SN17. (Large hoard of gold.)

212. *HAWICK (High Street), Roxburghshire, 1876   1555 x c.1557
> BD:SN2 (558 coins, mostly bawbees of Mary.)

213. ***GLASGOW (corner of High Street and Duke
Street), 1902   After 1556

> BD:SN3. (Mainly foreign gold.)

214. JEDBURGH (Castlehill), Roxburghshire, 1822   After 1556

> BD:SN21.

215. ABERDEEN (near Marischal College), 1847   1559?

> BD:SN5 = BD:SN11. (Uncertain, before 1860.)
> Three leather or canvas bags together containing
> several thousand billon coins. The counterfeit
> hardheads of Francis and Mary are from this
> find.

216. ISLAY (Ballynaughton), Argyllshire, 1901   After 1558

   BD:SN12. (Almost all English and Irish groats,
   hidden in chamber of neolithic cairn.)

217. KIRKCUDBRIGHT, 1912   After 1558

   BD:SN4 (108 billon and 2 silver coins, in a pirlie
   pig.)

218. PLUSCARDINE PRIORY or DUFF HOUSE, 1827 After 1558

   BD:SN22.

219. **LINLITHGOW, West Lothian, 1910   After 1559

   BD:SN6. (2 groats, 50 placks, 141 bawbees,
   and 1 nonsunt.)

220. NIGG, Ross and Cromarty, before 1793   After 1559

   BD:SN24.

221. PRESTONPANS (Birseley Brae), East Lothian, 1869 After 1559

   BD:SN7 (1 gold, 2 silver, and 109 billon coins,
   mostly bawbees.)

222. ABERNETHY, Perthshire, 1866   After 1560

   BD:SN8. (510 billon and 8 silver coins.)

223. KIRKMABRECK (Holecroft farm), Kirkcudbrightshire, 1871 After 1560

   BD:SN9.

224. NEWSTEAD, Roxburghshire, 1863   After 1560

   BD:SN10. (Mostly billon.)

225. AYR, 1793   After 1562

   BD:SN13. (Three miles from Ayr, in an old
   middenstead.)

226. ABERDEEN (Norman Dykes), 1841   1542 x 1567

   BD:SN14.

227. DRUMOAK (Dalmaik farm), Aberdeenshire, 1812 1542 x 1567

   BD:SN25.

228. DUMFRIES, before 1870   1542 x 1567

   BD:SN15.

229. DUNSCORE, Dumfriesshire, 1945   1542 x 1567
        W., p. 332, BD:SN34.

230. EARLSTON, Berwickshire, 1787   1542 x 1567
        BD:SN16.

231. ECKFORD (Easter Wooden), Roxburghshire, before 1793   1542 x 1567
        BD:SN26.

232. HADDINGTON, East Lothian, 1830   1542 x 1567
        BD:SN20.

233. JEDBURGH (Swinnie), Roxburghshire, 1834   1542 x 1567
        BD:SN28 (Cf. no. 167.)

234. KAMES, Argyllshire, 1966   1542 x 1567
        BD:SN29.

235. LOCHMABEN, Dumfriesshire, before 1845   1542 x 1567
        BD:SN33.   (Site-finds?)

236. MONTROSE, Angus, 1836   1542 x 1567
        BD:SN19.

237. PERTH, 1836   1542 x 1567
        BD:SN27.

238. TRANENT, East Lothian, 1828   1542 x 1567
        BD:SN30.

239. AYR, High Street, 1914   After 1567
        BD:SO26.   (In a recess in a ground-floor wall.)

240. STORNOWAY (Steinish), Lewis, 1876   After 1572
        BD:SO1.

241. HIGH BLANTYRE (Blantyre Well), Lanarkshire, 1797   After 1572
        BD:SO11. (Pot hoard. Terminus post quem
        from James VI half-marks.)

242. BRAESIDE, Greenock, Renfrewshire, 1955   After 1573
        BD:SO2. (In a cow's horn.)

243. *BEITH (Mossend farm), Ayrshire, 1958   After 1574

        BD:SO3. (19 coins, mostly half- and quarter-
        merks of James VI, 1572-4, showing little or
        no wear.)

244. EDINBURGH (Niddry Street), Midlothian, 1786   After 1583

        BD:SO24. (Just to the E. of South Bridge. Cf.
        no. 77 of about the same date. Brown and Dolley
        give the find-place as Leith. Cf. no. 117.)

245. ABERDEEN, 1858   After 1584

        BD:SO4.

246. NORANSIDE (Tannadice), Angus, 1962   After 1587

        BD:SO20. (Billon.)

247. EDZELL Castle, Angus, before 1852   After 1588

        BD:SO5. The castle is mentioned in a letter to
        R.W.C.-P.

248. ELGIN, Morayshire, 1759   After 1588

        BD:SO14. (Suppl.) (Gold coins, in the ruins of
        a religious house.)

249. BORERAY, North Uist, 1836   After 1592

        BD:SO6.

250. ANWOTH, Kirkcudbrightshire, 1784   After 1567

        BD:SO29.

251. BONNINGTON, Midlothian, 1853   After 1567

        BD:SO12.

252. EDINBURGH (Canongate), 1821   After 1567

        BD:SO13.

253. EDINBURGH (Arthur's Seat), 1831   After 1567

        BD:SO23.

254. JOHNSTONE (Kerse of Kinnel farm), Dumfriesshire, 1827   After 1567

        BD:SO30.

255. KELLS, Kirkcudbrightshire, 1828   After 1567

        BD:SO33.

256. KELSO, Roxburghshire, 1789   After 1567

    BD:SO15 (Gold coins, found in taking down an
    old house.)

257. KIRKPATRICK DURHAM, Kirkcudbrightshire, 1967   After 1567

    BD:SO32.

258. LINLITHGOW, West Lothian, 1789   After 1567

    BD:SO16 (Gold and silver, found "in an old house",
    or "under a house". See no. 172 above.)

259. NEWMILLS, Ayrshire, 1783   After 1567

    BD:SO19.

260. SORN, Ayrshire, 1837   After 1567

    BD:SO22.

261. WEST LINTON, Peeblesshire, 1808   After 1567

    BD:SO17.

Addendum

129.   PERTH (High Street), 1812

    T. H. Marshall, The History of Perth, 1849, p. 309 gives the following
fuller account of the coins found when the old Parliament House was pulled
down: " an immense number of small silver coins... adhered together in one
concrete mass, and many of them crumbled to pieces: on being heated, almost
to fusion, in charcoal, a great number of them were recovered, and the legend
quite distinct. Several of them were of Alexander of Scotland, and of Edward
of England; but the great majority were Flemish, bearing the names of different counts of Flanders; many also had the names of bishops, such as
Episcopus Guido, on the one side, and Moneta Montes on the other" . The
coins with Guido are in all probability of Gui de Collemède, bishop of Cambrai
(1296-1300). Those with Moneta Montis are probably of Jean d' Avesnes,
count of Hainaut, (1280-1304) from the mint of Mons. If there really were
coins naming different counts of Flanders (GCOMES, RCOMES), the hoard is
unlikely to be earlier than the time of Robert (1305-22), and thus cannot belong
with the group from ca. 1300. The account given in NSAS (with a find-date of
1818) implies a terminus post quem of 1318, but a predominantly Flemish
hoard of that date is to say the least unexpected. It may be that NSAS is
confusedly describing a different hoard.

INDEX OF HOARDS

There is no logical system in the naming of hoards. Sometimes the name of the parish is used, at other times that of the hamlet or farm. Where a name has become established by use, there is little point in attempting to change it merely for the sake of consistency. A few changes have, nevertheless, been ventured in the foregoing inventory, either because more exact information about provenance has become available, or in the interest of accuracy. Alternative and outdated names have been included in this index. Abbreviations: fm. = farm, psh. = parish.

THE EVIDENCE OF SITE-FINDS AND STRAY LOSSES
FOR THE CURRENCY OF MEDIEVAL SCOTLAND

S.E. Rigold

I found myself at a disadvantage when asked to repeat for Scotland my experiment of last year on England and Wales, viz: to attempt to reconstruct the mobile, as distinct from hoarded, currency from stray losses, or rejections. Medieval site-archaeology has little to show from Scotland and less published. There has been some urban excavation, but it is very recent and only available in 'interim' reports.[1] Most of the familiar categories of abandoned peasant site, with the exception of sand-blown littoral settlements, are little known, or little studied. The local literature is very restricted, and, though the Society of Antiquaries of Scotland has a long and splendid record of medieval publication, including many of the hoards that seem so plentiful a search through eighty years of Proceedings produced very little about site-finds. Furthermore, I have not been in regular contact on numismatic matters with excavations in Scotland, though my Edinburgh colleagues in the Inspectorate of Ancient Monuments occasionally send me problems. Having almost 'drawn a blank' from other sources, I asked my colleagues what records they had of finds from 'Guardianship' Monuments since 1913 - a prime, but not the only, source for my English investigations, and in England reasonably well carded, thanks to the labours of the late B.W. Pearce. I learned that there were no cards, but that the source was almost overwhelming - nine drawers of envelopes containing coins described in varying detail, but some clearly examined by competent numismatists and usable even if the descriptions are outdated. This huge deposit deserves much more attention that I could find time for and, while 'calling for volunteers' for the future, for the purpose in hand, being unable to visit Edinburgh or to obtain photostats of the full envelopes, I can only express my gratitude to Mr. P.J. Ashmore, who bore with my persistence and communicated to me what I am passing on to you - a random sample of the medieval and sub-medieval material (about half that available) to a total of 120 in three batches of 40. I was grateful to find that each 40 produced a similar and distinctive pattern, and that, presumably, we had a valid sample in the total. The selection includes jettons, of which there were few and these generally late, and everything down to James VI in copper, billon or silver, but stops short of post-Union turners, though admitting French pieces of like date. The total of 120, only about a quarter the size of the total English sample, must be compared with, rather than supplemented by, the few coins noted in the Antiquaries' Proceedings and elsewhere, usually in special circumstances. The specimens are all well provenanced, but coming as they do, largely from old-fashioned clearances, they are seldom precisely stratified.

The predominance of specimens from relatively wealthy monuments, castles and monasteries, is matched in England and the comparison is a straight one with the proviso that Scottish foundations are generally somewhat later than English, though not so much later as to leave the twelfth and early thirteenth centuries uncovered. David I and his immediate successors were strenuous planters of abbeys. The real lacuna is in urban sites, which in England show a very distinctive chronological distribution of coins, with the Old English phase well represented. Suffice it to say that when excavation in Perth has yielded but one medieval site-coin, though that of William the Lion. It is in fact the only early site-find known to me, after the rather surprising occurrence of Northumbrian 'stycas', especially in the west.

The first problems that the sample should illuminate are those posed by hoards: first, in view of the massive presence of Edwardian pennies in Scotland and the lesser, but noticeable, incidence of Long-cross English pennies, what evidence is there for a similar English presence in Short-cross and before (?); second, in view of the persistence of worn English groats, as a kind of bullion coinage, to a late date in Scotland, did the worn pence, so typical of late medieval scatters in England, have any place in Scotland? In both cases the answer of the sample is negative. Edwardian pence are plentiful (10 in all) and the absence of Alexander III sterlings is consistent with the proportion observed in the hoards. There are no Henry III Long-cross pence in the sample, but a few isolated finds are known from other sources. On the other hand, no Short-cross or earlier pence are known to me from any source, neither are any sterling silver pence from late Edward III onwards. The picture of the hoards is thus confirmed: the doubling or trebling of available currency in England during the Short-cross phase is not attested in Scotland even by cut fractions, but the gentle rise in Long-cross may be matched by a sudden access in Scotland some 50 years after that in England; the rise in the time of Edward I, even before his assault on Scotland, is proportionately much greater than that in England, but does not seem to include fractions. The situations is a primitive one, more like that of England 300 years earlier - much greater reserves of wealth, but not necessarily much more petty trade.

The remaining 110 pieces in the sample comprise 15 jettons (mainly Nuremberg, a few French 'derivatives'), 16 foreign coins, French, English and Dutch of the 16th and 17th centuries and 79 Scottish pieces, beginning with a Robert penny that needs closer examination. The rest nearly two-thirds of the total, or over 80% if jettons and later foreign pieces are excluded, is of the 15th and 16th centuries - a high proportion by English standards. They may be tabulated, but the uncertain descriptions call for some conflation and a margin of possible error.

I   Traditional types with bust in base silver or billon.
    a.   James I groats - 2;
    b.   Pennies, one or two called 'silver', the rest billon and two called
        'James II halfpennies' — 10; three ascribed to James II, four to
        James III and three to James IV.

II Placks of the earlier type — 6; three ascribed to James III, two to James
    IV and one to James V, but this may be unreliable.

III   Ecclesiastical issues, so-called 'Crossraguel pennies' — 12, but no moneta pauperum pieces. The supposedly rare pennies, if pennies they are, thus occur more frequently than any other early base money. It may reflect rejection rather than loss, but I have knowledge of 38 provenanced specimens from 20 sites, apart from the Crossraguel hoard.[2]

IV   Mary, including Francis and Mary — 18. Only one early Bawbee (and none of James V), but 5 placks of 1557, 2 nonsunts and 10 hardheads.

V   James VI before the Union — 30; 3 silver, including a half-merk, 2 placks of the 1580s and 25 hardheads from 1588.

The foreign coins are: English — 4 silver, 2d or 6d, of Elizabeth I, not necessarily introduced before the Union; Dutch — one duit; French — 2 billon doubles tournois of Francis I, and 9 copper, 7 apparently, doubles tournois of Henry III to Louis XIV and the rest liards. At least the copper doubles seem to have been regularly current in Scotland, and closely imitated in one issue of James VI.

Of the provenances, including those culled from the Antiquaries' Proceedings, there is little to say. Out of 14 Edwardian pennies 10 are from castles and great houses and only 4 from religious sites, but of the later material it is almost '50:50' between secular and religious sites, themselves increasingly assimilated - and Holyrood, the most prolific site of all, firmly 'in both camps'. There is a great chasm between these two groups and a complete lack of anything from the later fourteenth century and the first quarter of the fifteenth. We await the full publication of the excavations at Achanduin Castle, Lismore, with its reportedly well stratified numismatic evidence of this period.[3]

The few recorded hoards containing base money might seem to provide controls on the evidence of these stray finds, but one at least shares with certain other base hoards the possibility that it represents an attempt to make the most of rejected and demonetized material as scrap rather than a reserve of something that would keep its value. This is the celebrated cache from Crossraguel Abbey[4] from which Sir George MacDonald deduced, almost certainly incorrectly, that the ecclesiastical issues were produced there, and which, if the group was truly a unity, included pennies of James III's second type, bringing the concealment down at least to c. 1492. Glenluce Sands, in Galloway, has produced several dissociated so-called 'Crossraguel Pennies', yet there were none in the poor man's hoard from the same area, found by the amazing good fortune and observance of Professor and Mrs. Jope,[5] which ends just short of James III's second type. A natural inference might be that the ecclesiastical issues date from the very end of the century, yet other indications are against this and would rather suggest that they were already withdrawn by the time of the hoard from Glenluce Sands. Their frequency as stray finds may represent a wholesale and catastrophic rejection, rather than a long and plentiful currency.

At the other end is the 'pirlie pig', ripe for 'slaughter', from Kirkcudbright, dating at earliest from 1559:[6] such finds, all too rare, surely show, even better than the pockets of those unlucky enough to end up as Moorleichen in the peat, what money might come the way of the poor or of children. The Kircudbright 'pig' contained placks, at least back to James IV; bawbees of Mary but none of the earlier type; a Mary penny, but none of the older base pence, to say nothing of ecclesiastical issues, as though they were all clean gone; numerous fresh hardheads and two billon doubles tournois of Francis I, bearing strong witness that these as well as the later copper doubles, were accepted in Scotland.

NOTES

1. As in Med. Arch., xviii (1974), 207.

2. These are:

   Borders and Galloway: Crossraguel (outside the cache); Skirling Castle; Stevenston Sands; Foulden House; Glenluce Sands; Jedburgh.

   Lothian: Crichton Castle; Edinburgh Castle; Holyrood; Inchcolm; Traprain Law; Linlithgow Palace.

   Fife and the Midland Valley: Cambuskenneth Abbey, Dunfermline Abbey; St. Andrews Sands; St. Andrews Kirkheugh; Tantallon Castle.

   Moray: Balvenie Castle; Culbin Sands.

   England: Coventry.

3. Med. Arch., xviii (1974), 197.

4. PSAS, liv (1919-20), 20ff.

5. BNJ, xliv xxix (1960), 362-81.

6. PSAS, xliv (1912), 352.

THE VOLUME OF EARLY SCOTTISH COINAGE

Ian Stewart

When I was invited to contribute a paper on the volume of the Scottish coinage and currency in the sterling period, it quickly became clear to me that a great deal of evidence had first to be assembled about hoards containing Scottish coins of the twelfth to fourteenth centuries and about the number of dies involved in each issue. At the meeting I was able to present some broad conclusions in the context of a general survey of the coinage of the period. The written text, however, in covering the evidence as well as its interpretation, has out-grown the scale of other papers read at the Symposium and included in this volume. It therefore seems more appropriate for it to be published separately, but I welcome the Editor's request to contribute here a short summary of my principal findings about the size of the early Scottish coinage, since these constitute part of the basic evidence referred to by others. I.S.

INTRODUCTION

The year 1358 marks the end of a period of more than two centuries during which the basic coin in Scotland as in England was the silver penny, or sterling.[1] No Scottish mint accounts have been preserved from before that date. Indirect methods are therefore needed for obtaining information about the amount of coinage issued during the sterling period. Two kinds of evidence have been used in reaching the conclusions set out below, first, die-analysis of the extant material and, second, the percentages of Scottish coins present in hoards relative to English (or Irish) coins of which the mint output figures are known.

Medieval coins were struck from hand-made dies which, although in each series mostly made with the same or similar punches, usually differ sufficiently in minor details and in the exact arrangement of lettering and other elements of design to enable them to be identified and counted without undue difficulty. Since such dies eventually wore out (if they had not already broken or split) as a result of repeated hammering, they had frequently to be replaced, and the number of dies used is therefore a rough indicator of the size of a coinage. To date I have carried out a thorough die-analysis of all Scottish coins struck before 1250 that are accessible to me, and of substantial samples of the issues of 1250 to 1358. Statistical formulae have been evolved which permit the approximate number of dies used in a coinage to be estimated from the number of them actually observed in a sample of coins of given size.[2] This method gives the most accurate results when the coinage was continuous and sustained (so that dies were fully and more or less evenly used), when the extant sample is random and unbiased (ideally, when the coins are drawn from a number of hoards spread in time and place), and when the sample is large

65

enough for most of the known dies to be recorded from more than a single specimen. These conditions in general apply to Scottish coinage from the thirteenth century onwards, but in the twelfth century the coinage was patchy and the material is unevenly preserved.

When both are available, a figure for the number of dies used, multiplied by an estimate of their likely average output, will produce a reasonably reliable assessment of at least the order of magnitude of the original mintage. There are several well-documented calculations of die-output at English mints in the thirteenth and fourteenth centuries.[3] Average output of 25,000 coins per obverse die was commonly achieved, and figures two or even three times higher were not beyond the physical capability of the die at periods of intensive coinage, especially at temporary mints distant from the source of dies. In the twelfth century, when the volume of coinage was significantly lower and its production less centralised, minting was sporadic and often intermittent. The survival-rate of coins from different obverse dies varies widely before the Short Cross period, and this variation must reflect differences of die-output as well as circumstances and chance of survival. Although individual dies were sometimes used to exhaustion (as their later products demonstrate),[4] many others were in all probability used for much less than their productive capacity. In some cases this must have been due to premature breakage, but in others to discontinuous or occasional minting. It is therefore impossible, in our present state of knowledge, to decide by how much thirteenth century figures for average die-output should be scaled down to allow for this factor of under-use through circumstance, or for the (presumed) inferiority of twelfth century manufacturing techniques.

Hoard evidence[5] too is least satisfactory for the twelfth century. Although well recorded hoards from the period of the Short and Long Cross coinage (1195-c. 1280) are relatively few, several of them were very large and representative. From the Edwardian period the hoards are plentiful, although they are mainly from the 1320s or later by which time little coinage had been produced in Scotland for upwards of 30 years. The usefulness of hoard proportions for estimating the size of an issue depends upon the thoroughness and speed with which coins from the various mints in England, Scotland and Ireland became evenly mixed in the currency. After a brief initial phase of interchange in the Stephen period, Scottish and English coins appear to have become intergrated with each other in circulation only to a very limited degree in the second half of the twelfth century. The process of interchange quickly developed again in the thirteenth century and by the Edwardian period was rapid and thorough. Although there was always some delay in the intergration of coins from the peripheral mints of the sterling area (which of course included those from Scotland), neither this factor nor an element of selective bias in favour of or against Scottish coins that can sometimes be detected seems to have been of sufficient force to upset the general testimony of hoard proportions about the content of the currency, especially when several hoards are available for comparison. On all these counts the hoard evidence is most reliable for the Edwardian period; though less comprehensive it is also sufficient to be meaningful for the second and third quarters of the thirteenth century, but not for earlier coinages.

THE EARLY STERLINGS (1136- c. 1170)

Before the introduction of the Crescent type of William I (1165-1214) in c. 1170 (?), Scottish coinage was sporadic and intermittent. The surviving material is too uneven and incomplete for reliable estimates to be made of the number of dies used, except in a few of the series. The picture is complicated by the fact that the various mints do not always appear to have been striking coins of the same type. An approximate general sequence can be worked out, but the absolute dating is an open question in the absence of a satisfactory chronology for the fragmented coinage of England in the Stephen period.

Scottish coinage began as a result of the capture of Carlisle in January 1136 by David I (1124-53). Of the earliest coins (period a), a few are copied from the last type of Henry I but most from the first type of Stephen. They are of Carlisle (in Stephen's name), Corbridge (in Prince Henry's) and Edinburgh (in David's). I have counted 31 specimens from 15 obverse dies.

During period b, which falls between period a and. the introduction of a coinage of unified type (Cross Fleury) late in David's reign, a number of mints were operating, including Newcastle for Earl Henry (in Stephen's name). David's principal issues were from Carlisle (with reverse type a cross with pellet-in-annulet/crescent in each angle) and Edinburgh (still with Stephen's type), but each of these types is known from other mints. I have records of about 20 of the Carlisle coins, from 5 obverse dies, and a similar number of the Edinburgh ones from 7 (?) obverse dies. While these issues therefore seem to be quite thoroughly known to us, between 25 and 30 other coins are recorded from at least 15 obverse dies, many of them individually unique.

The early Cross Fleury coins (period c) are known of five mints, Berwick (28 coins, 4 obverse dies), Roxburgh (17 coins, 4 obverses), Carlisle (4 coins, 2 obverses), Aberdeen (1 coin) and Perth? (1 coin). It is impossible to assess the scale of the Cross Fleury coinage beyond the Border mints.

A derivative series of Cross Fleury coins may have continued after David's death, since it is represented in English hoards of the 1160s and 1170s. Among some eighty specimens I have noted about 30 obverse dies. Coins in the name of Malcolm IV (1153-65) and of the pre-Crescent issues of William I are extremely rare. Of Malcolm I have noted about 15, 7 from one obverse die, 2 from another and the rest all different. All seven early coins of William are from different dies. Roxburgh appears to have been the major, sometimes only, mint in the post-David period.

Even in the cases where a reasonable estimate can be made of the number of dies used, it is dangerous to attempt to calculate the size of the issues concerned because of the impossibility of assessing average die-output. Not only are we without information about the productive capacity of dies at this period, but there is reason to believe that many dies would not have been fully used.

THE CRESCENT COINAGE (1170s - 1195)

A coinage of uniform type was again established in the 1170s, with a pellet-in-crescent in each angle of the reverse cross. The only sequential division that can be made in a coinage that lasted for 20 years or more is according to the sceptre-head, at first a square cross like that on the 1158-80 coinage of Henry II of England, later a cross pommée as on the English Short Cross coinage from 1180 onwards. Roxburgh was much the largest mint, with Perth in the square cross series, and Edinburgh in the cross pommée series, the more active of the other mints.

I have records of nearly 300 Crescent sterlings, from about 55 obverse dies. Average die-output of 15-20,000 coins would mean an issue of about one million coins, or £4,000, assuming that we know most of the original dies, which seems likely but is only a provisional assumption in the absence of fuller hoard evidence. In the light of figures for the thirteenth century, higher die output is possible, especially since some obverse dies show signs of extensive use and renovation. On the other hand, others may have produced much less than the average as a result of imperfect technology and irregular patterns of minting.

THE SHORT CROSS COINAGE (1195-1250)

In Scotland the Short Cross coinage began long after the type had been introduced in England (1180). Five phases of the coinage have been identified: (a), the earliest, during William I's lifetime, struck at Roxburgh, Perth and Edinburgh; (b), mostly with the joint moneyers' names, Hue Walter, but without mint name, extending into the reign of Alexander II (1214-40), although still in William's name; (c), again in William's name, but certainly issued by Alexander, and struck at Roxburgh only; (d), in Alexander's name, and again almost entirely of Roxburgh; and (e), a tiny issue from Berwick, with an unbearded face and so presumably of Alexander III (1249-86) before the introduction of the Long Cross type in 1250.

Coins of phase a are scarce in English finds, chiefly because the main finds, like Eccles and Colchester, were buried late in the Short Cross period. However, they are well represented in the French hoards[6] of their own period and must have constituted an issue of respectable size. Among 95 coins checked, 33 obverse dies have been noted, 20 used exclusively at Roxburgh, 6 at Perth and 4 at Edinburgh, the other three dies being shared. If 35-40 obverse dies were originally used, an average die-output of 20-25,000 would mean an issue of £3-4,000.

Coins of phase b are the most plentiful. I have examined about 400 from 72 obverse dies, and the number of dies used is unlikely to have exceeded 80, even perhaps 75. The appearance of the coins suggest rather heavy die-output: an average of 25,000 coins per die would mean an issue of £7,500, or of 40,000 one of £12,000. Coins of phase b predominate in hoards buried from c. 1215 until the end of the Short Cross coinage.

57 coins of phase c are from only 8 dies and their relative abundance is largely due to Eccles (where they were the latest of the Scottish series) and Colchester. A central guess at the size of issue would be £1,000.

The autonomous coins of Alexander II (phase d) are very rare, and because hoards from the 1240s are few they are less thoroughly known than the coins of phases b and c. I have checked 33 specimens and found 13 obverse dies, but there are probably more to be found. An issue of between £1,500 and

£3,000 seems likely. Although several Berwick dies are known of phase e, with the head of Alexander III, all the Short Cross coins struck from them are individually unique, and they were apparently superseded before being much used. It is therefore impossible to estimate the size of the issue, but the extreme rarity of the coins suggests a few hundred pounds at most.

Adequate hoard evidence for the chronology of the early Short Cross coinage is lacking. Phase a may have lasted for 10/15 years and phase b for 15/20. Phase c began before the Eccles hoard (c. 1230) and phase d before Colchester (c. 1237). Approximate dates would therefore be: a, 1195-1205/10; b, 1205/10 - later 1220s; c, later 1220s to mid-1230s; d, mid 1230s to 1249. On this reckoning, the average annual volume of coinage would have been greatest during phase b, but at a very low level during phases c and d, when the London and Canterbury mints were at their most active. This explains the reduced proportion of Scottish to English coins in the later Short Cross hoards.

THE LONG CROSS COINAGE (1250- c. 1280)

Our knowledge of the Scottish Long Cross coinage is derived mainly from the Colchester (1969)[7] and Brussels hoards. The Scottish coins in Colchester (deposit summer 1256) amounted to 489 against about 11,300 English (4.3%) and in Brussels (c. 1264?) to about 2,200 (?) against about 80,000 (less than 3%), whilst an even lower proportion is found in some later, smaller hoards. It appears that the bulk of the Scottish Long Cross coinage took place during the recoinage of the early 1250s (which was completed by the date of Colchester); again the Scottish issues tailed off, as in the Short Cross period, while London and Canterbury continued to coin heavily in the later 1250s and 1260s.

Output figures are preserved for the mints of Shrewsbury (£7,167) and Dublin (£43,239) in the recoinage, and the obverse dies used at each have been counted (37 and 154). Based on the Colchester and Brussels proportions, these figures would suggest a Scottish coinage of some £50/60,000 up to 1256. A sample die-analysis of the coins of Aberdeen and Ayr indicates output of some 60,000 and 40,000 coins per obverse die respectively, compared with 70,000 at Dublin and 46,000 at Shrewsbury. In the following ten years another £5/10,000 may have been struck (all at Berwick); between 1265 and 1280, the coinage seems to have been at a low level, but in the absence of very late hoards it cannot be quantified.

A recoinage with named mints provides evidence for the distribution of the currency immediately before it. The Long Cross recoinage is the only instance of this kind in Scotland. 25% of the issue (and almost the whole of the coinage after the regional mints were closed) took place at Berwick; another 25% at Perth and Roxburgh; 20% at Dumfries, Edinburgh and Aberdeen; and the remainder divided between Glasgow, Ayr, Stirling, St Andrews, Forfar, Lanark, Inverness, Kinghorn, Renfrew and Montrose.

THE SINGLE CROSS COINAGE (c. 1280-1357)

The Scottish Single Cross sterlings were produced in five distinct phases: I, from c. 1280 until and probably beyond the death of Alexander III (1286), and in his name; II, in the name of John Balliol (1292-6); III, under Robert

Bruce (1306-29), after his recovery of the kingdom, not before 1313/4 and probably not until the recapture of Berwick in 1318; IV, in the 1330s and/or 1340s (halfpence and farthings only); and V, in the earlier 1350s, after Edward III had reduced the weight of the English penny to 18gr. in 1351. The volume of the coinage in these phases differed dramatically, and there were intervals without coinage in between. Output was substantial in phase I and modest in phase II; then, while Berwick was in English hands from 1296 and much of Scotland was occupied, there appears to have been no coinage at all for 20 years or so. Bruce's coinage was very small, and the issue of fractional coins in the earlier years of David II (1329-71) even smaller. The final issue of sterlings (phase V) met with resistance in England because of deficient weight, and was soon overshadowed in circulation by the new groat coinage of 1358.

Because of the wars, hoard evidence for the Edwardian era abounds, although there is little for the period before 1290 (phase I), when the bulk of the Scottish Single Cross coinage took place. Most of the Edwardian hoards were buried well into the fourteenth century, particularly in the 1320s and 1330s. Since virtually all the Scottish sterlings had been struck by 1296 while the bulk of the English coinage was produced in the first quarter of the fourteenth century, these later hoards show a small and diminishing percentage of Scottish coins.

The mint accounts for London and Canterbury are virtually complete for the whole Edwardian period, and figures are also known for six English provincial mints in the partial recoinage of 1300.[8] By reference to the early London and Canterbury issues in hoards, it is possible to obtain from the proportion of Scottish coins an idea of the size of the Alexandrian coinage relative to known English mint output up to 1290. These figures suggest a total for the issues of Alexander in the range of £130-180,000. A sample check has produced an estimated average die-output of 25/35,000 coins, which is exactly in line with the known English figures for the reigns of Edward I and II. There were also a few round halfpence and farthings of Alexander.

For the Balliol coinage comparison may also be made with the English figures for 1300 as well as with the early issues of London and Canterbury. About £9,000 worth of Balliol pence may have been struck, and since the halfpence of this reign (there are no farthings) are rather commoner than Alexander's, the overall total was probably about £10,000. Average output of the 55 obverse penny dies would be about 40,000 coins.

About 11 obverse dies for pennies of Robert Bruce have been noted among 55 coins checked, probably implying an issue of £2,000 or less. There were also 2 or 3 dies each for Bruce halfpence and farthings.

Only about 15 halfpence and farthings are recorded in all of the early coinage of David II (phase IV); since they include several die-duplicates, the issue must have been tiny. Thirty obverse dies for the post-1351 pennies have been noted among more than 150 specimens checked, so that few others seem likely to be found. Depending on the estimate for average die-output (presumably in the range 25,000 to 40,000), the size of this coinage (phase V) is likely to have been between £3,000 and £5,000.

No mint names, except that of the bishop's mint at St Andrews under John Balliol, appear on the Scottish Single Cross sterlings. But Berwick was probably the main mint of Alexander and John. It is also the likeliest candidate for Bruce's mint, but having been lost to the English in 1333, was unavailable to David II after that. Edinburgh, the prime mint from 1358, seems to have the strongest claim to have produced the coins of phases IV and V. Only in the Alexandrian recoinage were provincial mints (apparently) used, but we have no sure means of telling which were indicated by the code embodied in the combinations of stars and mullets on the reverse (six of which are found regularly).

Although we do not know where the mints were, we can be confident that most of the Alexandrian coinage resulted from reminting old (mostly English) Long Cross coins, and so may deduce that the volume of currency in Scotland had multiplied by two or three times between 1250 and 1280. The last twenty years of the thirteenth century were thus the high point of the Scottish sterling coinage. Output in the first half of the fourteenth century was economically insiginficant because the mints were kept idle at first by the English occupation and from the 1320s, when again available, by the sharp change in the availability of silver in the British Isles, from surplus to dearth. Silver was only brought back to English and Scottish mints after 1350 by reductions in the weight of the coins which permitted a more realistic mint price for bullion.

NOTES

1. The most extensive series of illustrations of Scottish sterlings is still that in E. Burns, The Coinage of Scotland, 1887. A more modern account of the coinage may be found in Stewart, The Scottish Coinage, 2nd. edn. 1967, but important revisions to the arrangement and chronology of twelfth and thirteenth century coinage have been made in Stewart, 'Scottish Mints', in Mints, Dies and Currency, ed. Carson, 1971, 165-289.

2. C. S. S. Lyon, "The Estimation of the Number of Dies Employed in a Coinage", Numismatic Circular, 1965, 180; cf. NC 1964, 298.

3. Stewart, "Medieval Die-Output" and "Second Thoughts on Medieval Die-Output", NC 1963, 97-106 and ibid., 1964, 293-303; M. Mate, "Coin Dies under Edward I and II", NC 1969, 209-18; J. D. Brand, "The Shrewsbury Mint, 1249-50", Mints, Dies and Currency, 129-50; for Dublin see BNJ XLIV (1974), 43-4.

4. Stewart, 'Mints', p. 259.

5. For lists of hoards and references see J. D. A. Thompson, Inventory of British Coin Hoards, A.D. 600-1500, 1956; M. Dolley and W. Seaby, SCBI Ulster Museum Belfast, Part I, 1958, pp. xlvii-lv; Dolley, "The Irish Mints of Edward I in the Light of the Coin-Hoards from Ireland and Great Britain", PRIA 1968, vol. 66, C3, 235-97; and D. M. Metcalf, "The Evidence of Scottish Coin Hoards for Monetary History, 1100-1600", in this volume, pp. 1-57.

6. J. Yvon, "Esterlins à la croix courte dans les trésors français de la fin du XIIe et de la première moitié du XIIIe siècle", BNJ XXXIX (1970), 24-60.

7. BNJ XLIV (1974), 39-61.

8. C. G. Crump and C. Johnson, " Tables of Bullion Coined under Edward
    I, II and III" , NC 1913, 200-45; cf. NC 1969, 217-8.

THE QUALITY OF SCOTTISH STERLING SILVER 1136-1280

D. M. Metcalf

If the speedometer of one's car reads 28 m.p.h., and one accelerates until it reads 30 m.p.h., one can accept as quite accurate the instrumental information that one is travelling 2 m.p.h. faster than before. But whether the speedometer is accurately calibrated is another question. It may be that in reality one was travelling at 28.4 and 30.4 m.p.h., or 27.7 and 29.7 m.p.h. The absolute accuracy of the instrument, to within such narrow limits, cannot be guaranteed, whereas the relative difference, of 2 m.p.h., is information of a higher quality, the main limitation on it being the practical difficulty of reading very small units off the dial of the speedometer. This analogy may help to explain the first difficulty encountered in attempting to determine the silver contents of Scottish twelfth- and thirteenth-century sterlings by non-destructive analysis, using a small X-ray fluorescence spectrometer.[1]

The procedure involves several separate measurements and calculations. The ratio of silver to copper is measured on the edge of the coin, and is compared with standards of known composition.[2] Let us say that it is found to be $1\frac{1}{2}\%$ higher than a standard containing 92.5% silver and 7.5% copper. The ratio in the coin, then, is 94% silver to 6% copper, and this information is accurate to within quite narrow limits. The practical difficulty here is not in distinguishing small instrumental differences, but in the construction of the calibration curve on graph paper. A curve drawn from fixed points (standards) at 90.5, 92.5, and 97.5% silver allows readings at intervals of about 0.25%, and the result should certainly be within ± 0.5%, with no reason to expect any systematic error (i.e. the average derived from analyses of a group of coins should be very accurate).

But the Scottish sterlings are not the product of modern technology. They contain adventitious traces of gold and lead, small additions of zinc, and almost certainly traces of other chemical elements too, such as bismuth, antimony, tin, and nickel. These various additions or contaminations may add up to 2 or 3% of the total alloy, and the silver ratio figure, calculated on the assumption that silver and copper together equal 100%, is to that extent in error. The silver and copper percentages need to be adjusted pro rata to allow for the trace elements.

Very small proportions, e.g. 1% or less, are difficult to measure accurately with the "Isoprobe", because the signal they emit is weak in relation to the background "noise". Any element, present in the coins, which is ignored in the analysis will cause the final result for silver to be that much too high. In the present series of analyses, for example, it was impracticable to measure bismuth, which was probably present in amounts of around 0.1%. From the point of view of any historical conclusions, this inaccuracy will not matter very much;

but greater errors in the silver figure could arise from inexact measurement of the lead in the sterlings, where the total may be around 1%.

Thus the trace-elements introduce a further small degree of uncertainty into the result, comparable to the uncertainty between 30 m.p.h. and 29.7 m.p.h. The best way to overcome this likely inaccuracy is to take care to draw one's conclusions from relative figures — the differences observed between one coin and another. Thus if one wishes to ask whether Scottish sterlings were any different in their alloy from the contemporary English coins, it is highly inadvisable to analyse some Scottish sterlings and then to compare the results with previously published figures for English coins. This would be to rely on two different speedometers, both possibly inaccurate, in order to establish a very small difference in speed. Similarly with the trace-elements: the calibration may unfortunately be slightly adrift, but comparisons should be substantially reliable.

In endeavouring to discover the intended fineness of the coins, the figure of consequence is not the percentage of the chemical element silver (Ag), but what the workmen of the time thought was silver, namely their refined metal which still included small amounts of copper, lead, gold, and bismuth. To approximate to this, the total observed quantities for silver plus lead plus gold have been quoted as the "silver" contents of each coin. Any inaccuracies in the lead results, arising for example from segregation in the alloy, will be largely discounted by the pro rata method of computation, as the percentage for silver is adjusted downwards by an amount almost equal to the lead percentage, and that same figure is subsequently added in to the total for "silver".

The next practical difficulty arises from the difference between the alloy of a medieval coin as it is now, and as it was when it was made. After lying in wet soil for several hundred years, the metal is likely to have been microscopically penetrated and corroded, and some elements may have been preferentially leached out of the alloy. Coins are usually "surface-enriched" in this way: that is to say, a thin surface zone is richer in silver than it originally was, because some of the copper has been dissolved out by ground-water. It is necessary for the analyst to file off this surface layer, to reach what he hopes is unaltered metal. The X-rays can be focussed onto an area of only 1 or 2 mm^2, and a cleaned patch on the edge of the coin is therefore ample. No damage is visible on the face of the coin. But failure to abrade the edge sufficiently — and, obviously, one does not want to do more damage to the coin than is essential for an accurate result — can lead to errors far greater than the errors of calibration discussed above.[3] So can a failure to position the cleaned area exactly so that the X-ray beam is centred on the centre line of the edge of the coin, since corrosion is liable to be greater at the corner (between the face and the edge). Care was taken in the analyses presented here to minimize any errors arising from the positioning of the coin. All in all, however, it must be said that the results (below) calculated to two decimal places should not mislead anyone into assuming that the measurements are that accurate. Re-measurement of the same coin by exactly the same procedure would give a slightly different result. An element of uncertainty will always remain with non-destructive analyses. Since there is no prospect of carrying out large-scale destructive analyses on thousands of pounds' worth of coins, many of which are historically too precious to sacrifice even if their financial value were of no consideration, one can only choose the lesser of two evils. It remains desirable, however, to correlate the X-ray fluorescence results with at least a few destructive analyses. No modern exact analyses of Scottish sterlings have been made, but there have been several scientific enquiries into the metal contents of English sterlings of the eleventh to thirteenth centuries. They indicate that the fineness was very reliably maintained in most reigns except that of Stephen, and that the coins tended to exceed the 92.5% prescription by up to 2 or even 3%. This excellent result was achieved to some extent by rule of thumb, for it was not commercially practicable to refine silver to 100% purity. The definition of sterling silver as 11 oz. 2 dwt. of pure silver to 18 dwt. of alloy may be a later rationalization of a traditional standard that had been evolved and established in the mid-eleventh century by the use of practical recipes and procedures that were modified or superseded in the late thirteenth century.[5]

For trace-elements, the most careful and exact analyses of sterlings are those published by Forbes and Dalladay. They are helpful as an indication of of the accuracy or otherwise of the "Isoprobe" in measuring elements present in fractions of one per cent.

Early Scottish coins, which were intended to be of the same quality as the English coins alongside which they circulated, have not hitherto been analysed in such a way as to provide statistically reliable averages of the standards achieved, nor of the parameters of variation in fineness. One coin in the name of David I from the Bute hoard is in fact the only analysis of a sterling that I have come across. It was found (by destructive or "wet chemical" analysis) to contain 86.4% silver, 7.75% copper, and 5.59% gold.[6] Such a large admixture of gold, one can now say, is very unusual indeed. Presumably it was unwitting, and entered the alloy with the silver; if so, the "silver" contents should be stated as 92.06%. The gold contents of the coin are enough to make one wonder whether it was a contemporary imitation, rather than the product of a regular Scottish mint.

Scottish silver plate of the sixteenth and seventeenth centuries has been analysed chemically,[7] but the results probably have very little bearing on mint practice before 1280.

It is hoped that the foregoing remarks will have served to make clear to readers not acquainted with the techniques of non-destructive analysis that one should not accept the percentages of various elements measured in a coin as infallibly true, and that elaborate procedural safeguards are advisable even when conclusions are going to be drawn only from within-sample variations.

Silver, copper, gold, lead, and zinc were measured in all the coins listed below, and tin was looked for in a selection of them but was not found in any measurable amounts.

I. Silver Contents

David's early coins, with ca. 93-94% "silver" adhere closely to the best English standard. The cross-fleury coins which followed them in the 1140s, however, fall as low as 86% "silver", and the issue seems to have been extensively debased by several percentage points. In this it was probably no worse than Stephen's first issue, which was of similarly variable quality. One coin of Malcolm IV was available for analysis: it falls within the pattern of the cross-fleury type.

William the Lion's crescent-pellet coinage is on a restored standard of 93-94½% "silver", which may be regarded as the norm. The earliest English Short cross sterlings exceed the standard, and contain 94-95½% "silver". (The figures published by Yvon, from neutron activation analyses by Gordus, are in effect silver-copper ratios. For the early Short cross coins they range around 95½-96%, thus marginally higher than the XRF results). The Scottish Short voided cross issue, begun in 1195, was likewise 94-95%, until the introduction of variety D (coins in the name of Alexander II, belonging to the late 1230's or the 1240's), when there was a distinct falling-off, to ca. 91½-94½%. The scarcity of variety D suggests that, if it was in issue for any length of time, there was little work for the Roxburgh mint (and virtually none for any of the other mints). The temporary decline in alloy thus probably coincides with a very slack period for the inflow of bullion.

The Long voided cross sterlings, introduced at the recoinage of 1250, contain 93-94½% "silver", and are apparently closely in line with the English coins.

II. Lead Contents

Lead persists in the silver from the refining process. Forbes and Dalladay found amounts ranging from 0.44 to 2.1% in English sterlings in the period under review, with an average of 1.07%. Very similar results were obtained from the Scottish and English sterlings analysed by XRF, with no obvious trends or differences between the two series.

III. Zinc Contents

Zinc was deliberately added to the coinage metal in England from the Anglo-Saxon period until the middle of the twelfth century, in order to improve its malleability. Forbes and Dalladay found as much as 4.0 and 4.7% in two coins of the 1130's. In another ten specimens ranging in date from ca. 1163 to c. 1300, however, zinc was virtually absent (less than 0.02%). It would seem, therefore, that there was a change in mint-practice at a date near to the middle of the twelfth century.

The measurement of small quantities of zinc using the "Isoprobe" is difficult, since the zinc peak occurs at a point in the spectrum in between the two copper peaks, and is swamped by them. The peak height can be measured, and it has been assumed that values of less than 5% of the height of the primary copper peak merely reflect background noise or scatter. Coins of Stephen, on the other hand, give values of up to ca. 10% peak height.

McKerrell's experiments have shown that cupellation readily removes zinc to below 0.1%.[8] The only Scottish sterlings which show zinc in quantities above this "floor" level are a few early coins from the Borders. It seems likely, therefore, that the practice of adding zinc was never regularly followed in Scotland. (Significant amounts of zinc were measured, on the other hand, in English short-cross sterlings minted in 1180-9; and conversely very little was found in the preceding cross-and-crosslets sterlings. This seems to run counter to Forbes and Dalladay's findings from four somewhat later short-cross coins, minted c. 1200-15. Further research is desirable).

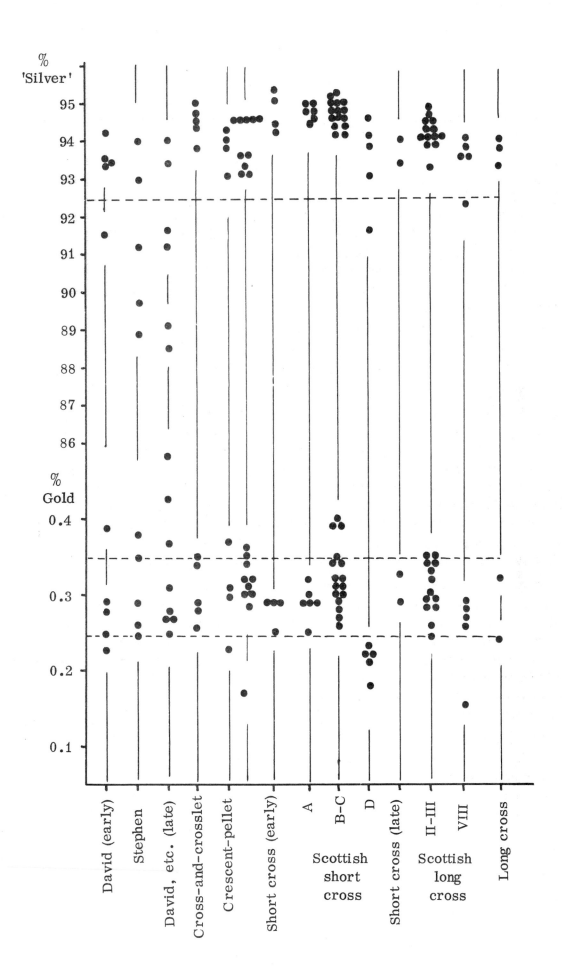

IV. Gold Contents

Gold, being a noble metal, may be expected to survive the cupellation process without loss, and any traces of gold in the coinage silver should therefore be in almost exactly the same proportion after reminting. If Scottish sterlings were struck by melting down old coins withdrawn from a currency that was predominantly made up of English coins, one might expect that the gold trace levels would coincide. In general this seems to be the case, although the experimental data are not of sufficiently high quality to stand on their own.

Forbes and Dalladay found 0.44% gold in a coin of Stephen, and 0.46% in a Cross-and-crosslets sterling. Four sterlings from the years 1200-25 contained 0.20-0.28% gold. Harris has also found an average of 0.55% gold in four coins of Stephen, but only 0.2% in a Short-cross sterling, and 0.1-0.25% in six coins of Edward I. Yvon has published clear evidence of a decline in the gold contents of Short-cross sterlings as between Groups I-II and III-IV. The "Isoprobe" results for Group I (0.25%, and three at 0.29%) are perhaps marginally higher than the neutron activation results by Gordus, which Yvon published (0.2-0.3%).

The English evidence in general is of a fall in the gold contents during the twelfth century (coinciding with a rapid supplementation of the national stock of bullion). The "new" silver with lower gold traces presumably came from the continent to balance the British export surplus.

The accurate measurement of gold by the "Isoprobe" is hampered when zinc is present in the alloy, as there is a secondary zinc peak in the spectrum coinciding closely with the primary gold peak at 9.7 keV. Discounting the contribution of the zinc to the combined peak introduces rather wide margins of error. With that proviso, it would seem that there was relatively little variation in the gold traces in Scottish sterlings, and that they correspond quite well with the English coins from which they might be assumed to have been reminted. Where there are differences, one may consider the possibility that the bullion for the Scottish coins was coming from continental rather than English money.

The graph, p. 77, illustrates the pattern of gold traces. The sterlings of David I match those of Stephen. William the Lion's crescent-pellet coinage, particularly in its second phase, shows a compact distribution. In the short voided cross series, phase b seems to be more scattered than a or c. Phase d sterlings (in the name of Alexander II) are conspicuous by their low gold traces, and there is no obvious reason to doubt the validity of this difference. The long voided cross coins revert to the normal value of around 0.3% gold, although the later issues of the type again seem to be lower.

Any future programme of study of the gold traces will obviously need to achieve a high degree of instrumental accuracy and consistency, and equally will need to be based on a large number of specimens. The coins of Alexander II deserve further study; and it may turn out that there are small differences between the distribution-patterns for some of the mints in the long voided cross coinage.

V. Other Trace Elements

Other elements were not measured. One may presume that the Scottish sterlings contain ca. 0.05% bismuth, ca. 0.01% antimony, and occasionally up to 0.1% tin. Of these, bismuth deserves study.

VI. Forgeries, etc.

One analysis has been excluded from the list below, as being uncertain. A crescent-pellet sterling of William the Lion was found to contain only ca. 77% silver. There is no obvious reason, however, to doubt the coin's authenticity.

VII. Summary

The quality of Scottish sterling silver corresponded very closely with its English counterpart. Its high standard faltered in the 1140's, but was restored by a reform undertaken in ca. 1174. There were signs of weakness again for a few years ca. 1240. Otherwise the alloy tended to be, if anything, above what we take to have been the legal prescription. The fineness was, however, to some extent governed by traditional, "rule-of-thumb" workshop procedures.

Of the trace-elements in the metal, gold is virtually unchanged in its proportion to silver by recycling of the coinage metal. The pattern of gold traces in Scottish sterlings generally seems to match the pattern in the contemporary or preceding English sterlings which one might have assumed to be the obvious and major source of bullion. Where the gold traces are different, and in particular lower than expected, the Scottish mints were perhaps re-striking foreign coins that came into the country through trade directly with the continent.

Zinc was not used in the Scottish sterlings, although they may have contained traces (deriving from English bullion) of up to ca. 0.1%, which cupellation had failed to remove. In the same way lead occurred in the silver in amounts of around 1%.

NOTES

1. The instrument used was the Isoprobe, for which see E. T. Hall, F. Schweizer, and P. A. Toller, "X-ray fluorescence analysis of museum objects: a new instrument", Archaeometry XV (1973), 53-78. The Isoprobe uses a lithium-drifted silicon detector, a miniature X-ray tube, and a multichannel analyser. For the detection limits, see F. Schweizer, "X-ray fluorescence analysis of museum objects: a new instrument and its application to the analysis of early Chinese white porcelain", Applicazione dei metodi nucleari nel campo delle opere d'arte, Rome, 1976, 227-45.

2. On the procedures using calibration curves and standards, see D. M. Metcalf and F. Schweizer, "The metal contents of the silver pennies of William II and Henry I (1087-1135)", Archaeometry XIII (1971), 177-90.

3. This became clear to my colleague, Mr. N. J. Mayhew, during his researches into the alloy of continental sterlings. In checking back I have found that some of the XRF coin results from the Oxford laboratory in the years 1966-76 failed fully to discount surface enrichment, because the sample surface was insufficiently abraded.

4. J. S. Forbes and D. B. Dalladay, "Composition of English silver coins (870-1300)", BNJ XXX (1960-1), 82-7; Metcalf and Schweizer, op. cit.; J. Yvon, "Esterlins à la croix courte dans les trésors français de la fin du XIIe et de la première moitié du XIIIe siècle, BNJ XXXIX (1970), 24-60, at pp. 37f. (analyses by A. A. Gordus); N. J. Mayhew and D. R. Walker, "Crockards and pollards: imitation and the problem of fineness in a silver coinage", Edwardian Monetary Affairs (1279-1344) (ed. N. J. Mayhew), 1977. I have deliberately re-analysed a few of the same coins listed by Mayhew and Walker, as an illustration of the "two speedometers" effect.

5. This is well brought out by Mayhew and Walker, op. cit.

6. E. Burns, The Coinage of Scotland, 1887, p. 40.

7. H. McKerrell, "Chemical analysis of the Cadboll Cup and the Watson Mazer", PSAS CIV (1971-2), 309-15.

8. H. McKerrell and R. B. K. Stevenson, "Some analyses of Anglo-Saxon and associated Oriental silver coinage", Methods of Chemical and Metallurgical Investigation of Ancient Coinage, ed. E. T. Hall and D. M. Metcalf, 1972, pp. 195-209.

A. England: Stephen 1135-54

BMC Type I			Ag	Cu	Au	Pb	Zn	"Silver"
1.	Oxford, Gahan.	SCBI 261	91.64	5.85	0.29	1.05	1.17	92.98
2.	—, Osbern.	262	90.31	7.32	0.25	0.65	1.46	91.21
3.	—, Swetig.	264	87.66	9.74	0.26	0.97	1.36	88.89
4.	York, Turstan.		88.51	10.27	0.35	0.86	n.d.	89.72
5.	—, Laisig.		92.54	5.49	0.38	1.12	0.47	94.04

B. Scotland: David I, 1124-53

Cross moline - fleury.

Cf. Stephen's BMC Type I

		Ag	Cu	Au	Pb	Zn	"Silver"
6.	Edinburgh, Erebald. 1.38g	92.03	6.66	0.25	1.07	n.d.	93.35
7.	—, —, (same obv.) 1.33g	92.46	6.43	0.28	0.85	n.d.	93.59
8.	—, moneyer? 1.33g	90.59	8.42	0.23	0.75	0.10	91.57
9.	Borders?, moneyer? 1.40g	92.62	5.39	0.39	1.23	0.47	94.24
10.	Durham, Fobund. SCBI 280	92.15	6.14	0.29	1.10	0.31	93.54

Cross-fleury type.

		Ag	Cu	Au	Pb	Zn	"Silver"
11.	Berwick, 1.26g	84.91	14.40	0.28	0.41	n.d.	85.60
12.	—, ... LT 1.24g	87.98	10.87	0.27	0.88	n.d.	89.13
13.	Carlisle? (HA), Riccart? 1.45g	87.26	11.34	0.27	1.03	0.10	88.56
14.	Roxburgh (degraded) 1.44g	89.8	8.34	0.43	1.42	n.d.	91.65

C. Earl Henry, 1136-52

		Ag	Cu	Au	Pb	Zn	"Silver"
15.	Carlisle, (cross-fleury) SCBI 292	92.98	5.41	0.25	0.82	0.54	94.05
16.	Bamburgh, Willelm (cross-crosslet) 291	91.66	6.37	0.37	1.41	0.19	93.44

D. Malcolm IV, 1153-65

		Ag	Cu	Au	Pb	Zn	"Silver"
17.	(Retrograde legend) 1.52g	89.20	8.82	0.31	1.67	n.d.	91.18

E. England: Cross-and Crosslets, 1158-80

		Ag	Cu	Au	Pb	Zn	"Silver"
18.	Class A. Canterbury. SCBI 298	93.28	5.22	0.34	1.15	n.d.	94.77
19.	A. London. 310	93.03	5.41	0.28	1.19	0.08	94.50
20.	A. Norwich. 312	93.73	4.62	0.26	1.06	0.32	95.05
21.	A. York. 321	93.10	5.52	0.29	1.01	0.08	94.40
22.	B. London. 332	92.20	6.09	0.35	1.28	0.09	93.83

F. Scotland: William I, 1165-1214

Crescent-pellet coinage, first
phase, from ca. 1174 (square head
to sceptre)

	Ag	Cu	Au	Pb	Zn	"Silver"
23. Perth, Fopolt. 1.46g	91.55	6.89	0.37	1.18	n.d.	93.10
24. —, —, 1.49g	92.25	6.41	0.30	1.02	n.d.	93.87
25. —, —, 1.51g	93.00	5.68	0.23	1.09	n.d.	94.32
26. Roxburgh, Raul 1.29g	92.65	5.91	0.31	1.12	n.d.	94.08

Second phase (cross pommée)

	Ag	Cu	Au	Pb	Zn	"Silver"
27. Berwick, Raul Derlig 1.38g	91.52	6.89	0.30	1.30	n.d.	93.12
28. —, William 1.47g	92.09	6.40	0.34	1.16	n.d.	93.59
29. Edinburgh, Hue. 1.39g	93.14	5.42	0.35	1.08	n.d.	94.57
30. Roxburgh, Raul. 1.42g	92.83	5.40	0.36	1.40	n.d.	94.59
31. —, —, 1.49g	92.37	6.40	0.31	0.90	n.d.	93.58
32. —, —, 1.54g	92.05	6.66	0.28	1.00	n.d.	93.33
33. 2 —, —, 1.34g	93.12	5.42	0.33	1.13	n.d.	94.58
34. Roxburgh?, Raul. 1.41g	93.05	5.42	0.30	1.24	n.d.	94.59
35. —, (Raul) Derlig 1.46g	92.26	6.94	0.17	0.63	n.d.	93.06
36. No mint name, (Raul) Derlig 1.46g	93.27	5.43	0.33	0.98	n.d.	94.58

G. England: Short cross, 1180-1247

Early coins (1180-89)

	Ag	Cu	Au	Pb	Zn	"Silver"
37. Ib. London, Aimer. SCBI 529	93.27	4.91	0.25	0.88	0.69	94.40
38. Ib. —, Alain. 530	93.66	4.41	0.29	1.10	0.53	95.05
39. Ib. —, Alward. 532	92.79	5.40	0.29	1.24	0.27	94.32
40. Ib. —, Davi. 534	93.88	4.42	0.29	0.97	0.43	95.14

Late coins (after 1217)

	Ag	Cu	Au	Pb	Zn	"Silver"
41. VIIa. London, Abel. 523	91.99	6.40	0.33	1.08	0.19	93.40
42. VII. —, Adam. 527	92.50	5.90	0.29	1.24	0.06	94.03

H. Scotland: Short voided cross, 1195-1250

Variety A.

	Ag	Cu	Au	Pb	Zn	"Silver"
43. Edinburgh, Hue 1.34g	93.69	4.93	0.32	0.99	0.07	95.00
44. Perth, Walter 1.42g	93.60	4.93	0.29	1.03	0.15	94.92
45. —, —, 1.20g	93.80	4.94	0.29	0.89	0.08	94.98
46. Roxburgh, Raul. 1.40g	93.68	5.19	0.25	0.88	n.d.	94.81
47. —, —, 1.21g	93.34	5.43	0.29	0.93	n.d.	94.56
48. —, —, 1.31g	93.32	5.17	0.30	1.13	0.08	94.75

Variety B.

	Ag	Cu	Au	Pb	Zn	"Silver"
49. Roxburgh, Hue, Walter (24 points) 1.18g	92.76	5.40	0.39	1.45	n.d.	94.60
50. —, —, —, 1.45g (24)	93.39	5.70	0.34	0.57	n.d.	94.30
51. Hue, Walter (24) 1.40g	92.56	5.91	0.35	1.18	n.d.	94.09
52. —, —, (24?) 1.41g	93.65	5.19	0.28	0.88	n.d.	94.81
53. —, —, (20) 1.40g	93.63	4.67	0.26	1.31	0.14	95.20
54. —, —, (20) 1.39g	92.85	5.40	0.32	1.35	0.08	94.52
55. —, —, (20) 1.31g	93.67	4.93	0.27	0.99	0.15	94.93
56. —, —, (20) 1.39g	93.67	4.93	0.30	1.04	0.07	95.01
57. —, —, (20) (1.27g)	93.37	4.66	0.40	0.93	0.64	94.70
58. —, —, (?) 1.30g	93.58	5.19	0.31	0.93	n.d.	94.82
59. Henri le rus. (24) 1.44g	93.60	4.67	0.39	1.20	0.14	95.19
60. Hue, Walter. Retrograde (24) 1.32g	93.35	5.17	0.34	1.13	n.d.	94.82

Variety C.

	Ag	Cu	Au	Pb	Zn	"Silver"
61. Roxburgh, Adam. 1.28g	93.17	5.42	0.33	1.08	n.d.	94.58
62. —, Peres, Adam. 1.23g	93.57	5.18	0.31	0.94	n.d.	94.82
63. —, —, —, 1.41g	92.67	5.92	0.29	1.12	n.d.	94.08
64. —, —, —, 1.23g	92.94	5.67	0.31	1.08	n.d.	94.33

Variety D. (Alexander II)

	Ag	Cu	Au	Pb	Zn	"Silver"
65. Roxburgh, Alain, Andrew. 1.46g	90.65	8.42	0.18	0.75	n.d.	91.58
66. —, —, —, 1.47g	91.74	6.91	0.21	1.14	n.d.	93.09
67. —, Pieres. 1.51g	92.50	6.17	0.22	1.11	n.d.	93.83
68. —, —, 1.15g	93.56	5.45	0.23	0.76	n.d.	94.55
69. —, —, 1.22g	92.90	5.93	0.22	0.95	n.d.	94.07

J. Englands: Long cross, 1247-79

	Ag	Cu	Au	Pb	Zn	"Silver"
70. Vg. London, Renaud. SCBI 886	92.10	6.67	0.24	1.00	n.d.	93.34
71. Vg. —, —, 887	91.85	6.12	0.80	1.22	n.d.	93.87
72. Vg. —, —, 888	93.03	5.94	0.32	0.71	n.d.	94.06

K. Scotland: Long voided cross, 1250-80

Class II

	Ag	Cu	Au	Pb	Zn	"Silver"
73. Aberdeen, Andreas. 1.39g	93.05	5.42	0.35	1.18	n.d.	94.58
74. Berwick, Robert. 1.28g	92.65	5.91	0.32	1.12	n.d.	94.09

Class III		Ag	Cu	Au	Pb	Zn	"Silver"
75. Aberdeen, Alex. 1.22g		92.16	6.67	0.24	0.93	n.d.	93.33
76. —, Ion. 1.41g		92.33	6.16	0.33	1.18	n.d.	93.84
77. Ayr, Simon. 1.42g		93.54	5.44	0.30	0.72	n.d.	94.56
78. Berwick, Robert. 1.47g		92.33	6.16	0.34	1.18	n.d.	93.85
79. —, Robert. 1.57g		93.59	4.93	0.35	0.99	0.15	94.93
80. —, Robert. 1.48g		92.80	5.92	0.34	0.94	n.d.	94.08
81. —, Walter. 1.40g		92.84	5.93	0.29	0.95	n.d.	94.08
82. —, Willem. 1.32g		93.00	5.41	0.33	1.08	0.18	94.41
83. Glasgow, Walter, 1.52g		93.00	5.94	0.29	0.77	n.d.	94.06
84. Inverness, Gefrai. 1.43g		93.60	5.34	0.26	0.81	n.d.	94.67
85. St. Andrews, Tomas. 1.50g		92.80	5.82	0.28	1.10	n.d.	94.18
Class VIII							
86. Berwick, Iohan. 1.70g		92.70	6.18	0.26	0.86	n.d.	93.82
87. —, —, 1.60g		91.41	7.68	0.28	0.63	n.d.	92.32
88. —, Walter. 1.46g		93.00	5.94	0.29	0.77	n.d.	94.06
89. —, —, 1.25g		92.47	6.43	0.27	0.83	n.d.	93.57
90. Perth, Rainald. 1.38g		92.68	6.44	0.15	0.73	n.d.	93.56

MONEY IN SCOTLAND IN THE THIRTEENTH CENTURY

N. J. Mayhew

This paper will attempt to review the principal trends in the monetary history of thirteenth-century Scotland, a period which saw an astonishing growth in the money supply enabling us to talk of an economic revolution. Mr. Stewart has estimated about 145 dies for the total Scottish Short Cross coinage which implies a tiny output at the beginning of this period; it cannot have amounted to more than £20,000. By the end of the century an estimate of £150,000 seems conservative.[1] We may be talking in terms of an eight- or ten-fold growth. This monetary explosion seems to have occurred some 50 years later in Scotland than in England. Nevertheless, throughout the century the role of English money in Scotland was of paramount importance. It is clear that large sums of English coin passed in and out of Scotland as a normal consequence of trade, long before the Wars of Independence brought English men and money north of the border. It will be shown that in the second half of the century there was enough money in Scotland to facilitate the same sort of monetary arrangements as those common in England, and there is documentary evidence to show that such arrangements were often in force.

Many of these trends are revealed by a consideration of the location of mints. There were only 4 Short Cross mints: Roxburgh, Perth, Edinburgh, and Berwick. Figure 1 shows the location and output of Scottish Long Cross mints.[2] Many more mints were then in operation and although the domination of the eastern seaboard mints is clear, illustrating the vital importance of foreign trade, it is significant that minting had spread inland to Forfar and Lanark, and to the western towns of Ayr, Renfrew, Glasgow and Dumfries.[3] This picture is not dissimilar to that obtaining in England where the eastern mints consistently outweigh the western.[4]

The establishment of a mint implies that there was coin in the region but the absence of a mint does not necessarily mean the absence of coin. There was surely money in prosperous Dundee in the 1250s but there was no mint; Dundee was not then a royal burgh. Nevertheless a comparison between the location of mints in the Short Cross and Long Cross periods does seem to suggest that the authorities were aware of a wider dispersal of coin by the middle of the century. The 1280 recoinage, however, seems to have required only 9 mints.[5] Apart from St. Andrews (the only mint named on the coins) they probably included the top five Long Cross mints: Berwick, Perth, Roxburgh, Edinburgh and Aberdeen. Stirling, a leading burgh but not a notably prolific mint in the Long Cross coinage, probably competes with Dumfries, Glasgow and Ayr for the last three available places. The reduced numbers of mints should not be interpreted as a contraction in the area using coin towards the end of the century. The authorities may simply have become aware that coinage could be moved considerable distances without undue inconvenience, and the expense of establishing and maintaining small mints was not altogether justified. It will be noticed that the numbers of mints contracted in England at the same time. Site finds indicate that although Oxford lost its mint at this there was no less money in use there at the end of the century.

Despite the difficulties of interpreting negative evidence, the location and relative size of mints in this century indicate the importance of international trade, and the extension of the areas using large quantities of coin. Given the importance of wool, and the parallel English experience at this time, it is probably fair to speak of export-led growth spreading into all the more populous regions of Scotland. The cash originally brought to Scotland by international trade spread, perhaps somewhat unevenly, through the economy into local trade and agriculture.

In the absence of mint records, so plentiful for England, much of the monetary history of thirteenth-century Scotland must be based on the evidence of hoards, stray-finds and die-identities which have been studied by Metcalf, Rigold, and Stewart elsewhere in this volume.

The most obvious point to be made about the thirteenth century hoard evidence is its scarcity. There are only twenty-three Scottish hoards with a terminus post quem in the thirteenth century.[6] The terminus post quem is in effect set by the date of manufacture of the most recent coin in the hoard. In attempting to date a hoard, the historian begins with the terminus post quem, and then goes on to consider other factors, such as the degree of wear on the coins or the length of time which it may have taken for the most recent coins to travel from their mint of origin to the place of deposit of the hoard. Negative evidence, although extremely difficult to use, should also be evaluated; for example if the coins of a nearby mint are totally absent from a hoard it may be that the hoard was concealed before that mint began to work. This is the case at Mellendean (Metcalf 25) where the absence of coins from Berwick suggests a date of deposit shortly before that mint was opened in 1296.[7]

Thus the terminus post quem is only the beginning of the process; this is particularly true of Scottish hoards when we often have only the vaguest information of what coins were found in a hoard. What, for example, are we to make of the Cockmuir Hill, Aberdeenshire hoard (M.20) which we are told consisted of "A bag of small silver coins...of Alexander I" (sic). There must be a strong possibility that we are really dealing with Alexander II or III and that this is really a thirteenth-century hoard, though when a hoard report becomes garbled it may be misleading to try to unravel it. Nevertheless, if one is making a point of the scarcity of thirteenth-century hoards it is probably best to base it on all possible material. The figure of twenty-three hoards also includes two hoards which may belong to the fourteenth century. Canonbie (M.30) is an ill-recorded find with a thirteenth-century terminus post quem, but it is probably a fourteenth-century hoard. Had it been concealed in the thirteenth century it seems likely that the proportion of Scots to English coins would have been higher, Scots coins becoming less plentiful in Scottish hoards as the great Alexandrian recoinage of the 1280s receded into the past. Nevertheless there remains a possibility that Canonbie is an odd thirteenth-century hoard so it has been numbered in the group of 23. The small hoard found at Fyvie (M.29) has also been included. The crucial coin in this case was a

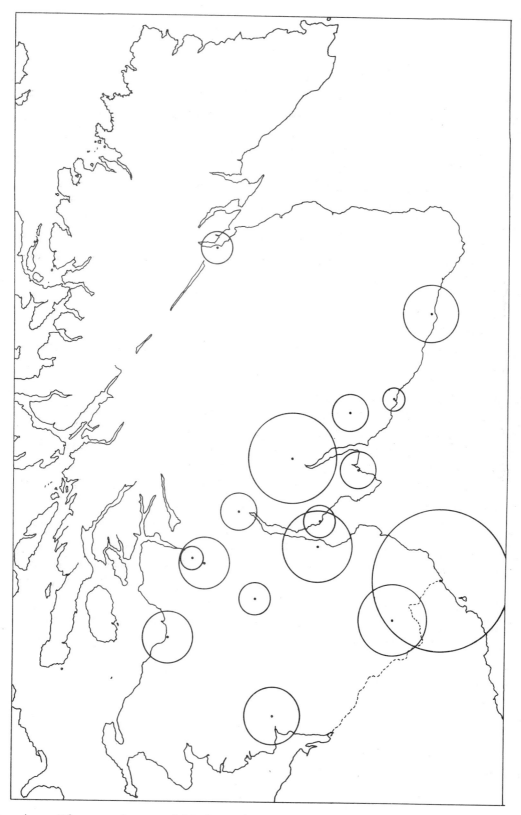

Fig. 1   The recoinage of 1250. The areas of the circles are proportional
to the estimated output of the mints.

sterling of Thibault, duke of Lorraine from 1303 to 1312. A date of c. 1305-c. 1310 was accordingly postulated for the hoard [8] but this date is probably too late. Thibault struck money before he became duke of Lorraine, and a date of 1300 is possible. [9] The Kinghornie hoard of 1902 (M. 110) is also included, as a thirteenth-century date for it may be indicated by the large number of John Baliol coins.

As the very scarcity of thirteenth century hoards is a major theme so the question of negative hoard-evidence needs detailed consideration. A good deal has already been written about the discovery of hoards. [10] There are three points to consider: why hoards were hidden; why they were not recovered by their owners; and why they were eventually discovered. Hoards may often have been hidden in times of danger, but the fear of theft or simple loss may sometimes have led men to bury their savings even in times of comparative peace. The facilities offered by abbeys for the safekeeping of larger sums may explain why hoards found today tend to be small. Warfare will have played a great role in preventing the owners of cash from recovering their property, but not plague: it is noteworthy that there is no group of hoards in Britain which can be associated with the Black Death. Death had to come suddenly to prevent a man passing on the whereabout of his savings to his heirs. Nevertheless, accidents do happen, and there are many isolated hoards for which the history of the time and place of their concealment offers no explanation. There is sometimes a danger that the circumstances of a hoard may be stretched to fit in with a suitably dramatic event, when in reality the hoard was hidden and lost by chance. However, where a series of hoards occur, clustered in time and place, some kind of strife is often a convincing explanation.

When examining the distribution of hoards, one must also consider the factors behind the accidents of discovery. Ploughing, building or more particularly the excavation of foundations, and marine erosion are the chief discoverers of hoards. Where these activities have not taken place in recent times the absence of hoards is not surprising, but in the future rescue archaeology may take over the role played hitherto by the builder's pick-axe, and the advent of the metal detector may lead to the discovery of more hoards in isolated parts.

Bearing all this in mind one may approach the question of the scarcity of thirteenth-century Scottish finds. Clearly scarcity of hoards does not necessarily imply scarcity of money. It may however be evidence of a long period of peaceful prosperity. On this point, of course, the numismatic evidence merely confirms the impression derived from various other forms of evidence that thirteenth-century Scotland enjoyed an unparalleled degree of security and wealth. The hoards from the end of the century illustrate the converse of the theorem, namely that troubled times leave an archaeological legacy in the form of more hoards. Of the 23 thirteenth century hoards, five [Mellendean, Kirkcudbright (M. 26), Galston (M. 27), Cleuchhead (M. 28) and Fyvie] may be dated to the last five years of the thirteenth century or to the earliest years of the fourteenth: that is to say, the earliest phase of the Scottish Wars of Independence.

These hoards are also important because of the very large quantities of continental imitation sterlings they contain. Fyvie, with only 4 coins, and Cleuchhead with 138, were composed entirely of continental sterlings, while Kirkcudbright and Galston both had a continental element of over 90 per cent. At Mellendean there were 103 continental coins out of a total of some 890. The English, Scots and continental coins all suggest that Mellendean may have been concealed rather earlier than the other hoards, so as Metcalf has suggested,[11] the picture is one of high continental sterling content in the currency of c. 1296, for which there is ample documentary evidence from England,[12] followed by a veritable flood of imitations into Scotland soon after the demonetisation of crockards and pollards in England in 1300. It is not inconceivable that the English authorities themselves may have sent crockards and pollards north with their armies. Governments were inclined to adopt a rather ambivalent attitude to these coins - in other people's hands they were base and had to be re-coined; in their own coffers they were often declared to be sterling fine.[13] It is tempting to suggest that the poorer continental imitations were welcomed in Scotland because of the scarcity of better coin there, or because of the lower standards of a poorer and less sophisticated economy. However, it should be pointed out that these coins were only eliminated in England by vigorous government action, while the administration in Scotland was hardly in a position to concern itself with such matters.

Unfortunately, the surviving details of many of the 23 possible thirteenth-century hoards are often hopelessly inadequate. Usually we can make only the most approximate guess at the date of the hoard; often only a few of the coins were properly examined, so we have no idea of the total numbers found, or of the proportions of Scots and English coins. Nevertheless, even these few ill-recorded finds tell us a good deal.

The discovery of small change in even the remotest regions of Scotland is significant. There are halfpennies and farthings in four of the hoards of of this century - Tom a' Bhuraich (M.13), Dun Lagaidh (M.15), Glenluce Sands c. 1880 (M.16), and Glasserton (M.23). Although coins may have been taken into the country-side to be hidden in time of trouble the distances involved will necessarily have been small; Tom a' Bhuraich and Dun Lagaidh can certainly be taken at face value as indicating the use of fractional coins in the far north in petty transactions requiring the smallest denominations. Such evidence is an important supplement to documentary evidence for the use of larger quantities of cash involved in the payment of taxes or ransoms and in the sale of land. It is not suggested that money had totally supplanted older arrangements. Barter and small-scale credit may be presumed to have stretched the money supply, and the payment of rents and dues in kind will certainly have continued alongside a growing monetary sector. The sale of tithes by the bishop of Aberdeen is an interesting illustration from the second half of the thirteenth century of the conversion of an income in kind to cash.[14] But small change shows that it was a convenience to be able to convert goods and services of the smallest value, presumably at the lowest levels of society.

The survival of a mould for lead tokens from Dundrennan Abbey, Kirkcudbrightshire, is also worthy of note in the context of small change.[15] Much uncertainty attaches to the question of lead tokens, both their date and their original purpose being in doubt. Lead tokens can be divided into two main types: those of crude fabric and design, and those of much neater execution. More is known about the neat types. The mould from Dundrennan, which is very similar to a mould taken from the Thames near Osney Abbey[16] is for tokens of the neat type, and corresponds to the groups of tokens found last century in London, and more recently in Dublin.[17] A token of this type has recently been found in Perth.[18] The circumstances of these finds of neat tokens indicate a thirteenth-century date and a definite monetary use particularly associated with taverns. It thus seems possible that in Scotland, as in England and Ireland (and also incidentally in France)[19] lead tokens were used to augment the supply of small change.

The crude types are more varied. They are generally thicker and often have a design composed of some arrangement of strokes and pellets. In England there are probably a large number of local varieties, dating from medieval times into the eighteenth century, and little further will be known about them until they are more generally collected and find spots systematically recorded. Tokens of this type are, I understand, absent from Scotland. This may imply a later medieval date for the crude types - in Scotland, they would not have been required because of the official billon coinage.

The next point to emerge from the hoard evidence concerns the ratio of Scots to English coins. Despite the inadequacies of the hoard reports it is quite apparent that Scottish minting was completely overshadowed by English. Except at a time of recoinage, Scottish coins, even when most plentiful, were outnumbered by English coins by at least ten to one in Scotland. This figure is based on the Mellendean hoard, concealed just over a decade after Alexander III's second recoinage. Where the hoard evidence is richest, that is in the early fourteenth century, a more sophisticated analysis is possible which indicates that the Scottish element in the currency of Scotland dwindled steadily as the years passed after each Scots recoinage. A Scottish hoard from the 1280s, should one be discovered, may be expected to have a higher Scottish content since presumably all the coin in the country, except the very newest English coin, was recoined. This pattern of mint activity is confirmed by the coins themselves; considerable activity at a series of mints at the time of recoinage was followed by a long period of very little work at only one or two surviving mints. For most of the thirteenth century less than a tenth of Scotland's currency was Scottish made.

Thus it is clear that the dominance of English coinage in Scotland predates the payment of troops and the purchase of supplies in Scotland during the wars of the fourteenth century. It was a natural consequence of the healthy and peaceful commerce which characterised one of Britain's most prosperous centuries. The thorough mix of all sterling coinages so admirably illustrated by the Colchester and Brussels hoards indicates the operation of a Sterling Trading Area in which the geographical location of hoards had surprisingly little influence on their contents. English provincial mints when local to the find spot are sometimes more fully represented in a hoard by a factor of perhaps 5%, but the local colouring of the circulation often faded within a few years of the closure of the local mint. Also Anglo-Irish coins tend to outnumber Scots coins in Irish finds, while the reverse is true in Scotland. It may be that this reflects under-representation of Scots coins in Ireland, as much as over representation of local Anglo-Irish coins. It is possible that as a rule most Scottish coins went to Ireland via England as part of the English circulation, while similarly most Anglo-Irish coin found its way to Scotland through England. In general, however, the sterling hoards of the British Isles in the thirteenth and fourteenth centuries are remarkably homogeneous.

All this implies a vigorous circulation of coin in a Sterling Area which extended throughout the British Isles, and also excercised very great influence in Northern Europe. Within this Sterling Area, the strengths and weaknesses of English coin were of paramount importance, and the growth of the English money supply may be expected to have had repercussions on the Scottish economy.

At the Symposium held here in Oxford at this time last year it was argued by Michael Metcalf, on the basis of die-numbers and mint output figures, that late twelfth- and thirteenth-century England experienced an astonishing growth in the money supply.[20] The evidence of stray finds confirmed this growth but also suggested a further growth in the Edwardian period.[21] The problems of interpreting stray-find evidence will be considered later, but in spite of the difficulties of exactly matching stray find evidence with the other sources, the general trend in the English money supply seems clear; that is, rapid expansion in the early thirteenth century and sustained output thereafter. Since English coin so thoroughly dominated the Sterling Area, it seems likely that the money supply in Scotland also grew very considerably in the thirteenth century as a result of the monetary explosion in England. Even if the percentage of the total sterling money supply circulating in Scotland fell in the thirteenth century - and there is no evidence that it did - a reduced share of a very much enlarged cake will still suggest an absolute increase in the quantity of money in Scotland.

Once the central role of English money in Scotland is fully grasped, it is clear that we need a proper understanding of the patterns of circulation and the relationship between the two coinages. To this end it is important to distinguish between the general recoinage of earlier types of coinage - for example when English and Scots Short Cross types were replaced by Long Cross types - and the recoinage of foreign coin at frontier ports as an inescapable part of trade. The English not only recoined all money from time to time with a change of type, but constantly recoined foreign silver brought to England by the sale of exports, pricipally wool. This practice goes some way towards explaining the consistently high level of output which characterised the work of the English mints of London and Canterbury in the thirteenth century. However there seems to have been no attempt to recoin Scottish sterlings whose weight and fineness were designed to allow their circulation alongside the English coin. Similarly there was no general attempt to recoin English sterling in Scotland except at the three major recoinages introducing the Short and Long Cross and 1280 types. This mutual tolerance of English and Scottish coins is apparent from the hoards and is central to the notion of a British Sterling Area. It is not impossible that very small quantities of English coin might occasionally have been recoined in Scotland, to provide sums of money in Scottish coin for making diplomatic payments when the use of Scottish dies might have been a matter of some prestige. The pre-eminence of the Roxburgh mint, that is of a political rather than economic centre, in the Short Cross period may support this idea, though one should not underestimate the economic importance of Roxburgh fair. However the order of precedence for the Long Cross mints which is established by the Brussels and Colchester hoards and elucidated by Stewart [22] makes it clear that by the middle of the thirteenth century Scottish coinage had a primarily economic rather than political role.

Once economic factors gain the upper hand in matters of coinage a number of assumptions follow. In the first place no one ever takes their silver coins to the mint to be recoined unless the coins are not acceptable in trade. This could occur if they are noticeably more deficient in weight or fineness than the rest of the circulating medium, but was more usually only brought about by official decree against foreign money or coins of obsolete type at a time of general recoinage. I think it may be assumed that the vast majority of Scottish Long Cross coin made after the general recoinage was largely complete, will have been struck from foreign (principally Flemish) silver brought mainly to Berwick.

Of course this foreign silver, amounting to no more than a few thousand pounds will not represent all the profit earned by Scotland from the Continent. We may assume that many Flemish bills will have been paid in English sterling. Moreover much of Scotland's export trade will have been with England, and English and Scots coin will have become quickly mixed. It is possible that what was in effect monetary union in Britain will have removed one obstacle to the equalisation of prices in Scotland and England. Obviously local and seasonal variations in supply will have occurred and if cash was more plentiful in England this too will have caused higher prices in richer districts. Nevertheless a common currency will have encouraged trade and the prices of commodities may be presumed to have moved in fairly constant relation to one another north and south of the border. Any disparity of prices greater than the costs of transport would have been prevented by free trade. Ultimately of course the level of agricultural commodity prices will have been reflected in land prices. Thus a growing money supply in Scotland, together with rising prices in England may be presumed to have contributed to a rise in prices in Scotland. Since so little Scottish coin was struck between recoinages (and even this can be readily identified and excluded from calculations) an assessment of the size of a recoinage gives us a minimum estimate of the quantity of coin in that region at the time.

Stewart's estimates for the thirteenth-century Scottish coinage may be summarised as follows. The Scottish Short Cross coinage was very small, and mint output for the Long Cross coinage of the 1250s probably lay somewhere between £50,000 and £80,000; Alexander's recoinage of the 1280s was larger, involving something like £130,000-£180,000. John Baliol's coinage may have involved a further £10,000. It is important when using these estimates not to lose sight of the reservations with which they were originally put forward. Nevertheless, the techniques of die- and hoard-analysis are well established. These estimates represent the best state of our knowledge at the moment: all the evidence suggests a significant increase in the volume of Scottish coinage in the thirteenth century. The very small Short Cross issues were replaced by a respectable Long Cross coinage, and towards the end of the century the Rex Scottorum issue greatly increased on the Long Cross coinage.

These recoinages can only be a rough guide to the quantity of silver in Scotland at the time since we cannot know how much silver may have escaped recoinage or how much coin, once struck, was rapidly exported. Ideally we would like several large hoards from central Scotland concealed in the 1250s to check the thoroughness of the Scottish recoinage. It seems likely that any new English long cross coin crossing into Scotland would not have been recoined in the 1250s because it will already have conformed to the new designs. Nevertheless the two recoinages of Alexander III appear to show that the quantity of coin in Scotland was much larger in 1280 than in 1250. English mint output[23] in contrast seems to have risen sharply late in the twelfth and early in the thirteenth century, and to have been maintained at a fairly high level throughout the century with spurts at times of recoinage. The pattern of English output — rising sharply to a high plateau - mirrors fairly accurately the behaviour of English prices in the thirteenth century. The Scottish monetary pattern of growth throughout the century seems to be different, but with so little data one should perhaps be more cautious. It should also be remembered that since the Scots made no attempt to recoin the incoming English coin which must have formed the bulk of the credit side of the Scottish balance of payments, comparison between English and Scots patterns of mint output are likely to be misleading. Bearing these reservations in mind however, it is worth noting that that the rise in the Scottish money supply seems to have occurred more gradually than that in England, and some 50 years later.

Scottish prices are also much less fully documented than English, and it is difficult to be sure how they behaved in the thirteenth century beyond the general observation that they were rising. Professor Duncan has suggested that rents rose steeply before 1250 and more slowly thereafter, and by the end of the century high rents are explained in terms of high building costs rather than excessive demand for land; this seems to be the only explanation of high rents side by side with vacant plots in the Berwick survey of 1297.[24] Sometime in the second half of the thirteenth century there seems to have been a fairly general upward review of rents.[25] Frequently there are parallels with England. Indeed, the late thirteenth-century rental of Kelso Abbey looks very like English rentals of similar period. Week-work survives at the grange of Revenden, while commuted rents of 6s 8d were paid for husbandlands in the town of Bolden with only the lightest boon services. In England a rent of the sort found at Bolden would suggest fairly early commutation of week-work. It has been suggested that " as landlords the monks preferred to obtain a cash rent rather than labour services" . Heriots were generally converted to cash, and Abbot Richard has been particularly identified with commutation. Except for the granges, demesne land was increasingly leased.[26] In southern Scotland at least, there was enough cash available in the thirteenth century to permit the same sort of economic changes that were taking place in England.

With only fairly limited knowledge of the behaviour of Scottish rents and even less data on prices, we cannot really take a comparison of prices and money supply much further. Even the estimates of money supply only give us two rather approximate fixed points, from which it might be rash to attempt to establish anything more precise than a general rise. Nevertheless, a general picture of rising rents and rising money supply does seem to mirror the English experience. Of course, this was also a period of rising population, but happily, for the thirteenth century at least, monetary and demographic explanations of the behaviour of prices are not necessarily incompatible.

However, an examination of Scottish and English demographic evidence is necessary if we are to evaluate the monetary estimates properly. Debate about the size of England's pre-Black Death population has raged long and furiously with little sign of agreement in sight. In Scotland there seems hardly enough evidence even to begin debate. J. C. Russell comments: "The indications about Scotland are rather vague".[27] His extremely tentative conclusions are as follows:

1066	275,000
1348	550,000
1377	348,000

Not very far removed from this estimate Professor Nicholson has used Lord Cooper's estimate of an early fourteenth century population of about 400,000, 90 per cent of whom seem to have lived in the countryside as opposed to the burghs.[28] Professor Barrow further stresses the role of the Highlands[29] as a home for very nearly as many people as the rest of Scotland, although the density of Highland settlement per square mile would certainly have been lower than that of lowland Scotland. Professor Duncan is frankly agnostic about Scottish population, figures of half a million and a million both seeming to him to be equally reasonable and equally unsupported by evidence.[30]

With such uncertainty attaching to the population estimates, I shall offer both maximum and minimum figures: for England 6 and 3 million: for Scotland 1 million and 500,000. It will be noticed that whether one uses the maximum (Postan-Titow)[31] or the minimum (J. C. Russel) English estimate, the corresponding Scottish maximum and minimum are both 1/6th of the English totals. Estimates of English and Scots money supply in the 1280s are more precise than the population figures, but are not without difficulties of their own. The Scottish estimates have already been discussed and £130,000 is a conservative figure. For England Marion Archibald has offered a figure of £1,172,655 of pence struck at all mints in England between the beginning of Edward's new coinage in 1279 and July 1290.[32] This English figure does not include halfpence and farthings. Nevertheless, it probably gives too large an impression of the amount of silver in England in the 1280s, since it includes all the foreign silver brought to England in that decade (c. £450,000), without making any allowance for English silver exported. £200,000 may easily have left the country in the same period, so a figure of c. £1,000,000 for silver in England in the 1280s seems reasonable:

	Money	Population in Millions	
		Maximum	Minimum
England	£1,000,000	6	3
Scotland	£130,000	1	$\frac{1}{2}$

In pleasingly round terms, which may convey the approximate nature of the calculation, one can say that Scotland may have had a seventh or eighth of England's money supply and 1/6th of her population. The implication is that if every Scotsman had 2s 7d in his pocket, every Englishman had 3s 4d. The difference is perhaps not as large as some may have expected, and yet if anything, the Scottish monetary figure may be an underestimate. Working on the upper of Stewart's figures £180,000 it would appear that the Scot had more money than his English counterpart. It should also be remembered that the money supply was by no means stable, and Englishmen may have had to manage on a good deal less cash in periods of low mint output in the fourteenth century. Thus Scotland's thirteenth-century money supply may have exceeded English money per head of the population at times in the fourteenth century. It must be remembered that this high period of Scottish money was of shorter duration than the English, but it seems clear that Scotland was by no means as poverty-stricken as has sometimes been suggested.

Perhaps the stories of James VI's amazement at the wealth of England compared with Scotland are too well known to be set aside easily. Yet the prosperity of thirteenth-century Scotland is well attested. Vast tracts of Scottish countryside were well suited to the production of Britain's prime export, wool. The Kelso rental lists pasture for over 6,000 sheep and Kelso wool features in Pegolotti's list.[33] Conversely, by the late thirteenth century we are told, the English economy may have passed its peak of performance, and growing population, previously the foundation of English prosperity, was apparently bringing its share of problems. Neither should the disadvantages of Scottish soil and climate be overstated. The highly organised ecclesiastical estates sited in the richest lands of southern England rarely managed a four fold return on wheat,[34] while the Scottish preference for oat and barley crops may betoken a more realistic attitude to the capacity of the available land and techniques. The Wars of Independence clearly demonstrate that Scotland was by no means a contemptible prize.

It is tempting, and not entirely untrue, to suggest that there was more spare money in thirteenth-century Scotland than at any time till the oil came on stream. More seriously, it is clear that by the second half of the thirteenth century, the nature of the Scottish monetary experience was not widely different from that of England, and that despite its dependence on the products of English mints for much of the time, Scotland was not monetarily backward. The evidence does not permit one to speak of changes in the coinage as the cause of changes in social and economic patterns. The policy of individual landowners regarding direct exploitation or the leasing of demesnes was probably central to the question of wage labour and money rents. However, without the development of the money supply many choices would not have been available, and it is clear that Scottish economic life could not have developed as it did without a plentiful supply of coin.

The size of Scotland's money supply in the 1280s in relation to its population is an important index of the health of Scottish trade. A very close correspondence between mint output and trade has long been presumed for England, and has recently been documented in detail by T.H. Lloyd.[35] Scottish mint output patterns were different from the English, but the comparable amounts of coin per head of the population in England and Scotland in the 1280s imply a very considerable degree of prosperity for Scottish merchants and their European colleagues resident in Scotland. That Alexander III felt able to tax exports would seem to be further evidence of the health of the Scottish economy. In the late thirteenth century at least Scotland was not a poor neighbour to England, and the size of the 1280 recoinage compared with the Long Cross recoinage indicates that Scotland was very definitely in balance of payments surplus.

The documentary and monetary evidence all seem to suggest that the reign of Alexander III was a high point, but the archaeological evidence of single coin finds, from excavated sites or found by chance does not fully confirm this.[36] Professor Duncan has asked " should not isolated finds of individual coins weigh more as evidence of urban trade than deliberately concealed hoards usually in rural places? Is the absence of reported finds at, say, Edinburgh and Perth rightly taken as evidence that they were not towns before the twelfth century?"[37] Equally in the thirteenth century, isolated finds are much rarer in Scotland than one might expect, especially if one is proposing a similar degree of monetisation to that existing in England. Yet finds of the later middle ages are much more common. Can it be that the monetary economy did not take off till much later than the evidence of hoards and output figures suggest? Is it not possible that in the first few decades of relatively plentiful money, the habit of using coin was only slowly acquired by small folk, while large quantities of cash were concentrated in the coffers of monastic houses, the royal administration and a merchant élite?

There is probably some truth in this. After all it will be remembered that medieval contracts of almost all types in England and Scotland usually stipulate easy-payment terms of a certain sum per year or half year, which seems to recognise the difficulties of putting together even quite small sums of money quickly. Moreover stray finds may be expected to present a better picture than that suggested by the hoards for a number of reasons. Hoards tend to exclude the smaller denominations; if anything, stray finds may favour fractional coins since they are more easily lost. Hoards may sometimes have been deliberately moved to lonely spots; stray finds were lost in the course of ordinary use. For these reasons the answer to Professor Duncan's question seems to be, yes, stray finds do make better evidence. On the other hand, stray finds may be difficult to date in the sense that a coin made in 1280 may have circulated for well over 100 years after that date; it is much more difficult to put in context, whereas a hoard can in principle be dated to within quite narrow limits. The other problem with stray finds is their scarcity. The evidence comes to us by chance, but it is not statistically speaking random, making the data from this source very difficult to evaluate. Moreover, each archaeological site needs to be judged as a whole. Two apparently comparable sites may have been excavated in different ways. The relationship between the amount of coin used, and the amount lost or rejected, may not have been constant over the centuries, and similarly the relationship between the amounts lost and the amounts found is also variable. It is for this reason that Rigold told us in his paper last year on English stray finds that " It is not claimed that the sample shows how much coinage existed in one phase relatively to another, or even how much was circulating and not hoarded."[38]

However, even bearing in mind the different nature of evidence from stray finds it is still difficult to explain the different patterns of growth in the English and S ottish money supply exhibited by stray finds, compared with that suggested by mint output figures or estimates. Partly, the unexpectedly high number of Edwardian stray finds in England can be explained by the long period of circulation for Edwardian coins, but this may also be evidence of changing patterns of use of coin in England at this time. In Scotland, the high number of Edwardian stray finds may be partly explained in terms of the Wars of Independence. The relatively plentiful finds from the late medieval period may be explained in terms of the lower monetary value of the billon coinage. In a sense one would not expect thirteenth-century silver pennies to be lost very often. Each coin represented a day's labour and if mislaid would be eagerly searched for. Moreover, although comparisons of per capita income may show Scotland to have been fairly prosperous, the quantities of money per acre are less impressive. In absolute terms there was obviously much less money in Scotland than in England. Thus there is no need to invoke the notion of Scottish thrift to explain the scarcity of thirteenth-century stray losses. If negative evidence from hoards can be treacherous and misleading, it can be even more so with stray finds.[39] But there are other factors which may lead us to question or at least qualify the assertion of monetary expansion and prosperity in Scotland. For example it is surprising that there is not much evidence of credit facilities at this time. If Scotland was really as prosperous as I have suggested might we not expect to see more Lombards and Jews at work in high Scottish finance?[40] Moreover comparisons between the incomes of English and Scottish barons, where this is possible, suggests that the English aristocracy was more prosperous. Taking his English and Scottish incomes together, Roger de Quincy, Earl of Winchester and Constable of Scotland, was one of the four richest barons in Scotland though he would probably not have been among the top ten in England.[41]

Such comparisons can give only an impressionistic picture. Moreover, it should be remembered that the numismatic estimates of money supply indicate that the existence of large quantities of cash in Scotland in the 1280s was a relatively recent phenomenon. The scarcity of Scottish thirteenth-century stray finds, and the apparent absence of advanced money-lending facilities are not so surprising when it is recalled that Scotland had only just achieved a monetary take-off when the Wars of Independence began to inflict such damage on the country. The relative figures of baronial wealth may also need to be seen in this context. Monetarily, Scotland was some fifty years behind England; might Scottish baronial exploitation of estates also have been lagging behind the English example? A further illustration of the delayed development of the Scottish currency is the absence of contemporary counterfeits in the Short and Long Cross periods. It is only in the Edwardian period that counterfeits of the Scottish coinage appear in any numbers.

With these qualifications in mind, the monetary evidence for thirteenth-century Scotland would seem to indicate that this was a time of prosperity and rapid growth. The role of English money is clearly a dominant one, and the quantities of Scottish coins recovered in England and on the continent are evidence of thriving trade. Moreover the volume of the Scottish recoinages seems to indicate that any Scottish money taken out of Scotland was more than replaced

by other money coming in. The Scottish money supply expanded greatly,
while population and prices were also rising. We are seeing a golden Alexandrian age.

NOTES

1. See Stewart, above pp. 68-71.

2. For the data on which this map is based see Ian Stewart, 'Scottish Mints'
   in Mints, Dies and Currency: Essays dedicated to the Memory of Albert
   Baldwin (1971) ed. R. A. G. Carson, 209. It should be remembered that
   Berwick struck over a much longer period than the other mints. During
   the recoinage its output was roughly equivalent to that of Perth and
   Edinburgh together.

3. The mint signatures of Dun and Fres are here assumed to be Dumfries.

4. D. M. Metcalf, " Geographical patterns of minting in medieval England",
   Seaby's Coin and Medal Bulletin 1977, 314-17.

5. Mints, Dies and Currency, 216.

6. The possible thirteenth-century hoards are Metcalf nos. 9-30 inclusive
   and 110. Metcalf nos. 58-114 are inadequately described Edward hoards
   which must have been deposited at some time between 1280 and 1360. A
   few of them may be thirteenth-century.

7. G. Macdonald, ' Two hoards of Edward pennies recently found in Scotland',
   NC 1913, 57-118.

8. M. Dolley 'A small find of Continental Sterlings from Aberdeenshire'
   NC 1961, 170.

9. The coin of Thibault is a crockard, that is an imitation of an English
   sterling of a type tolerated in England in the 1290s but finally demonetised
   in the spring of 1300. It is unlikely that such coins would have been struck
   for long after this date. It should also be noted that the coin was not struck
   by Thibault as Duke of Lorraine, but was minted at Florennes, which
   Thibault held by right of his wife Isabella de Rumigny. We know that the
   bishop of Liège granted Thibault the privilege of minting at Florennes in
   1300, and there must be a possibility that this permission merely regu-
   larised an existing state of affairs.

10. J. P. Kent ' Interpreting Coin-Finds', in Coins and the Archaeologist,
    eds. Casey and Reece.

11. See Metcalf above, pp. 12-13 and 27.

12. M. Prestwich, ' Edward I's monetary policies and their consequences',
    Econ. Hist. Rev. 1969, 406-16 and M. Mate, ' Monetary policies in
    England, 1272-1307', BNJ XLI (1972), 34-79.

13. M. Prestwich in Edwardian Monetary Affairs (1279-1344) ed. N. J.
    Mayhew, 1977, 55 n. 29.

14. <u>Registrum Episcopatus Aberdonensis</u> I, 17.

15. National Museum of Antiquities of Scotland, Edinburgh.

16. Department of Antiquities, Ashmolean Museum, Oxford.

17. J. Y. Akerman, <u>NC</u> 1846, 116-7; C. Roach Smith, <u>Catalogue of the Museum of London Antiquities</u> (1854) 156-7; M. Dolley and W. Seaby, <u>NCirc</u> 1971, 446-8.

18. I am grateful to Messrs. R. B. K. Stevenson and Nicholas Bogdan for this information.

19. A. Forgeais, <u>Numismatique des Corporations Parisiennes Métiers, etc. d'après les Plombs Histories trouvés dans la Seine.</u>

20. D. M. Metcalf, 'A survey of numismatic research into the pennies of the first three Edwards', in <u>Edwardian Monetary Affairs</u>, 7 thus: "It is very clear that, leaving aside any short-term fluctuations, the volume of English currency was rising like a rocket between 1180 and 1280."

21. S. E. Rigold, 'Small change in the light of medieval site finds', <u>ibid.</u>, 59-80.

22. An order of precedence among the Long Cross mints is given by Stewart in <u>Mints, Dies and Currency</u>, 209.

23. C. E. Blunt and J. D. Brand, 'Mint output of Henry III', <u>BNJ XXXIX</u> (1970), 61-6; C. G. Crump and C. Johnson, 'Tables of bullion coined under Edward I, II and III', <u>NC</u> 1913, 200-45.

24. A. A. M. Duncan, <u>Scotland: The Making of the Kingdom,</u> Edinburgh (1975), pp. 516-7.

25. A. McKerral, 'Ancient denominations of agricultural land in Scotland', <u>PSAS</u> LXXIX 68.

26. <u>An Historical Atlas of Scotland c. 400-c.1600</u> eds. McNeill and Nicholson, St. Andrews (1975), 43-4.

27. J. C. Russell, <u>British Medieval Population</u>, 319, 362.

28. R. Nicholson, <u>Scotland: The Later Middle Ages,</u> Edinburgh (1974), 2.

29. G. W. S. Barrow, <u>The Kingdom of the Scots: Government, Church, and Society from the Eleventh to the Fourteenth century</u> (1973), esp. Chapter 13, 'The Highlands in the lifetime of Robert the Bruce, .

30. A. A. M. Duncan, <u>op. cit.</u>, 309.

31. J. Z. Titow, <u>English Rural Society, 1200-1350</u> (1969).

32. M. M. Archibald in <u>Edwardian Monetary Affairs,</u> 182.

33. <u>Historical Atlas of Scotland</u>, 44.

34. J. Z. Titow, <u>Winchester Yields : A Study in Medieval Productivity.</u>

35. T. H. Lloyd, 'Overseas Trade and the English Money Supply in the Fourteenth Century', in <u>Edwardian Monetary Affairs,</u> 96-124.

36. See Rigold, above pp. 61-4.

37. A. A. M. Duncan, op. cit., 464-5.

38. S. E. Rigold, in Edwardian Monetary Affairs 61.

39. See Appendix pp. 101-2.

40. On this point, I am grateful to Professor Barrow. There was some
    Jewish activity, however: Alexander, steward of Scotland obtained a
    Jewish loan of £200 in 1262. See Grant G. Simpson, An Anglo-Scottish
    Baron of the Thirteenth Century: The Acts of Roger de Quincy, Earl of
    Winchester and Constable of Scotland, D.Phil. Thesis for University of
    Edinburgh 1965, 216.

41. Grant C. Simpson, op. cit., 214-6. I am particularly grateful to Dr.
    Simpson for his advice, and for making sections of his thesis available
    to me.

APPENDIX

LATE-TWELFTH AND THIRTEENTH-CENTURY STRAY FINDS IN SCOTLAND

This is not a comprehensive list, but rather a brief note of the finds which I have come across without any systematic search. With the exception of the Walston House find, for which I am indebted to David Cauldwell of NMAS, all the references come from one of two sources:

(a) The Proceedings of the Society of Antiquaries of Scotland.
(b) 'Coin Finds and Hoards from Dumfriesshire and Galloway', by James Williams in NCirc 1970.

Stray finds are not often noted in PSAS unless they occurred in the course of an archaeological excavation, or were donated to NMAS. Williams' paper illustrates how much more material can be found by thorough search especially in regions served by a good local archaeological journal.

Edward pence have been included in this list only if there is good reason to believe that they were struck in the thirteenth century. However it should be noted that some, if not most, of the early Edward I coins found may have been lost well into the fourteenth century.

1. Dun Beag, Skye. Penny of Henry II, PSAS 55, p. 127-8.

2. Mote of Hawick. Short Cross penny of Henry II, PSAS 48, p. 23.

3. Old Luce. Short Cross, probably twelfth century, Williams, p. 492.

4. Luce Sands. Penny of William the Lion, Williams, p. 492.

5. Strathdon. Penny of William the Lion, PSAS 5, p. 31.

6. Mortlach, Banffshire. Penny of Henry III, PSAS 29, p. 61.

7. Howden Farm, Lauriston Scaurs, near Selkirk. Penny of Henry III, London, PSAS 61, p. 111.

8. Walston House near Carnwath, Lanarkshire. Irish Long Cross penny of Henry III.

9. Kildrummy Castle, Aberdeenshire. Long Cross penny of Henry III, 1251. Ion at Bury St. Edmunds. PSAS 96, p. 233.

10. Tentsmuir, Fife. Long Cross cut halfpenny of Henry III, 1248. PSAS 93, p. 253.

11. Freswick, Caithness. Long Cross penny of Henry III, 1258-72, Willem at London PSAS 73, pp. 86 and 102.

12. Dryfesdale, Dam Farm, Dumfriesshire. Long Cross penny of Henry III, 1248, London. Williams, p. 331.

13. Monifieth, Forfarshire. Penny of Alexander III, PSAS 3, p. 246.

14. Dumfries. Penny of Edward I, 1279-80, London, Williams, p. 332.

15. Moffat, Dumfriesshire. Penny of Edward I, 1279-80, Williams p. 388.

16. Penpont, Dumfriesshire. Penny of Edward I, 1279-80, London, Williams, p. 388.

17. Castle Douglas, Dumfriesshire. Penny of Edward I, 1279-80 London, Williams, p. 443.

18. Kirkgunzeon, Dumfriesshire. Irish penny of Edward I, Dublin, Williams, p. 443.

19. Donald's Isle, Loch Doon. Penny of Edward I, 1260 (?), London, PSAS 71, p. 327.

20. Gorten Bay, Kentra, Ardnamurchan. Penny of Edward I, thirteenth century, London, PSAS 59, pp. 106, 108.

21. Dun Beag, Skye. Penny of Edward I, Canterbury, PSAS 55, pp. 127-8.

22. Auchlishie, Kirriemuir, Forfarshire. Penny of John Baliol, PSAS 3, p. 246.

SCOTTISH MONETARY PROBLEMS
IN THE FOURTEENTH AND FIFTEENTH CENTURIES

Ranald Nicholson

The return of David II to Scotland in 1357, after eleven years of captivity in England, is one of the landmarks of Scottish history. Among the changes that rapidly ensued was a great recoinage, when groats and gold nobles were first minted in Scotland.[1] Until 1355, when Edward III had ordered that a coinage recently issued by Robert the Steward should be received only as bullion, the parity and interchangeability of English, Scottish and Anglo-Irish coins had been recognised. Through his great recoinage David II hoped to bring Scotland back to the 'sterling area' of the British Isles: in 1358 he is said to have successfully petitioned Edward III that Scottish coins be again accepted at par.[2]

Circumstances had altered by the late 1360s, when financial stringency, associated with the king's ransom, though scarcely caused by it, was apparent in Scotland.[3] To meet the stringency various measures were taken, of which three deserve particular attention. It would be convenient to consider them in reverse chronological order. The last of the three was an ordinance of the three estates in 1368 which stated that the customs duties should pay for the king's ransom; simultaneously the duties on the export of staple commodities — wool, fleeces and hides — were again raised, so that they were four times as high as they had been in 1357, the charge on a sack of wool being set at 26s. 8d.[4] Export duties were to stay at the level of 1368 for over two centuries.[5] For a few years they did not lessen foreign demand for Scottish exports; in the sluggish trading conditions of the 1400s they may have discouraged demand and contributed to a trade deficit. Another measure, adopted in 1367, was a decision to coin a further ten pence from the pound weight (Scots) of silver. This seems to have meant that the Scots minted $23\frac{1}{2}$ pennies from the ounce of silver while the English minted only $22\frac{1}{2}$ pennies.[6] The reduction in the intrinsic value of the Scots penny was slight. Perhaps it was hoped that it would go unnoticed, though it did not; nor did a second reduction under Robert III in 1373; Scotland was evicted from the 'sterling area'.[7] The third notable measure of the 1360s preceded the other two. It was a general assessment in 1366 of all lands and rents within the realm, both ecclesiastical and lay. The obvious intent was to levy contributions for the king. Indeed conceivably the only intent behind all three measures was to swell King David's revenues (which did swell)[8] though one cannot discount the possibility that consideration of the public weal may also have been involved.

It is the general assessment of 1366 which raises this possibility. It set side by side the Antiqua Taxatio, an assessment of the time of Alexander III, with the Verus Valor — the 'true' or current value according to the assessors of 1366. If the two sets of figures are compared it would seem that there had been a general fall in landed income from the later years of Alexander III to those of David II: according to the Antiqua Taxatio the assessment of the Scottish bishoprics amounted to £15,002 16s. 0d.; by the Verus Valor it amounted to only £9,396 6s. 6d.; the returns for twenty-two sheriffdoms give the Antiqua Taxatio as £48,249 7s. 8d., while the Verus Valor, though not fully certified, came to about £23,250.[9] Thus one historian has stated that 'evidence of the poverty of the country appears from the taxations [assessments] which the estates imposed to pay off the ransom.'[10]

If we assume that 'poverty' in this context signifies a fall in the production of goods and services — 'real' wealth — it must be questioned what caused the fall. Plague, which I shall discuss later in this paper, does not seem to provide the answer. An explanation that also comes readily to mind is the destruction of warfare. This, and the accompanying dislocation, certainly brought at least temporary poverty to the areas ravaged by the rival armies.[11] Yet warfare cannot be regarded as the basic explanation for the drop in monetary assessments from Antiqua Taxatio to Verus Valor: in the case of the sheriffdom of Perth, last devastated in 1339, the drop was markedly greater than in the case of the sheriffdom of Edinburgh, devastated not only in the 1330s but more recently in the 'Burnt Candlemas' of 1356; and in the case of the lands of the barons of Argyll, not known to have been devastated at all, at least since 1309, the drop was even greater than in the case of Perth.[12]

The difficulty in finding an explanation for a wholesale fall in the production of goods and services — a fall of about 50% in the gross national product, to use the terminology of modern economists — suggests that perhaps no such fall took place. The assessments, it must be recalled, are expressed in monetary terms; and money, though the measure of wealth, is a variable measure. The measure must vary, to some extent at least, according to the plentifulness of money on the one hand and goods and services on the other, not to mention what has been styled 'the long-term increase in the demand for money, resulting from the long-term growth of population and/or of income and/or of the "monetization" of the economy.'[13] Thus the assessments need not be taken as evidence of 'poverty' but may be taken as symptomatic of falling rents, falling prices,[14] and wholesale deflation, with regional differences in the extent of the deflation. In short, the supply of money in Scotland had decreased relative to demand — thanks to causes that affected most of western Europe.

Deflation was not a word that figured in the economic vocabulary of fourteenth-century Europe. Yet the symptons were felt. What was apparent was a shortage of money. There was an awareness that extra money could be created by reducing the weight of coins or their bullion content. David II cannot have lacked advice from the talented John Mercer, burgess of Perth,[15] or Bonagio, a Florentine employed as moneyer from 1364 to 1393.[16] Hence, perhaps, the slight reduction in the weight of Scottish coins in 1367 was an experiment in what would now be styled reflation. The experiment — if experiment it was — was a cautious one. Further changes in the weight or bullion content of coins under Robert II and his successors ended deflation and introduced inflation. Thus in 1409 the abbot of Dunfermline considered that 'all things are dearer than they were in times past' and granted forty shillings a

104

year to each monk to buy clothing.[17] In 1454 the bishop of Moray lamented that 'three marks present money scarcely equal one mark of old money, so that formerly where six marks sufficed for the sustentation of a vicar of the choir, today ten marks scarcely suffice.'[18] The inaccuracy of the bishop's comparative statistics perhaps testifies to his vexed exasperation.

How is the historian of today to respond to such cris de coeur from the past? Certainly not, given recent experience of inflation, with the self-assurance and prejudice of his predecessors in the age of laissez-faire. Carlo Cipolla, in an article on 'Currency Depreciation in Medieval Europe' amusingly draws attention to the remarks of two economic historians whose nationality seems apparent. One, C. J. Shive, writing in 1871, affirmed that 'in England they went more honestly to work than elsewhere, and the coins kept their proper weight'; the other, R. G. Hawtrey, writing in 1923, stated that 'of all countries England was (during the Middle Ages) the freest from illegitimate debasements.'[19] What one might conveniently style the 'Shive-Hawtrey thesis' was that debasement of the coinage represented economic failure, whereas an unaltered coinage represented all the economic virtues, not to mention some national and moral ones as well. There would be no point in belabouring the 'Shive-Hawtrey thesis' but for the fact that it is still with us and may colour our interpretation of the monetary problems of Scotland during the later Middle Ages. Thus in a very recent and admirable work, Dr. William Ferguson's Scotland's Relations with England: a Survey to 1707, it is stated that 'in the late Middle Ages the economy of Scotland stagnated, a sure index of this being the dramatic fall in the value of Scottish currency. Until about 1360 Scottish and English money stood at the same value, but thereafter Scottish currency steadily depreciated.'[20] This statement elicits two comments. Firstly, if the economy of Scotland stagnated during the late Middle Ages was there any other economy in western Europe that did not — relative to its performance in the thirteenth century — also stagnate? Secondly, it is natural for a Scottish historian to draw comparisons with England — and in this paper I shall be as guilty as any other — yet the comparison is, I think, misleading. It is clear that in matters of currency, as in many other aspects, social, economic and political, England was the odd-man-out in a western European context. Explanations for at least the monetary abnormality are fairly obvious[21] and need not involve any unduly high estimation of the quality of management of the economy by English governments in the later Middle Ages. I have used the word 'abnormality' deliberately; for it is the fate of Scotland to be perpetually measured by historians against the standards set by her abnormal southern neighbour. The contrasts that thereby appear might not necessarily be so apparent were conditions compared with those in many parts of continental Europe.

This seems particularly the case in regard to the monetary problems of the later Middle Ages, though so far as I am aware no one has yet completed the daunting task of producing a statistical synthesis. Some useful figures are, however, given by Cipolla. On the basis of the number of grammes of pure silver corresponding to a pound-tale of 240 pennies he shows that between 1250 and 1500 the English pound depreciated by about 47%, that the French livre tournois depreciated by about 72%, that the lire of Genoa, Milan, Venice and Florence depreciated by about 81½%, 87%, 70% and 83% respectively.[22]

Following the 'Shive-Hawtrey thesis' we might conclude that if the Scottish depreciation approximated that of France the landscape of Scotland was dotted with large and gracious châteaux that reflected the fertility of the soil. If it approximated that of Florence we might conclude that Scotland enjoyed a high degree of urbanisation, coupled with intense sophistication in trade and industry. These conclusions would, of course, be ridiculous. They serve as a warning that international comparisons on the basis of currency depreciation are meaningless as a guide to social and economic conditions. Cipolla lists no less than seven economic 'causes' which, 'singly or in various combinations' led to currency debasements in the Middle Ages.[23] Between 1250 and and 1500 it would seem that the depreciation of Scottish coinage, about 82%,[24] was much the same as that of Florence; yet it cannot be supposed that it was exactly the same combination of Cipolla's economic 'causes' that produced this result. Each country, to a greater or less extent, faced monetary problems in the later Middle Ages; each attempted its own solutions and the outcome was haphazard.

The basic problem common to all western lands was, as is well known, a shortage of silver and gold, the only respectable sources of currency; hence the need for various expedients to avoid deflation, or, to put it in contemporary language, to remedy the type of situation that existed in Scotland in 1473 when the king's lieges were described as being 'bare of money'.[25] A subsidiary problem common to all western lands was the demographic change occasioned by the Black Death. But this change seems to have reacted upon the various economies in different ways. In an article on 'Wage Labour in France in the Later Middle Ages'[26] E. Perroy notes that the effect of epidemics on both France and England was to bring about a fall of both population and production, but 'the relative importance of the two phenomena was different in each country. In England, the demographic contraction was more accentuated than the fall of production; therefore wages rose. In France, the economic disruption due to wars and other as yet unknown factors was so complete as to limit production faster than population. In spite of a great fall in the number of men the magnitude of the recession kept wages low all through our period.'[27]

The interpretation of statistics regarding the fall of population resulting from the Black Death and subsequent epidemics is notoriously controversial, and in the case of Scotland statistics are almost wholly absent. Scottish chroniclers note the coming of the Black Death — which was at first called 'the Foul Death of the English' — but in a less emotional way than their English counterparts.[28] Later visitations, the second, third and fourth mortalities, which may not all have been of a bubonic nature, briefly attract the attention of the chroniclers and do leave a trace in the records;[29] yet there seem to be no signs of a dramatic drop in population. A hypothesis may be advanced, though one of an impressionistic nature, that in the fourteenth and fifteenth centuries Scotland suffered less loss of manpower than neighbouring lands and that therefore the plague had less drastic economic consequences. Some incidental facts may serve to support this impression. In Scotland there was no legislation comparable to the English statute of labourers. In contrast to England, where the labour shortage made landlords reluctant to see the end of villeinage, the last known legal suit for the recovery of runaway nativi occurred in 1364; and even before that date it may be presumed that unfreedom on the land had simply become a thing of the past; and in Scotland there was no Peasants' Revolt.[30] In accordance with this line of thought it may be supposed that Scotland did not undergo to the same extent as neighbouring lands the strains and stresses of rapid demographic change. A certain stability seems to be indicated, conceivably even coupled with some growth of population in the fifteenth century.

Did wages rise, as in England, or fall, as in France? Certainly they did rise in monetary terms in the case of the labourers and artisans who were normally paid daily wages - a minority operating mainly in, or from, urban centres. Thus the artisan could expect to earn 3d., 4d., even 8d., a day in the 1330s,[31] but 1s., 1s. 4d., even 1s. 6d by 1500, while by the same time an unskilled workman could expect 8d. or even 1s.[32] The variation of wage rates for what seems to be the same class of labour, makes deductions awkward. Nonetheless it seems likely that the rise in daily wages at least compensated for the fall in the intrinsic value of the coinage (by two-thirds between the 1330s and 1500). It remains an enigma whether the higher wages of 1500 could buy as much as their counterpart in the 1330s. Possibly a dedicated graduate student might find an answer; more probably the compilation of relative indices of the cost of living and of 'real' wages is a task beyond achievement.

If these problems face us in dealing with those urban workers who were paid a daily wage there are greater problems in dealing with the rural classes who comprised the bulk of the population. Their income was basically in produce. The rents they paid to their landlords were often a combination of both cash and produce. The historian tends to assume, perhaps wrongly, that the portion of rent expressed in cash was more significant than the 'bolls' or 'chalders' of cereals or the ubiquitous 'marts' — salted beef carcases. The latter, at least, represented a portion of rent that was immune from monetary problems, though doubtless even the 'marts' were subject to inflation. Despite periods of stability rents certainly did rise throughout the course of the fifteenth century,[33] probably to an extent that at least compensated for the intrinsic fall in the value of currency, though the corresponding rise in the cost of living is unknown. Certainly the agricultural tenant of the fifteenth century was not oblivious of the significance of inflation, at least in the form of higher rents: following the alteration of domestic and foreign exchange rates in 1467 there was 'grete romour... because of diversiteis of payment within the realme throu the takking in of the rentis be the auld payment and gevis it oute agane be a derrar price.' To 'content the commons' the domestic rate of exchange was soon restored to the previous level.[34]

Probably conditions of land tenure favoured acceptance of inflation — so long as it was not too sudden, as in 1467 or 1482. For agricultural tenants did not usually enjoy security of tenure beyond a 'tack' (lease), which depended upon a contract 'set' every three years on payment of a 'grassum' to the landlord. The latter might adjust his income (depending upon the relative shortage or abundance of prospective tenants) either by keeping the rent unchanged, or by raising the grassum, or by raising the rent, or by raising both grassum and rent. Hence, perhaps, the suspicion that the barons entertained towards the new-fangled system of feuing that James II seems to have advocated in the parliament of 1458. They pointedly advised that the king should 'begyne and gif exempill'.[35] In the following reign the monarchy <u>did</u> begin to set an example on the crown lands, initially to its advantage, later to its disadvantage when the fixed and perpetual feu-duties fell in real value with continuing inflation.

Feuing gave heritable security of tenure, hence an incentive to invest in the land and improve husbandry. At first, however, when feuing was widely applied to the crown lands by James IV, it was usually entrepreneurs of some standing who paid the lump sum needed to obtain a feu charter. To redeem their investment they seem to have rack-rented the working tenants under them, who continued to labour under the normal conditions of a three-year tack.[36] Thus feuing was not, in its initial stages, the panacea for agrarian ills that it was presumed to be by John Major, who argued strongly in its favour in his History of Greater Britain (1521).[37] Insecurity of tenure and the resulting poor husbandry and poverty were characteristics of later medieval Scotland. It was, so says the anonymous writer of 'The Harp' — a didactic Scottish poem of the 1460s — ' a barane land, fertile of folk, with gret scantnes of fude'.[38] This description may safely be taken as a fundamental synopsis of the Scottish economy in the later Middle Ages. Land was by far the major source of wealth, and increased wealth was attainable less by increased productivity upon the land than by control over a greater extent of land. The whole population was land-hungry; and from 1424 onwards it was the king himself who was the hungriest — hence the forfeitures that augmented the crown lands and made their rentals normally the most abundant source of royal revenue.[39]

What of trade and industry? The latter was doubtless of some significance in providing hand-made goods for the domestic market. Perhaps domestic trade, in contrast to external trade, was growing in the fifteenth century. Perhaps the sizable rural population, although it does not seem to have enjoyed the golden age of its English counterpart in the fifteenth century, was making rapid use of the new billon and copper coins thoughtfully put at its disposal by the government. Perhaps this was an underlying reason for the hopeful creation of so many burghs of barony[40] that could never aspire to more than a local significance. For, apart from legal disabilities, there was nothing in the landward areas really comparable to the flourishing English cloth industry that sent out tentacles to overseas markets.

Overseas trade was almost wholly the monopoly of the royal burghs; yet the products that they exported — wool, fleeces and hides — were raw materials forthcoming from the countryside. The intricacy and elaborate organisation of burghal life as revealed in the records of Edinburgh and Aberdeen tend to make historians over-estimate the economic significance of the burghs and burgesses — after 1472 the burghs no longer paid their way as one of the three estates; formerly they had paid one-third of contributions, thereafter they paid only one-fifth.[41] Nor should the meanderings of the Scottish staple in the Low Countries, which are relatively well documented,[42] be invested with an importance greater than the small volume of trade that was involved. Certainly overseas trade provided openings for entrepreneurs, from John Mercer in the days of David II to Robert Barton in the days of James IV; but Scotland, like the rest of Europe, suffered from a trade recession.

This is well documented from the statistics of the great customs levied upon Scottish exports. The export trade reached a peak at the end of the reign of David II and the beginning of the reign of Robert II, when the great customs brought in more than £9,000 a year[43] at a time when Scottish and English coins were almost at par. By 1500, levied at the same rate, they scarcely brought in £3,000 Scots, about the same as what James IV received from either feudal profits or judicial profits.[44] The export trade that was flourishing in 1371 dwindled and dwindled, not necessarily because of decreased productivity in Scotland but more likely because of a shrinking demand in foreign markets.

The vessels that left Scottish ports with wool, fleeces and hides came back with miscellaneous cargoes that included luxury goods. Since there was no general tariff upon imported goods until 1597 there are no useful statistics to indicate the volume of imports. That there was an imbalance of trade and a drainage of bullion overseas may be gathered as early as 1385, and more clearly from the enactments of James I's first parliament in 1424 which put a tax of 3s.4d. on each pound's worth of gold or silver exported from the realm.[45] In 1436 there was an act that not only forbade all export of gold, silver and jewels but put Scottish merchants under a troublesome obligation: for each exported sack of wool and its equivalent in hides and salted fish they were to bring back three ounces of bullion to be minted in Scotland.[46] Similar measures were re-enacted in the 1460s and 1470s, when 'sercheouris' and 'inquisitouris' were appointed to stop illicit export of bullion — but to no avail.[47]

Apart from a probable trade imbalance there were other international money movements of significance. Neither the ransom of David II nor the 'fynance' of James I to pay for his involuntary upbringing in England was paid in full, yet each meant a loss of bullion — 76,000 marks in the first case, 9,500 marks in the second.[48] There were also incalculable remittances for the upkeep of hostages — and Malise Graham, earl of Menteith, lay unredeemed in England for twenty-five years.[49] One might add the consequences of the skirmish at Homildon Hill in 1402 when it was ' as if the flower of the chivalry of the whole realm of Scotland was captured and held to ransom.'[50]

In an English context it is usual to write of the profits of war. In a Scottish context it would be more appropriate to write of the losses of war. The heaviest loss was doubtless the ravaging and partial occupation of southern Scotland, which, in monetary terms alone, meant a loss to the export trade. On the credit side were the 40,000 deniers d'or a l'escu brought by the sire de Garencières in 1355. This money, which the writer of the Scalacronica reckoned as worth 10,000 marks, was ' to be given among the prelates and barons of Scotland upon condition that they should break their truce with the king of England and make war upon him.'[51] Perhaps this influx of gold provided the wherewithal for David II's nobles, the first Scottish gold coins.[52] Similarly in 1385 Jean de Vienne, admiral of France, brought 50,000 gold francs to be shared out among the king, Cardinal Wardlaw and the more bellicose barons.[53] Perhaps under Robert III this influx sustained the regular coinage of gold crowns inspired by the French écu à la couronne.[54] Then there were the dowries of royal brides: Mary of Guelders brought 60,000 crowns;[55] in place of a stipulated dowry of 60,000 Rhenish florins Margaret of Denmark brought only 2,000 florins and many islands;[56] yet Margaret Tudor brought James IV a dowry of £10,000 sterling — then equated with £30,000 Scots — which was by far the chief contribution to the royal revenues between 1502 and 1505.[57]

Dowries, ransoms, the profits and losses of war, all these must have affected the supply of bullion. Yet these things were erratic and unpredictable; there remained another influence that was constant and pervasive, one that brought monetary debits and no monetary credits — payments to the Roman <u>camera</u> in connection with papal provisions to ecclesiastical benefices. These payments were systematised during the Babylonish captivity of the papacy at Avignon and received a new lease of life after the election of Martin V in 1417. By Scottish standards large sums of money were involved: when Alexander Bur was provided to the bishopric of Moray in 1364 he had to pay more than 650 florins of gold under pain of excommunication;[58] when Bishop Kennedy was translated to St. Andrews in 1440 he was unable to raise the usual 'common services' of 3,300 gold florins but was favoured by remission of half the sum.[59] James I liked neither papal control of ecclesiastical appointments nor the consequent outflow of bullion, hence in 1428 the new and undefined offence of 'barratry' which undoubtedly signified the purchase of benefices at the Roman <u>curia</u>.[60] Thanks to a papal indult of 1487 the Scottish crown obtained virtual control of appointments to the higher benefices but did not succeed in reducing the financial charges that had become traditional since the 1300s: in 1471 parliament complained of the 'gret dampnage and skaith dayli donne to al the realme' by trafficking at the <u>curia</u>, 'considering the innowmerable riches that is had out of the realme thar throw';[61] in 1484 parliament again complained of the 'grete skaith and damage' caused by the export of money by prelates and clerks 'for promociouns and pleis in the court of Rome' and it was envisaged that the way to stop the outflow of bullion was to force clerics to subsidise their transactions by taking out only merchandise to be converted into bullion on the continent.[62]

This was one expedient ordained by the parliaments of James III for the 'in halding' (conservation) of bullion. Other expedients were ordained for the 'in bringing' of bullion so that 'thare sulde sudanly cum bullioune in the realme in gret quantite.'[63] One means to this end was the attemped alteration of exchange rates in 1467 to attract foreign specie. Even when the scheme was first proposed there was an awareness that it might affect the cost of living, which it did: 'the penny worthis ar rysin with the penny and mekle derrar than thai war wont to be.'[64] Hence the project was abandoned. Parliament was, it seems, responsive to public opinion in its attempts to manage the currency — or to manage the king's management of the currency. It was recognised that 'the mater is gret and tuechis the hail body of the realme in gret nernes.'[65]

This was particularly the case in regard to copper small change and 'placks'. A conservative outlook upon monetary innovations made the introduction of a copper coinage an especially thorny political problem, quite apart from its economic consequences. In 1466 parliament approved the minting of £3,000 worth of copper coins, ostensibly for the ease and sustentation of the king's lieges and for the encouragement of almsgiving, yet within a year the copper coins were evidently so unpopular that it was ordained that 'thar be nane strikyn in tyme to cum under the payne of dede'; similarly in 1473 it was ordained that the striking of placks 'be cessit'.[66] Nonetheless experimentation in 'black money' continued and was a factor in the political crisis of 1482 when Cochrane's placks were cried down.[67] Their issue, which was itself inflationary, had come at a time of dearth. Thus a contemporary chronicler relates that 'thar was ane gret hungyr and deld ln Scotland, for the boll of meill was for four punds; for thar was blak cunye [coinage] in the realm, strikkin and ordinyt be King James the thred, half-pennys and three-penny pennys innumerabill of coppir...and mony pur folk delt of hungar.'[68] It was a copper coinage, so says Bishop Lesley, 'unmelt to have course or passage ln ony realme, quhairwith the pepill grudgeit.'[69] Perhaps the grudgings of. the people were inconsiderate, for by 1487 the realm was supposedly 'wastit of money'.[70]

'The mater of the mone', so runs the parliamentary record of 1474, 'is rycht subtile'.[71] What are we to make of the efforts of king and parliament to cope with the subtlety? They did, as we should expect, regard bullion as real wealth. Yet it must be conceded that the functions of money as a measure of wealth and as a means of exchange were also perceived. We may describe the monetary policies that were pursued but can scarcely criticise them or even subject them to realistic economic analysis. Far too many factors are unknown — population, whether falling, growing or static; the balance of trade; the extent of cash flow to the papacy. It was an age of trade recession and this, at least, can be shown to have reduced by two-thirds the external demand for the raw materials that Scotland exported. Clearly monetary problems were real and not imaginary.

The attempts made to solve them had political consequences, not solely of a domestic character. After the departure of Scotland from the 'sterling area' of the British Isles management of a separate currency became a notable function of a government that chose, or was forced, to abandon imitation of English monetary practices. In this respect, as in others, the distinctiveness of later medieval Scotland found expression.

NOTES

1. Ian Stewart, "Scottish Mints" in Mints, Dies and Currency, ed. R. A. G. Carson, pp. 165-289, at 179, 226, 227-8.

2. G. Burnett, The Exchequer Rolls of Scotland, ed. J. Stuart and others (1878-1908), II, xcvi-xcvii.

3. Ranald Nicholson, Scotland: the Later Middle Ages (1974), pp. 164-83, passim.

4. Ibid., p. 176.

5. See Athol Murray, "Foreign Trade and Scottish Ports, 1471 and 1542", An Historical Atlas of Scotland c. 400-c. 1600, ed. Peter McNeill and Ranald Nicholson (1975), pp. 74-5.

6. G. Burnett, Exchequer Rolls, II, xcv-xcviii.

7. Ibid.; Rotuli Scotiae, ed. D. Macpherson and others (1814-19), I, 964.

8. Nicholson, Later Middle Ages, p. 177.

9. Acts of the Parliaments of Scotland, ed. T. Thomson and C. Innes (1814-75), I, 499-501.

10. J. D. Mackie, History of Scotland (1964), p. 88.

11. Nicholson, Later Middle Ages, pp. 106-7 and Edward III and the Scots (1965), pp. 226-7.

12. The figures are :

	Antiqua Taxatio	Verus Valor
Perth	£6,192 2s. 6d.	£3,087 1s. 7d.
Edinburgh	£4,029 16s 10d.	£3,030 12s. 9d.
Argyll (barons)	£600 0s. 0d.	£133 6s. 8d.

13. Carlo Cipolla, "Currency Depreciation in Medieval Europe", in Change in Medieval Society, ed. Sylvia L. Thrupp (1964), pp. 227-36, at 228, first published in The Economic History Review (1963).

14. These, at least, can be demonstrated: see G. Burnett, Exchequer Rolls, II, xcix-c.

15. Ibid., xlii and note. See also the index sub nomine.

16. Ibid., xcv; Stewart, op. cit., p. 229.

17. Registrum de Dunfermelyn (Bannatyne Club, 1842), No. 399.

18. The Apostolic Camera and Scottish Benefices, ed. A. I. Cameron (1934), p. lvi, note 1.

19. Cipolla, op. cit., p. 233.

20. William Ferguson, Scotland's Relations with England (1977), p. 43.

21. See Cipolla, op. cit., pp. 234-5.

22. Ibid., p. 235.

23. Ibid., p. 228.

24. This figure is calculated from Cipolla's statistics (ibid., p. 235) and the fact that in connection with the dowry and dower of Margaret Tudor in 1502 £1 sterling was equated with £3 Scots (Nicholson, Later Middle Ages, p. 554).

25. Acts of the Parliaments, II, 100, c. 8; 105, cc. 12, 15.

26. First published in The Economic History Review (1955), conveniently reprinted in Change in Medieval Society, ed. Sylvia L. Thrupp (1964), pp. 237-46.

27. Ibid., p. 245.

28. Nicholson, Later Middle Ages, pp. 148-9.

29. Ibid., pp. 168, 252 (note), 319, 326, 375, 423 (note), 564, 601.

30. Ibid., pp. 109, 261-3.

31. See the accounts for the rebuilding of Edinburgh castle in 1335 in Calendar of Documents relating to Scotland, ed. J. Bain (1881-8), III, appendix iv, 347-59.

32. I am indebted to Mr. David I. Howie of the University of Guelph for allowing me to consult his research on this topic. The most readily available statistics are in the Accounts of the Lord High Treasurer of Scotland, ed. T. Dickson and Sir J. Balfour Paul (1877-1916), e.g. I, 245, 330, 347, 349, 350, 355, 378, 379; II, 20, 115.

33. Statistics concerning the crown lands are those most readily available. See Nicholson, Later Middle Ages, pp. 378-9, 408-9, 455-6, 570-1.

34. Acts of the Parliaments, II, 92, c. 1.

35. Ibid., II, 49, c. 15.

36. Ranald Nicholson, "Feudal Developments in Late Medieval Scotland", The Juridical Review: Law Journal of Scottish Universities, (1973), pp. 1-21, at 3-8.

37. Scottish History Society edition, p. 31.

38. Liber Pluscardensis, ed. F. J. H. Skene (1877-80), I, 392-400.

39. Nicholson, Later Middle Ages, pp. 285, 318-9, 378-80, 454-5, 570-1.

40. 44 between 1400 and 1500; a further 28 between 1500 and 1513. See G. S. Pryde, The Burghs of Scotland: a Critical List (1965), pp. 48-57.

41. Nicholson, Later Middle Ages, pp. 452-3.

42. See J. Davidson and A. Gray, The Scottish Staple at Veere (1909) and M. P. Rooseboom, The Scottish Staple in the Netherlands (1910).

43. Nicholson, Later Middle Ages, pp. 177, 187-8.

44. Ibid., pp. 565-67.

45. Acts of the Parliaments, I, 554, 572; II, 5.

46. Ibid., II, 23, 24.

47. Ibid., II, 105, cc. 11, 16.

48. Nicholson, Later Middle Ages, pp. 194 and note, 290.

49. Ibid., pp. 320, 368.

50. Johannis de Fordun Scotichronicon cum Supplementis et Continuatione Walteri Bower, ed. W. Goodall (1759), II, 433-5.

51. Nicholson, Later Middle Ages, p. 160.

52. Stewart, op. cit., pp. 226, 227-8.

53. Foedera...accurante Thoma Rymer, 3rd edn. (The Hague, 1739-45), III, pt. iii, 188.

54. Stewart, op. cit., p. 230.

55. Nicholson, Later Middle Ages, p. 348.

56. Ibid., pp. 415-16.

57. Ibid., pp. 554, 566.

58. <u>Registrum Episcopatus Moraviensis</u> (Bannatyne Club, 1837), Nos. 144, 145.

59. Annie I. Dunlop, <u>The Life and Times of James Kennedy, Bishop of St. Andrews</u> (1950), pp. 39-41.

60. Nicholson, <u>Later Middle Ages</u>, p. 294.

61. <u>Acts of the Parliaments</u>, II, 99, c. 4.

62. <u>Ibid.</u>, II, 166, c. 11.

63. <u>Ibid.</u>, II, 90, c.8; 92, c. 1; 105, c. 11.

64. <u>Ibid.</u>, II, 92, c. 1.

65. <u>Ibid.</u>, II, 100, c. 8; 105, cc. 12, 15.

66. Nicholson, <u>Later Middle Ages</u>, p. 436.

67. <u>Ibid.</u>, p. 505.

68. Brit. Museum Royal MSS. 17 DXX, edited in J. Pinkerton, <u>History of Scotland</u> (1797), I, 503.

69. J. Lesley, <u>History of Scotland</u> (Bannatyne Club, 1830), p. 48.

70. <u>Acts of the Parliaments</u>, II, 118, c. 3.

71. <u>Ibid.</u>, II, 106, c. 4.

THE BLACK MONEY OF JAMES III

Joan E. L. Murray

The black money of James III which was cried down after the Lauder episode in 1482 is of obvious interest to Scottish historians. In the absence of any detailed records of that coinage, and in particular of the royal profit from it, it is natural to hope that numismatists might throw some light on the subject, but one may say that they have instead tended to obscure it. The editor of the Exchequer Rolls quoted R. W. Cochran-Patrick, 'that very high authority', who considered that the billon placks were part of this black money, a view which now appears to be untenable — and indeed the editor appreciated some of the difficulties of accepting this.[1] The following is an attempt to fill in some of the gaps, while explaining the numismatic problems. It has been prepared hurriedly, after more than one aspect of the subject had come up in the discussions at the Symposium, and I am very conscious that further research would be an advantage. I also regret that there has not been time for consultation since then, although I have had the benefit of exchange of ideas and material in the past. In 1967 Dr. Norman Macdougall, who was then writing his Glasgow doctoral thesis on the political history of James III's reign, enquired about the black money, and discussion with him drew my attention to the desirability of a revised numismatic treatment of the subject. It was Mr. Ian Stewart who soon afterwards tentatively suggested to me the possible identification of the black money which I here advocate (with his permission), but his attitude to it at the Symposium was decidedly more cautious than mine and the responsibility for opinions expressed here is of course my own.

It would be helpful if contemporary usage of the terms white and black money could be accurately defined, but the fact is that there was no universal dividing line between the two types. In England, where the native coinage was then only in fine gold and silver, white money meant silver, and the French billon 'blanks' could be referred to as being of copper. In France, because of severe debasement and frequent mutations during the Hundred Years' War, the standard of fineness for the officially black money on a return to <u>monnaie forte</u> could be higher than the most recent standard for the <u>blancs</u>, although there was a considerable difference between the standards for the black and white coins at any one time.[2] It is thus necessary to rely mainly on the few Scottish records, not too far from the relevant date, which use the terms unequivocally. The copper farthings authorised in 1466 were certainly described as black in the mint accounts and in later acts of parliament,[3] although some brass specimens are known, which would hardly have been black in appearance. The particular coins of other realms which were named in 1469, as black money which was not to be current in Scotland,[4] were however of base billon. The French deniers were then about 8% silver, while the mailles were baser, and the mites of Flanders were still worse, at 2% silver in 1466. The white Scottish pennies which in 1468 were to be full legal tender until the next parliament[5]

were certainly of good billon, at about 50% on the evidence quoted below.
There was probably no distinction between the terms 'black money' and 'black
silver': certainly the meaning of money in general for the word silver is indicated in the case of James IV's gifts of drinksilver and bridlesilver, which
were generally in gold, judging by the sums of money involved.

Even if we knew what was considered to be the boundary between white and
black money at that date, it would often be difficult to tell from the look of a
billon coin now whether it qualified as white. In other cases, however, chemical cleaning may have left it as silvery in appearance as when issued. The
standard minting processes caused surface enrichment, because the copper in
the alloy oxidises more readily than the silver, particularly when heated, and
it was normal practice to remove oxidisation by blanching in weak acid. This
left depressions in the surface of the coin blank, between silver prominences,
and subsequent striking spread these prominences to give an almost continuous
surface layer of silver, an effect which would apply in coins as base as about
80% copper, according to one authority.[6] Quantitative analysis of the metal is
of course greatly to be preferred to even the most expert judgment by inspec-
tion, but it is necessary to eliminate the effect of surface enrichment first.
It had been hoped to analyse some of the coins in the Oxford collection non-
destructively, following the discussions at the Symposium, but most unfortunately the X-ray fluorescence equipment at the Research Laboratory developed
a fault very soon afterwards, putting it out of commission for some months.

The narrative source which gives most detail about the black money in 1482
is a short anonymous chronicle appended to one manuscript of Wyntoun's history and printed in Pinkerton's History of Scotland.[7] This contemporary chronicle, ending in the autumn of 1482, is generally considered to be reliable.
The relevant passage reads a follows:-

> Thir was ane gret hungyr and deid in Scotland for the boll of
> meill was for four pundis, for thir was blak cunyhe in the realme
> strikkin and ordinyt be king James the thred, half pennys and three
> penny pennys innumerabill of coppir, and thai yeid twa yere and
> mair ... And that sammyn yere in the monetht of Julij the king
> of Scotland purposyt till haif passyt in Ingland with the power
> of Scotland and passyt on gaitwart to Lawdyr, and thar the lordis
> of Scotland held thair consaill in the kirk of Lauder and cryit
> downe the blak silver.

The Edinburgh custumar's account for October 1482 to July 1483 includes a
payment of £180 16s. on the king's behalf 'to the werkmen that wrocht the blac
money of oure command', which confirms that this was indeed a regal coinage.[8]
This is in any case easier to accept than Pitscottie's version, that the king had
authorised 'ane new courteour start wpe callit Couchren ... to straik conye of
his awin as he had ben ane prince'[9] There is no need to quote the other early
historians, as the number of those who associated Cochrane with this black
money is no confirmation of the truth of that association. The writer of the
Hopetoun manuscript entitled 'Anent Cunyie ane ample discourss' also referred
to 'sa bass money as the lyke wes never sen Cochranis dayis', writing about
a century later, but there is no reason to believe that he had reliable evidence,
e.g. in mint books, for that distant period.[10] Pitscottie continues: 'And quhen

the wyffis wald refuse the said cunyie quhilk wes callit ane Couchrinis plak
and said to him that it wald be cryit doun ...', and there is ample record evidence of refusal of the black money, at a higher level than 'the wives', both in
the Exchequer Rolls and in legal actions before the lords auditors or the lords
of council — sources which numismatists have apparently not previously taken
into account in this context.

Several of the legal records referring to the time of the black money do not
necessarily concern payments in that form, but they are informative about the
valuation of the gold and fine silver coin at that time. One of the most clearly
phrased decisions was in April 1485, specifying payment in gold and silver
'as it had course in the tym of the blac mone/ that is to say the Inglis groit for
ij<u>s</u>. & gold and al vthir money as it was proclamyt to the said tym or the avale:
thairof';[11] and the phrase about the English groat occurs in several other
cases of 'solutio post declamationem nigrae monete'. It is fairly certain that
this was the heavier pre-1464 English groat, which was the commonest silver
coin in circulation in Scotland at the time, as shown by hoards and documents.
One example, which details the gold and silver coins for a payment of 100
crowns in 1485, has no silver coins except £14 of English groats at 16d. each
and £4 of English Edward groats at 12d. each.[12] Another case, in 1483, doubtless referred to the pre-Lauder valuation although not specifically mentioning
the time of the black money; the decision included that payment of £15 should
be made in 'auld hare (Harry) grotis, outher Lundon or Calise, ilk grote for
ij<u>s</u>., like as he is bund .... be his obligacioun'.[13] Known currency values
of this old English groat and of one representative gold coin, the Scottish demy,
are tabulated below, to illustrate the complex revaluations of James III's reign.[14]

Date		Old English groat	Demy	Comments
Oct	1451	12d	9s	
Oct	1456	–	10s	
Oct	1467	16d	12s	
	1468	13d	10s	As before October 1467.
July	1471	–	–	Some 'excrescencia antique monete' since July 1470.
April	1474	–	12s	
Nov	1475	–	13s 4d	
Before July	1482	2s	–	At the time of the black money.
July	1483	–	14s	
Jan	1485	16d	–	
	1488	–	14s	

In the actions mentioned above the judgments were clearly in accordance
with the act of parliament of October 1467, which ordained that any debt incurred
before the revaluation of that date was to be paid in money of the same intrinsic
value — 'the samyn sowmis in substance as was intendyt ... and proporcionally
in pundis and schillingis of the recknynge that sal be in tyme to cum to ryse
with the money lik as it geide of befor'.[15] On the same principle some refusal
of black money was held to have been justified. Thus in October 1483, although
a case was referred to the spiritual court for determination the lords stated

the legal position 'becaus it concernis our soverane & the hale realme anent the offering & payment of blac mone ... becaus the dait of the contract ... was befor the cours of ony blac mone and pament profferit in blac mone ... thairfor ordanis that payment be made of the said soumez of the mone that had cours the tyme of the makin of the contract or ellis of the mone that now rynnis'.[16] In a case the previous March, payment of £90 had been accepted but the remaining £90 which was offered in black money refused.[17] This might suggest that the black money was legal tender for not more than ten shillings in the pound, but there is no indication of any such restriction in the other cases and the explanation could well be that the obligation in this case had specified half gold and silver and the rest in usual money of Scotland: the 1467 act of parliament had in fact laid down the same principle of maintaining the intrinsic value of payments when this clause was used, but there was perhaps more scope for doubt about the legal position in such a case. In an action in Aberdeen burgh court, concerning £4 in black money, 'the said Henry grantit him that the said money was sufficient payment quhen he ressavit it, as he understude'.[18] Altogether the evidence that this black money was full legal tender appears to be strong, although such a state of affairs would be surprising at that period, particularly in view of the cessation of the earlier coinage of copper farthings in 1467 and the restrictions on their passage: in 1466 they were only required to be taken for one shilling in the pound for large sums, this limit being raised to three shillings in 1468.[19]

The 1482 crying down of the black money appears to have been either complete demonetisation (but see Appendix for the hoard evidence), or else a particularly drastic devaluation. It probably coincided with a return to the rates in force in the late 1470's for the gold and silver coins, and perhaps a bigger change for the billon. The best evidence about the virtual if not complete demonetisation is in the Exchequer Rolls. In October 1482, the record mentions £51 of the ferms of Carrick 'quas asserit compotans recipisse in nigra moneta, licet non solverit in tempore'.[20] Likewise the custumar of Edinburgh had part of the customs in his hands in black money when that was 'subito declamata' so that he could not spend it for the king's use nor his own, for which reasons he was allowed £440 of his arrears in 1484.[21] His total arrears from the previous account were £484 13s. 2½d. (and over £1500 from 1482), and it is highly probable that the full sum of black money involved was this £484 odd, the £44 13s. 2½d. which was not written off being either the intrinsic value of the demonetised coin or at least an upper bound to this. (The 1474 cost of brass, quoted below, in fact suggests a much lower intrinsic value.) A revaluation which rated all the black coins at farthings would fit this evidence, with most of the money included in the total being the threepenny pieces, as one would expect; and with the natural assumption of a return to limited tender for the copper pieces it might also be considered to fit the other records showing that this money could not be used. Another of these concerned the ferms of Kinclavin for Whitsun 1482, which the comptroller had refused 'ex eo quod noluerunt dare nisi nigram monetam' and 'illa moneta erat declamata et sic deperdita'; here the arrears were cancelled in 1487 'ex consideracione dominorum concilii et auditorum'.[22] The lords of council also dealt with an action about the mails of Strathearn, in March 1483, and proof was to be made that some payment was offered in black money and refused.[23]

There are strong reasons against identifying the billon placks as part of the black money. They were certainly officially current coin in 1485, although apparently viewed with some suspicion, since the king in parliament needed to command that they should 'pas & have cours universally throw out the realme'.[24] Both old and new placks were withdrawn in 1486, 'declamatis pro duabus partibus' and to be taken at the mint at twopence each, counterfeits too.[25] This surely indicates that their intrinsic value was no less than twopence in 1486, which does not agree with the black money being almost valueless after Lauder. Numismatists have remarked on the James III placks being much finer than those of James IV and V, and their judgment that these were white money is confirmed by analysis of the metal, carried out by the British Museum Research Laboratory.[26] Small samples from each of four placks of the first issue showed silver percentages of 37.5, 43.0, 42.2 and 16.1 respectively. The first three figures agree with the standard quoted in 1473 as five shillings of fine silver in the ounce,[27] which I interpret as five-twelfths or 41%, on the assumption that the fine silver was already priced as in 1475. The much lower percentage of silver for the fourth plack may possibly be due to a debasement, particularly as this coin is from one of the two latest obverse dies, distinguished by mixed saltire and colon stops, but one would need further analyses of these later placks before accepting this, as the explanation may lie in non-uniformity within the coin; this is unavoidable with alloys, except in the particular proportion known as the eutectic, and could affect such small-scale analyses. In the case of the placks referred to as new in 1486, of which the type was first identified in 1955,[28] no analysis is available, but visual examination of the very few known specimens suggests that the alloy was much the same as for the first issue. Finally, there is documentary evidence that the distinctly baser placks of James IV were classified by the Scots as white money in 1514, when £30 out of a sum of 100 merks was paid 'in moneta alba viz. plakkis and penneis'.[29]

The small billon pennies of James III are more varied in fineness than the placks. In this case no analysis is available, but some years ago Mr. R. B. K. Stevenson consulted Professor Bell of Heriot-Watt College on the subject, and they made some tests with a fluid which reacts by different colour changes to contact with silver of varying fineness. Mr. Stevenson emphasised that the results are only indications, and that many more coins would need to be tested to get the best results possible by this method, because of the variation found and difficulties like surface enrichment. Nevertheless I believe that these results are worth quoting here.[30]

Pennies	% silver
Corresponding to crown groats	50+
James III class A	c. 50
B	(Near to the indication listed for copper)
C	(Distinctly more coppery than A)
D	50 to 80
James IV, class I and II	(The indication listed for copper, although they have quite a silvery look)

There are difficulties over dating some of the changes in these pennies. Class D ones, which are very rare, by their portrait certainly correspond to the groats with three-quarter face portrait, at the weight standard introduced in February 1484, and these pennies are probably later than May 1485, as the authorisation to strike pennies then, limited to one ounce in fourty of silver,[31] probably means that the coinage of billon pennies had been interrupted, perhaps since 1482. A reversion dated March 1489 mentions payment in 'halfpenys quhilk wer umquhile pennys' of £22 out of £200, but no pennies,[32] so presumably very few pennies had been struck since this devaluation to halfpennies. It may be assumed to have affected all billon pennies of the standard type, i.e. the first two of the table above as well as the baser class C, which is much commoner. Class B pennies, which have a distinctive reverse type, appear to be contemporary with late class C ones, and it is possible that they were issued as halfpennies, since the latest known halfpenny at half the weight of a penny belongs in class A, contemporary with the first issue placks and the earlier light groats. Although the pennies of classes B and C do not as obviously qualify as white money as do the placks and the other classes of billon penny before 1482, the combination of the 1514 record of pennies as white money and the 1489 one of the current value of what were formerly pennies makes it very unlikely that these could have been part of the notorious black money.

Having thus found reasons, over and above the chronicler's description of the black money as copper, against identifying any of the billon coins of James III as black, it remains to consider the coins of that period which have always been accepted as of copper, or (less frequently) of brass. Although here too it would be more satisfactory to determine by analysis whether there is any trace of silver, there is no doubt that these were black money to the Scots of the time. There are four types of coin known as farthings, two being associated with the 'coppir money, four to the penny' ordered in 1466. Neither type exactly fits the description in that act of parliament. The first (Stewart fig. 113)[33] has the St. Andrew's cross and the crown on opposite sides as seems to be intended, but nothing to fit the phrase 'ane R with James on the tother part'; the second (Stewart fig. 114) has IR crowned on the obverse and the saltire environed with a cross on the reverse, which is perhaps as intended in the act. Possibly some of the copper coins, perhaps the first of these two types, were struck before this act in 1466, since the mint accounts in 1468 refer to a part of the copper coins having 'in principio fabricacionis' had course as halfpennies, not farthings. The remaining two types of copper coin of about the same size have been called ecclesiastical farthings. They were first published in 1919, from the find at Crosraguel Abbey, and Macdonald (later Sir George) ascribed them to a mint there,[34] on evidence later discounted. The reverse types of both are related to that of the light groats of James III, perhaps introduced in 1467, in having mullets in the angles of a long cross, partly reviving the common type of the pre-1393 silver. What is presumably the earlier of these copper issues has IR crowned on the obverse, like the undoubted farthing, and mullets alternating with crowns on the reverse (Stewart fig. 100). The other (Stewart fig. 101) has a very distinctive obverse with no inscription, the main feature being three fleurs-de-lis within a trefoil, with central mullet: the reverse has mullets in all four angles of the cross, in this case a cross fleury reminiscent of that on the placks. Both carry the reverse legend MONETA

PAUPERUM, abbreviated. Either or both of these might be the 'halfpenny penny' of the contemporary chronicle, particularly as the weight of such a coin could reasonably be expected to agree with that of the earlier farthings, since the currency value of the old English groat was practically doubled between 1466 and the time of the black money. Of the two, the distinctive tretrefoil-lis type is perhaps the more likely, as the old farthings might still have retained their original value.

A larger and commoner copper coin of the period has been named Crosraguel penny or, more recently, Bishop Kennedy penny; it is here referred to as Crux Pellit penny, after the reverse legend. The obverse type is orb and cross, the latter extending into the legendary circle and serving also as initial mark, while the reverse type is a Latin cross in a tressure of four arcs, with varying ornament on the cusps and in the spandrels. Stewart figs. 95 to 99 show the main classes, distinguished chiefly by the tilt of the orb, as shown by the curve of the bands, and by its decoration. The weight is about four times that of the farthings, with a wide range of weights for both denominations, as is natural for such small base coins, cut by hand. The Crux Pellit pennies may well have been struck at 16 to the ounce, the recorded weight standard of the billon bawbees introduced in 1538 and of Mary's placks in 1557, and perhaps that of the earlier placks too (for which 15 to the ounce was suggested by Burns). These pennies are smaller and thicker than the James III placks, but are certainly the only copper coins to which the name Cochrane's placks could plausibly be given, since plack, like groat, was a name applied to a large coin. There is, of course, no certainty that this was indeed the contemporary popular name, but there are later cases where a personal name other than that of a mint official was attached to a coin type.[35] Following Mr. Stewart's suggestion, I am fairly confidently identifying the Crux Pellit pennies as the 'threepenny pennies' of the contemporary chronicle. One point which might be argued against this is easily covered: the Crux Pellit coins do not appear to have been struck at six times the weight of the possible black halfpennies, but for a coinage of such negligible intrinsic value it was clearly unnecessary for the official currency values of the different denominations to be in accordance with the relative weights — if a coinage of only token nature was acceptable at all, which was of course the difficulty. It was already necessary to distinguish the fine silver groats, the baser ones, and the placks by type rather than by size.

It is perhaps necessary first to explain the probable reasons why numismatists have largely neglected this possible identification, when the attraction of fitting a large, inadequately explained and apparently undocumented coinage to one of much the same period for which we have only documentary evidence (itself inadequate) appears so obvious, once the idea has been put forward. The inscription on the obverse normally reads IACOBUS DEI GRA REX without the country, although one specimen with S for Scottorum has now come to light, and this partly explains how it was possible for a variety of wrong attributions to be current in the nineteenth century. Two earlier antiquaries had in fact described these coins as Scottish: George Martine, who attributed them to Bishop Kennedy,[36] and Ralph Thoresby, who in 1715 listed one under James III. The latter, who could not read the reverse legend further than Crux, wrote:[37] 'Quaere, Whether this be one of the Fardinges Statute for the

Ease and Sustentation of the Kingis Lieges' (in 1466), 'or one of the Black Pennies so odious to the vulgar' cried down in 1482. Cochran-Patrick certainly knew this work of Thoresby's, and this may have prompted his enquiry to George Sim, to which the latter replied in April 1873:[38]

> The small copper coins are of James II of Aragon 1291-1327. The rev. begins with "Crux", but after that word there are varied readings ...
>
> These coins are very often found in Scotland mixed with Placks of Scottish kings of the same name and I have greatly disappointed some collectors when I have convinced them that these coins are really foreigners. Perhaps they circulated in Scotland at a time when some people would not know any difference between them and the Scottish coins. ... The late Prof[r] Christmas was the first who told me what they were.

It now seems remarkable that both these distinguished Scottish amateurs should have deferred to received opinion, in the face of the find evidence. Sim acted as honorary curator of coins for the National Museum of Antiquities of Scotland, and was obviously well placed to know about these minor finds, as well as studying hoards which reached the Exchequer. Cochran-Patrick did not hesitate to put forward his own arguments about the attribution of Scottish coins, when interpreting the records which he so usefully assembled, but I know of no evidence in his other incoming numismatic correspondence nor in his published works that he pursued any further the subject of these copper coins. Edward Burns was the first to publish the early black farthings with their correct attribution, but his Coinage of Scotland gives no specific consideration to the later black money and understandably ignores the Crux Pellit coins.

In publishing the Crosraguel find and establishing as Scottish the Crux Pellit coins and the remaining types of black 'farthing', Macdonald considered at some length the documentary evidence about the early farthings and quoted the contemporary chronicle about the black money cried down in 1482. He pointed out that the placks and pennies were of white billon and claimed that Cochran-Patrick's explanation of the allusions to black money as referring merely to those had now been swept away. Although he 'positively asserted that during the fifteenth century copper coins were current in Scotland to a much larger extent' than previously suspected, Macdonald did not offer any identification of the regal black money decried in 1482, because he believed his theory of an ecclesiastical mint at the abbey, and even considered the coins of known regal types in the find as likely to be contemporary imitations.

In 1950 Mr. Stevenson reattributed the Crux Pellit pennies to Bishop Kennedy, which is far more satisfactory - if an ecclesiastical origin is to be sought - since the bishops of St. Andrews did have the privilege of striking coins, and the orb and cross was the principal charge of the arms of St. Salvator's college founded by Bishop Kennedy, He also discounted what Macdonald had claimed to be evidence of minting, in the finds associated with the coins.[39] Doubt has already been cast on this attribution in its turn: although Mr. Stewart adopted it in The Scottish Coinage (1955), he has since then written that 'it is questionable whether episcopal issues would have been on such a large scale as is implied by the variety and dispersion of these copper pennies, even if they were continued by Kennedy's successors'.[40] The coinage rights of the bishops of St. Andrews, which may not have been exercised later than John Balliol's reign, need not be understood as more extensive than those of some English sees, to strike silver coin at the same standard as the king's mints, retaining the seigniorage or profit.

There are some objections to dating the Crux Pellit pennies as early as Bishop Kennedy, although the evidence is somewhat tenuous. In general, close numismatic dating is possible only by comparison with other coins for which the date range is determined by other means; a good example is the use of the episcopal marks on Durham coins to date other Edwardian sterlings, the dies being made at a common centre, London. Hoard evidence can also be valuable, but it does not help for these copper coins, which typically occur as site finds in excavations, as considered by Mr. Rigold supra, or have been picked up from sands round the Scottish coast. Even if these were regal, as I believe, they did not necessarily share any punches for the lettering and ornamentation of the dies with the more datable silver and gold, nor indeed with the billon pennies. However, there are some details of the Crux Pellit pennies which 'perhaps reflect the ornamentation of Scottish regal coinage as late as the 1470s or 1480s'.[41] One frequent feature of their lettering, which is not found on the silver before 1475, is a peaked top to the Gothic A, and a similar peak inside the C; but admittedly a similarly peaked O is found on the placks dating from before 1473. Both the open and closed form of C are found on the Crux Pellit pennies, whereas the closed form is regular on the undoubted coins of James III after the end of the crown groat coinage (perhaps in 1467), but it is perhaps easier to accept a continuation of an out-of-date style of lettering on the petty coins than that an innovation should originate there. Macdonald in fact used a similar argument to give a later date, as he assumed that the use of the cross which tops the orb as the initial mark of the inscription too was copied from the three-quarter face portrait groats introduced about 1485 (the preferred date is now 1484). I discount this, because the natural positioning of the orb in the centre of the coin almost forces the designer to extend the cross into the legendary circle, and I do not think it necessary to look for a precedent.

Various calculations may be made, in an attempt to discover the likely profit to the king from the black money, but naturally they largely depend on the identification of the coins themselves. One further record of an action before the lords of council appears to be highly relevant to the question of how much the coins cost to mint. In April 1485 Gilbert Fish claimed from George Robison £104 'for certane stuff of copper' extending to 21 stone 11 pounds weight, and £64 for graving of irons, but the case was dismissed because Fish admitted that it was in the king's name that Robison took delivery of this copper stuff and at the king's command that he had 'prentit the said irnis'.[42] Coinage dies were normally referred to as irons; Gilbert Fish was a known coiner in this reign, being associated with Berwick groats; and the Treasurer's accounts and Exchequer Rolls have no mention in the Index of any use of copper, although brazen guns or gun parts occur. The conjunction of these facts pointing to this being a reference to the black money is strengthened by the knowledge that Robison (not yet serving as Comptroller) was the same Edinburgh customer whose account in 1483 included payment to the workmen who made the black money.[43] The sum of £104 is almost exactly at the rate of six shillings per pound of copper, which is a plausible rate for the fabrication, or possibly for the metal itself. We have for comparison the coiner's expenses for striking groats from the queen's silver in the accounting period 1459-64, at the rate of 2s 8d per pound,[44] and the 1557 figure of 10s per pound for pennies and testoons alike.[45]

I have not been able to find a record of the price of copper around 1482, but 35 pounds of brass for the artillery cost 40s in 1474, including carriage,[46] With some allowance for revaluation, the price of copper at the time of the black money can hardly have been more than 2s per pound. Adding 6s for the work, there would be about 56s profit per pound weight, or seven-eighths of the official currency value of 64s. It is obvious that these calculations involve several weak links, but that small adjustments to the fabrication charge or to the cost of the metal (where a lower estimate might easily have been taken) would not make much difference to the proportion of profit. It is certainly higher than that given for the base billon pennies of Mary's reign, at about three-eighths as recalculated by Burns,[47] but probably quite comparable to that for the basest issue of hardheads of that reign.

One would also like to be able to estimate the size of the issue of black money, or at least of the Crux Pellit pennies. In the last two decades numismatists have given considerable attention to the two aspects of using the extant coins to calculate output, namely what was the average number of coins struck per die in periods for which there are bullion figures, and how should the number of dies be estimated. For the latter, the established statistical method requires analysis of a sufficiently large sample of coins to give a reliable estimate of the proportion of dies used more than once i.e. of the number to be expected in another sample of similar size.[48] Unfortunately no such analysis is available for the Crux Pellit pennies, let alone the smaller copper coins of the period, for which the sample would probably be too small to allow this. What is available to me is a catalogue prepared by the late Mr. Kerr, listing 104 Crux Pellit coins by orb type, form of inscription, stops and ornaments. Discarding half of these because the form of the inscription is queried and considering the obverse dies only, they fall into 35 categories, of which 9 have more than one specimen. Doubtless some of the multi-specimen categories include more than one die, and three - with 5, 4 and 4 specimens - could conceivably yield extra non-singleton dies, but more of these categories are likely to provide extra singletons on full analysis, and reduce the number of non-singletons. I shall thus quote the figure obtained on the basis of 9 repeated dies among 35, which is about 200 "effective dies", without stating confidence limits - the normal statistical treatment would deal with variability between samples, rather than with the uncertainty about the true number of non-singleton dies within this sample. Two points may be made which suggest that this is an underestimate. Of the 35 categories, 19 have unusual obverse inscriptions, either spelling mistakes or use of some form of the reverse inscription, or have exceptional ornament on the orb, and these represent only 21 specimens. I have also done a full comparison of 19 specimens, not overlapping with the 21 unusual ones in Kerr's list, and there is only one obverse die occurring more than once among these. The effective number of dies is a convenient term to express the number which would account for the whole output, if their average output was the same as for the known dies.

Average outputs per obverse die have been determined for some periods of the English sterling coinages, as 39,031 for Edward I's reign and 28,187 for Edward II's, but much higher figures were possible. There are various caveats about applying these figures to the Crux Pellit coinage. Copper is a harder metal than silver, and the quality of steel used for the dies might not be the same in our case, while it is not certain that what we call the obverse, because it bears the king's name, was actually the pile die, which lasted longer on average than the trussel. If however we assume 20,000 coins per die, for the sake of argument, then we are considering 4 million coins and (at three-pence each) a sum of £50,000

The tentative figure produced above can be examined for plausibility in several ways. At 16 coins to the ounce, it represents 250,000 ounces or about 1000 stone weight. If the die-sinker was still paid at a penny for every 12 ounces coined, as at the beginning of the reign, this would come to about £92 This may be compared with the sum of £66 which Fish claimed for graving the irons, but of course that sum would not necessarily be the total charge over the period of this coinage, and on the other hand it might include other denominations and special payment for the punches and dies of a new coinage, as was customary towards the end of the sixteenth century. In comparison with the figures for the silver coinage, in the mint accounts for the reign, this would be a very high yearly mint output, if concentrated in something over two years, but in 1466 the intention was to strike £3000 of farthings 'countande to the silver', making 2,880,000 pieces - not necessarily completed, since this farthing coinage was discontinued by parliament in 1467. Output figures for hardheads in 1558,[49] when nearly 600 stones were struck in four months, indicate that the suggested rate of output could have been achieved without difficulty, together with a smaller number of halfpennies.

I hope that the degree of uncertainty in the above calculations will be fully appreciated. I should also point out that the quoted sum of money is in pre-Lauder terms. If the king's profit is taken to be seven-eighths of that sum, and if it could be realised in gold and silver which lost only about a third of its value in 1482, then the post-Lauder figure would be about £29,000; but pre-sumably there were in fact more losses at the devaluation than are recorded in the Exchequer Rolls, from black money already in the hands of the Treasurer or Comptroller, and some of the profit was expended on the war with England.

We who are accustomed to the idea of coinages of little intrinsic value may think that copper was a better medium for a petty coinage than very base billon, which may be considered a wasteful use of scarce silver. In discussing the Crosraguel find, Macdonald compared the Moneta Pauperum coins and the other copper money with tokens like the late seventeenth century ones in England, which fulfilled a genuine requirement for small change. He did make the caveat that the authors of this Scottish black money may have gone beyond regarding it as a token issue, when stating that it had 'the same economic justification as our copper coinage of to-day', but was condemned because it 'shared the obloquy which rightly fell' on the debased silver.[50] I have little doubt myself that the black money of James III was condemned on its own de-merits, although earlier experience of revaluations may have contributed to distrust of it. There may have been a devaluation of the placks when their coinage ceased in 1473 and they were to pass 'as thai ar of avale' after they had been assayed,[51] but I suspect that the later difficulties about their circulation may have been a result of the traumatic experience of the black money more than of the existence of counterfeits and the standards of the placks themselves.

ABBREVIATIONS

ADA	The Acts of the Lords Anditors of Causes and Complaints, 1466-94
ADC	The Acts of the Lords of Council in Civil Causes
APS	Acts of the Parliaments of Scotland
ER	The Exchequer Rolls of Scotland
RCS	R.W. Cochran-Patrick, Records of the Coinage of Scotland, I (1874)

NOTES

1. ER IX, p.lxvi.

2. Some examples of French usage are: a. In referring to bullion in 1351, 'marc d'argent blanc, alloyé à 4d 8gr... et au dessus... marc d'argent en billon noir, à 2d 8 grains de loy et au dessoubz'. b. 'Blancs à la fleur... à 1d 6gr.' in 1360. c. 'Deniers doubles noirs, qui seront à 3d. A.R.' in July 1364.

3. ER VII, 580-1; RCS, 44. APS II, 88, 90, 97; RCS, 32, 34, 35.

4. APS II, 97; RCS, 35.

5. APS II, 88; RCS, 34.

6. L. Cope, "Surface-silvered Ancient Coins" in Methods of Chemical and Metallurgical Investigation of Ancient Coinage, ed. E.T. Hall and D.M. Metcalf, Royal Numismatic Society Special Publication no. 8 (1972), p. 261-278.

7. B.M. Royal MSS. 17 DXX in J. Pinkerton, The History of Scotland (London, 1797).

8. ER IX, 219.

9. R. Lindsay of Pitscottie, The Historie and Chronicles of Scotland (S.T.S., 1899-1911), I, 169.

10. RCS, 106.

11. ADC I, 115.*

12. ADC I, 94.*

13. ADC II, p. cxvi.

14. APS for 1451 to 1468. ER VIII, 23 for 1471. TA I, 69 for 1474. APS for 1475. ADA, 122* for 1483. TA I passim for 1488.

15. APS II, 88; RCS, 33.

16. <u>ADA</u>, 122*

17. <u>ADC</u> II, cxxv.

18. <u>Extracts from the Council Register of the Burgh of Aberdeen 1398-1570</u> (Spalding Club, 1844), 413.

19. <u>APS</u>, II, 86, 88, 92; <u>RCS</u>, 32, 35.

20. <u>ER</u> IX, 196.

21. <u>ER</u> IX, 286.

22. <u>ER</u> IX, 480.

23. <u>ADC</u> II, p. cxxii.

24. <u>APS</u> II, 172; <u>RCS</u>, 41.

25. <u>ER</u> IX, 449. <u>APS</u> II, 174; <u>RCS</u>, 41.

26. I am most grateful to Miss M. Archibald for arranging for this analysis, in 1973. It was by atomic absorption spectrometry, on small samples scraped from the edges of the coins, avoiding the inclusion of corroded metal as far as possible. Besides the copper which was more than half in all 4 coins, tin and zinc were the most prominent metals, accounting for 2.3 and 6.0% respectively in the analysis of the fourth plack. The specimens were fragmentary coins from Perth hoard (1920), by kind permission of the then curator of Perth Museum, Mr. W. Davidson.

27. <u>APS</u> II, 105; <u>RCS</u>, 36.

28. I. Stewart, <u>The Scottish Coinage</u> (1955), 166, and "The Identity of 'The New Plakkis...'", <u>BNJ</u> XXVIII, 1955-57, p. 317-329.

29. <u>Protocol Book of James Young 1485-1515</u> (Scottish Record Society, 1952), No. 2066.

30. Letters dated 31 December 1965 and 20 January 1966.

31. <u>APS</u> II, 172; <u>RCS</u>, 40.

32. <u>RCS</u> p. cxxix, f.n. 3.

33. Stewart figure references are to <u>The Scottish Coinage</u> (1955 or later edition).

34. G. Macdonald, 'The Mint of Crosraguel Abbey', <u>Numismatic Chronicle</u> 4th ser. XIX (1919), 269-311. Reprinted from <u>PSAS</u> LIV, Session 1918-19, 20-44.

35. Groats of James V were called Douglas groats, e.g. in 1554 - <u>Acts of the Lords of Council in Public Affairs 1501-1554</u>, 634. The coin name bodle is supposed to be derived from Bothwell, presumably Fran is Stewart earl of Bothwell in the late sixteenth century.

36. <u>Reliquae Divi Andreae</u>, p. 108; pub. 1797, but with dedication dated 1683. Quoted in R.B.K. Stevenson, "'Crosraguel' Pennies - Reattribution to Bishop Kennedy", <u>PSAS</u> LXXIV, Session 1949-50, p. 111.

37. R. Thoresby, Ducatus Leodiensis, 391.

38. Letters to R.W. Cochran-Patrick on numismatic subjects are preserved in the family, and his great-grandson, Hunter of Hunterston, most kindly gave us the opportunity to study them.

39. Op. cit. (note 36), p. 110.

40. I. Stewart, "Scottish Mints", Mints, Dies and Currency ed. R.A.G. Carson (London, 1971), 242.

41. I. Stewart, The Scottish Coinage, Supplement 1966, 197.

42. ADC I, 116*, 117*.

43. Another possible connection of Robison with the coinage is the case decided a few days earlier, where the master coiner Thomas Tod and the same Gilbert Fish were required to pay him £110, according to their obligation, in good money at the pre-Lauder rates - ADC I, 115*. The king also instructed the auditors of Exchequer in 1483 'that ye allow to the saide George' £146 'that he had in keping of ouris and that was takin fra him at Lawdre and withhaldin' - ER IX, 219.

44. ER VII, 292.

45. RCS, 99 (Hopetoun ms.)

46. ER VII, 216.

47. E. Burns, The Coinage of Scotland, I, 313-314.

48. 'The only simple approach... is by way of a relationship which does not depend on the assumption of equal output per die, but relies instead on the assumption that every coin struck had an equal chance of surviving to be included in the corpus. When this assumption is valid, the proportion of the surviving coins of a given type which are not the only representatives of the obverse (or reverse) dies from which they were struck is a good estimate of the proportion of the total output of the type which was was struck from the known obverse (or reverse) dies'- S. Lyon, in The Lincoln Mint c.890-1279 by H.R. Mossop (Newcastle, 1970), p. 16. Bias against repeated dies may sometimes be suspected in museum or other collections, but at least there is no reason to worry about this in the sample used for the Crux Pellit pennies. Nearly half of these were from the Crosraguel find, unselected, and most of the others in small numbers from several sources, particularly local Scottish nuseums.

49. RCS, p. cxxxix.

50. Op. cit., p. 306.

51. APS II, 105; RCS, 36.

APPENDIX

Although hoard evidence for the Crux Pellit pennies and the four types of farthing is scanty, and of negligible value for dating their striking, it is enough to make it fairly certain that these copper coins retained some monetary value after 1482. There are three adequately recorded hoards or putative ones, i.e. closely associated finds, in which these copper coins occurred with billon or silver ones, and all three included billon pennies of James IV. The earliest is Glenluce hoard (1956), with a single black farthing of the first issue, the latest coins being first coinage pennies of James IV. The other two were probably deposited not before 1500, because of the second coinage pennies included: the Crosraguel find contained all five types of copper, while there were five farthings among the nine associated pieces found at Glenluce Abbey. There is also Sim's statement, in the letter quoted, that the Crux Pellit coins were often found mixed with placks of Scottish kings of that name (James); his use of the plural implies some cases of placks later than James III, a conclusion unaffected by errors in the attributions which were then current.

Further consideration ought to be given to the question of how the black money, if struck on the scale indicated, could be put into circulation and the profits realised in assets of greater intrinsic value. An answer is suggested by one 1483 record, when taken in conjunction with the approximately parallel case of another overvalued copper coinage, the light turners of 1632 to 1639, the profits of which were assigned to Sir William Alexander, first Earl of Stirling. A contemporary described the system adopted for the latter.

> For some tyme no money was to be seen almost but Turnors, which for ease of the receipt, were put in many little baggs and this way compted in dollars. The merchants did hurt the countrey much by this meanes, for some of the wealthyer sort did buy them from Sir William Alexanders factors by weight in barrells and entysed the ruder sorte of people to chaunge them for silver coyne, giving to the poorer sort some few Turnors of gaine.

(J. Gordon of Rothiemay, History of Scots Affairs (Spalding Club, 1841), III, 88. Quoted in R. B. K. Stevenson, "The 'Stirling' Turners of Charles I", BNJ XXIX, 1959.) Likewise in England the Harrington farthing tokens were initially exchanged at 21s of farthings for 20s sterling, in 1613. The 1483 record shows that 8 Henry nobles had been 'wissilit and changit' for £24 of black silver. The claim of Lady Ruthven that these nobles were only pledged ('laid in wed') was dismissed (ADC II, p. cxxx). As the currency value of a Henry noble was 31s in 1475 and 32s in 1488, it should have passed for about 48s in the time of the black money, so that it would be superficially very attractive to exchange one for £3 of black money in bulk. Doubtless the dealers' profits and expenses would also reduce the king's profit, but it is hard to conceive of so much black money entering circulation and being offered for sums as high as £90 in one recorded individual payment, without some such special measures being adopted. For comparison, the highest rate recorded for silver bullion coined in this reign was 181 pounds in just over 10 months to August 1487, making about £1270 in groats.

THE USUAL MONEY OF SCOTLAND AND EXCHANGE RATES AGAINST FOREIGN COIN

Compiled[1] by
John M. Gilbert

A. Summary of Table of References to Sterling and Usual Money of Scotland, 1320-1450.

Before 1380 no example of a sum of money being described as usual money of Scotland has been found. The entries for 1320 and 1380 refer to 'usualis monete' but omit 'Scocie' and that of 1377 refers to 'currentis monete' and likewise omits 'Scocie'. The first reference to usual money of Scotland listed is in 1386. From then till 1410 sums of money were described either as usual money of Scotland or as sterling. In this transitional period there is an example in 1387 of both coinages being mentioned in the one charter.[2] There is also in 1387 mention of 'sterlyngis of the payment of Scotlande' which is obviously distinguishing between Scots and English sterlings. In 1423 another charter mentions both sterling and Scots money.[3] There was, therefore, no clear cut change from sterling to the usual money of Scotland. Before 1390 sterling was more common than usual money of Scotland and after 1400 usual money of Scotland was more common than sterling. Sterling continued to be mentioned occasionally in the fifteenth century. Bearing in mind that this table is not exhaustive one can say that sterling was replaced by the usual money of Scotland between 1380 and 1410 and probably between 1390 and 1400. One must also remember that not all sums of money were described either as sterling or as usual money of Scotland. Some were simply described as 'argenti' and many had no description at all.

Having established that money was more commonly described as usual money of Scotland than as sterling after 1400 one must determine the significance of this alteration. Money of account was simply a means of counting coins. 1s meant 12 coins and £1 a score of dozens.[4] At some stage every money of account system was linked to an actual coin. Sterling was the name given to the silver penny which was the universal medium of trade in northern Europe.[5] English sterlings were the most reliable in the thirteenth and fourteenth centuries. Since the sterling was so popular it was subject to forgery and debasement. Usual money of Scotland meant what it said. Any coin could in theory be the usual money of Scotland though in practice this must have described coins minted in Scotland. When, therefore, a sum is given in a Scottish source as £5 6s 8d sterling this means £5 6s 8d of silver sterling pennies of Scots or English origin presumably, or their equivalent value. The importance of specifying the coin was that it ensured one obtained the correct amount. If one received debased pennies rather than good pennies £5 6s 8d would not be worth as much. If the coinage was debased the value of the money of account was reduced. That usual money of Scotland replaced sterling implies that Scottish sterling no longer matched English sterling. As the table of the relative values of Scots and English currency shows Scots money started to be devalued in relation to English from the middle of the fourteenth century. As this coinage became more debased and ousted good money, it had to be differentiated from the good sterling penny and so it became known as the usual money of Scotland.

B. Anglo-Scots Exchange Rates

The exchange rates are listed alphabetically under the name of the English coin concerned and are given in the form, one or more English coins equals so much in Scots money of account. Additional information concerning the minting of English coins and their currency value has been inserted either to draw attention to uncertainty or to clarify the tables.

C. Relative Values of Scots and English Coins

The relative values of these currencies have been tabulated in the following manner. In 1385 the English noble was worth 7s 8d Scots. In England the noble had a value of 6s 8d. Taking the English coin as 1 the Scots equivalent is 1 & 3/20ths. The relative value of the Scots and English coinage on the basis of this evidence in 1385 was 1 to 1 & 3/20ths or 1 : 1 & 3/20ths. Where the rate cannot be expressed neatly an approximation is given in the form 1 : 3½ c. where c. stands for circa. No relative value has been tabulated for an English coin when that coin or a very close equivalent had ceased to be minted.

Coins could stay in circulation long after that type of coin had ceased to be minted. Since English currency was devalued in the fourteenth and fifteenth centuries, coins often rose in value the longer they stayed in circulation since the new coins were not of such good weight. Consequently, although the old and new English groats in 1467 both had a currency value of 4d they had different exchange rates. Obviously when examining the relative value of Scots and English currency one must use the exchange rates of English coins which had not increased in value as a result of age or else of coins whose increasing currency values are known. The angel is a case in point. From 1526 onwards the currency value of the angel ceased to be 6s 8d but rose gradually to 10s. Since the weight of the angel remained constant, the changes in face value after 1526 can be taken as the new currency value of the old 6s 8d angel. The relative values of the angel, therefore, are based on its new currency values of 7s 6d, 8s and then 10s. Generally, the only way in which one could work out an accurate relative value from the exchange rates of coins which were no longer minted would be by comparison of their intrinsic values.

This table can be used firstly to illustrate more clearly the devaluation of Scots as compared with English currency. It can be seen that Scots devaluation began around the middle of the fourteenth century and became more marked in the last quarter of the century descending to the rate of 1:2 by 1398 during the period when sterling was replaced by usual money of Scotland as the appellation of the Scots coinage. A general downward trend with fluctuations is noticeable throughout the fifteenth century but the most marked decline of the

Scots coinage can be seen between 1560 and 1620. This table corresponds fairly closely to Pinkerton's shorter list of relative values printed by Cochrane Patrick.[6]

Secondly, in conjunction with English Coins by G. C. Brooke and The Scottish Coinage by I. H. Stewart, this table can be used by the historian as an approximate guide to the value of foreign coin whose Scottish exchange rates are not recorded, as in the following example. In 1512-16 the English angel was worth 28s Scots. The currency value of the angel in England was 6s 8d.[7] The value of the sovereign in England was 20s.[8] Therefore, the English sovereign was worth approximately £4 4s Scots. It must be stressed that the results obtained by this method are only an approximation. While the relative values of different coins can agree as in 1466, they do frequently vary not only because of the existence of a bi-metallic currency but also because of the fiscal policies of the governments and mints concerned. It is hoped, nonetheless, that this table will prove to be a useful tool for the historian.

D. French Exchange Rates

The exchange rates of French coins are presented in the same manner as the exchange rates of English coins.

E. Relative Values of Scots and French Coins

The major difficulty in compiling this list was the identification of the various crowns or écus. The crown of weight has been given the value of the écu soleil, and the écu soleil after it ceased to be minted has been given the value of the current écus which were of approximately the same weight as the écu soleil.

F. Other Exchange Rates

The exchange rates of Flemish and Spanish coins are listed without any additional information or tables of relative values since no suitable printed lists of these currencies have been consulted. The exchange rates of certain papal coins are listed here. Where the exchange rate is given in sous tournois the Franco-Scottish exchange rate of 1398, that is 1:4 3/4, was used to determine the Scots equivalent. Similarly the Anglo-Scots exchange rates were used when the equivalent of a papal coin was given in £ sterling. It is also possible to obtain Scottish equivalents when the exchange rate of a papal coin is given in sous parisis since the relation of parisis and tournois was 4:5, that is 1d parisis equalled 1 1/4 tournois.[9]

TABLES

A. Table of References to Sterling and Usual Money of Scotland, 1320-1450.

Since the purpose of this table is to try to show when 'usual money of Scotland' replaced sterling, only the source of each reference to these terms is tabulated and not the amount of money. All sums of money were of course given in money of account, that is in £ s d or in merks. For the purposes of this table the dates between 1 January and 25 March are modernised. Where a reference can only be dated to a period of two or three years it is allocated to the middle of the three or the later of the two. Where a reference was stated to be _circa_ a certain date it is tabulated opposite that date. The one reference dated to a broader period than three years was omitted. It was 12 merks sterling in 1327 x 1364 in CA, 110.

Year	Sterling	Usual Money of Scotland
1320	CA, 101	SHS M, 7, 8 (No 'Scocie')
1321	CA, 102	
1322		
1323		
1324		
1325	CA, 103	
1326	CA, 107	
1327	GR, 275, 276	
1328	SHS M, 10-12	
1329	AL, 3	
1330	RP, 31; AL, 5, 6, 8	
1331	AL, 10.	
1332	CA, 113	
1333	AL, 15; RK, 113, 114, 115	
1334		
1335		
1336		
1337		
1338		
1339		
1340		
1341		
1342	AL, 18, 19	
1343	GR, 288; FD, 17	
1344		
1345	GR, 293	
1346	AL, 21	
1347	APS, 491	
1348	AL, 22	
1349		
1350	AL, 23	
1351		
1352		
1353		
1354		
1355		
1356	FA, 16	
1357		
1358		
1359		
1360		
1361	GR, 297	
1362	GR, 299; SGR, 6	

Year	Sterling	Usual Money of Scotland
1363	SGR, 10	
1364	AL, 30	
1365	GR, 302	
1366	AL, 31	
1367	GR, 309	
1368	AL, 32; GR, 308,310; FD, 26	
1369	GR, 311, 312	
1370	AL, 33	
1371	WCC, 8; GR, 313	
1372	GR, 314	
1373		
1374	RP, 46	
1375	AL, 34	
1376	AL, 35	
1377	GR, 315; SGR, 14	FD, 30 (No 'Scocie')
1378		
1379	AL, 36	
1380	SHS M, 30-32	SHS M, 30-32 (No 'Scocie')
1381	FD, 36	
1382	AL, 38	
1383		
1384		
1385	FD, 38	
1386	YW, 34; FM, 19	FC, 23
1387	SGR, 17, 18	SGR, 17
1388	AL, 39	
1389	CA, 119	
1390	AL, 42; SGR, 18; WCC, 826A	
1391		
1392	SGR, 19	
1393		
1394		
1395		SGR, 21, 24
1396		
1397		
1398		
1399	AR, 111	SHS M, 45, 46; FM, 20
1400	YW, 43	
1401		SHS M, 46, 47
1402		PR, 184
1403		
1404		
1405		CA, 122; SGR, 27
1406		
1407		
1408	CA, 123	
1409		YW, 45
1410		YW, 46

Year	Sterling	Usual Money of Scotland
1411		SGR, 29
1412		FM, 25
1413		GR, 323
1414		AL, 52
1415		
1416		
1417		GR, 328
1418		
1419		
1420		
1421		
1422		
1423	SGR, 30	AL, 58; SGR, 30
1424		
1425		WCC, 714
1426		SGR, 32, 33, app. 1
1427		AL, 60; SGR, 34; FD, 66
1428		SGR, 35; FD, 67
1429		GR, 338; CA, 129; SGR, 39
1430		AL, 64; GR, 340
1431		
1432	GR, 341	GR, 341
1433		AL, 66; SGR, 40
1434		AL, 68, 70, 71; SGR, 41
1435		AL, 72; SGR, 42; FD, 71
1436		AL, 77
1437		
1438		AL, 81; SGR, 45
1439		
1440	GR, 345	
1441		
1442		GR, 346; SGR, 49
1443		AL, 86; SGR, 52
1444		
1445		
1446		GR, 348
1447		SGR, 56, 57
1448		CA, 135; FD, 79
1449		SGR, 61; AL, 89; GR, 457
1450		AL, 91; SGR, 67

B. Anglo-Scottish Exchange Rates

Angel Noble

1475	Angel Noble	23s	(APS, ii, 112) The Angel, worth 6s 8d, was first minted in 1464 and replaced the old noble.[10]
1488	Angel Noble	24s	(TA, i, 105, 117)

1492	Angel Noble	30s 6d	(ADC, 227)
1502-1506	Angel Noble	23s 4d	(TA, ii, 68, 190; iii, 31)
1507	Angel Noble	24s	(TA, iv, 72)
1512-1516	Angel Noble	28s	(TA, iv, 398; v, 93, 95)
1521	Angel Noble	28s	(Hopetoun MSS, no. xxxiii, p. 67)
1524	Angel Noble	30s	(APS, xii, 41)
1532	Angel Noble	32s	(TA, vi, 43, 46) From 1526 the angel had a currency value of 7s 6d.[11]
1534	Angel Noble	31s	(TA, vi, 232)
1536-1538	Angel Noble	30s	(TA, vi, 285, 288; viii, 151, 152)
1539	Angel Noble	33s	(TA, vii, 275)
1544	Angel Noble	34s	(TA, viii, 290) From 1544 the angel was minted at the value of 8s.[12]
1555	Angel Noble	36s	(Hopetoun MSS, no. 1, p.98). From 1550 the angel was minted at the value of 10s.[13]
1561	Angel Noble	40s	(Hopetoun MSS, no. 1, p. 101)
1566	Angel Noble	55s	(TA, xi, 460)
1569	Angel Noble	56s	(TA, xii, 155)
ante 1582	Angel Noble	£3 6s 8d	(Hopetoun MSS, no. 1, p. 105)
1582	Angel Noble	£3 16s	(Hopetoun MSS, no. 1, p. 105)
1590	Angel Noble	£5 4s	(CP, i, p. xcii)
1597	Old Angel Noble	£5 0s 4d	(Hopetoun MSS, p. xcv)

Groat

1451	English Groat	8d	(APS, ii, 39-41) The revaluation which would have made the groat worth 8d was never carried out. The English groat had a currency value of 4d.[14]
1466	New Groat	10d	(APS, ii, 86)
1467	Old English Groat	1s 4d	(APS, ii, 88, c.1)
	New English Groat	12d	(APS, ii, 88, c.1)
1468	English Groat	1s 2d	(APS, ii, 91, 92, c.1)
	Old English Groat	11d	(APS, ii, 91, 92, c.1)
1483	Groat	2s	(ADA, 115*) This applies to the time of black money before 1482.
1485	Groat	1s 4d	(ADC, 94*) Presumably the old groat.
	Groat	2s	(ADC, 115*) This applies to the time of black money before 1482.
	Edward Groat	1s	(ADC, 94*) Presumably the old groat.
1503	Groat	1s 4d	(TA, ii, 384) The old groat.
1506	Groat	1s 2d	(TA, iii, 181) The new groat.
1512	Groat	1s 4d	(TA, iv, 245) Perhaps the new groat.
1547	Groat	1s	(APC, i, 571; CP, i, 86) The Bagcheek. Groat, a debased coin of Henry VIII.

Noble

1385	Noble	7s 8d	(APS, i, 554) The noble was worth 6s 8d in England.[15]
1393	Noble	9s 6d	(APS, i, 569; ER, iii, 320)
1422	Noble	10s	(CSSR, i, 301)

ante 1430	Noble	13s 4d	(ER, iv, 656)
1430	Noble	16s	(ER, iv, 651)
1434	Noble	15s/18s	(ER, iv, 578, 656)
1452	Harry Noble	22s	(APS, ii, 46) Not minted after 1464.[16]
1467	Harry Noble	27s 6d	(APS, ii, 88, c.1)
1468	Harry Noble	24s	(APS, ii, 91, 92, c.1)
1474	Harry Noble	26s 8d	(TA, i, 24)
1474	Noble	30s	(TA, i, 25)
1475	Harry Noble	31s	(APS, ii, 112)
1483	Harry Noble	£3	(ADC, ii, cxxx) Referring to the time of the black money before 1482.
1488-1489	Harry Noble	32s	(TA, i, 111, 167)
1501-1503	Harry Noble	31s	(TA, ii, 62, 383)
1511	Harry Noble	38s	(TA, iv, 315)
1524	Harry Noble	40s	(APS, xii, 41)
1526	Harry Noble	36s	(Hopetoun MSS, no. 1, p. 95)
1536	Harry Noble	54s 9d	(TA, viii, 234)
1540	Harry Noble	48s	(SHS M, v, 31)
1544	Harry Noble	42s	(Hopetoun MSS, no. 1, p. 96)
1555	Harry Noble	48s	(Hopetoun MSS, no. 1, p. 96)
1561	Harry Noble	53s 4d	(Hopetoun MSS, no. 1, p. 101)
1565	Noble	50s	(SRO, E 14/1. f. 209 v)
1590	Harry Noble	£7 10s	(CP, i, p. xcii)
1597	Harry Noble	£7 0s 10d	(Hopetoun MSS, p. xcv)

Pennies

1374	3 English	4d	(Statutes, 43, Edw. 3, c.18) This was in fact more than the reduction in the weight of Scots coins justified.
1387	3 English	4d	(CP, i, 11, no. 12)
1390	2 English	4d	(Statutes, 14, Rich. 2, c.19) This also was more than the reduction in weight justified and marked an attempt to remove the Scots coins from circulation in England.
1398	2 English	4d	(Statutes, 7 and 8, Henry 4, c.135)
1452	1 English	3d	(APS, ii, 41)
1467	Old English Penny	4d	(APS, ii, 90, c.4)
	New English Penny	3d	(APS, ii, 90, c.4)

Rose Noble or Royal

1466	New Rose Noble	25s	(APS, ii, 86) The rose noble was valued at 10s in England.[17]
1467	Rose Noble	32s	(APS, ii, 88, c.1)
	Old Edward Noble	32s	(APS, ii, 88, c.1) This was the noble of Edward III which was the same weight as the noble of Edward IV.
1468	Old Edward Noble	28s	(APS, ii, 91, 92, c.1)
1475	Rose Noble	35s	(APS, ii, 112)

1488	Rose Noble	35s	(TA, i, 167) Not minted after 1490.[18]
1488-1494	Rose Noble	36s	(TA, i, 90,96,117,167,172,228)
1508	Rose Noble	35s	(TA, iv, 93)
1522	Rose Noble	42s	(Prot. Bk. Ros., no. 590)
1524	Rose Noble	44s	(APS, xii, 41)
1539	Rose Noble	50s	(TA, vii, 145, 166)
1539-1545	Rose Noble	53s	(TA, vii, 249,428,442,449; viii, 143, 417)
1554	Rose Noble	66s 8d	(ADCP, 634)
1555	Rose Noble	54s	(Hopetoun MSS, no. 1, p. 98)
1561	Rose Noble	£3	(Hopetoun MSS, no. 1, p. 101)
1571	Rose Noble	93s	(TA, xii, 279)
ante 1582	Rose Noble	£5	(Hopetoun MSS, no. 1, p. 105)
1582	Rose Noble	£6 or more	(Hopetoun MSS, no. 1, p. 105)
1591	Old Rose Noble	£6 13s 4d	(APS, iii, 526)
1597	Old Rose Noble	£7 16s	(Hopetoun MSS, p. xcv)

Sterling

1483	£1 Sterling	£5 Scots	(Apostolic Camera, lxxxvii, note 1) This may relate to the time of black money.
1485	£9 Sterling	45 Merks Scots	(Apostolic Camera, lxxxvii, note 1)
1486	£1 Sterling	£3 Scots	(ER, ix, 448)
1487	£15 Sterling	100 merks Scots	(Apostolic Camera, lxxxvii, note 1)
	£7 Sterling	30 Merks Scots	(Apostolic Camera, lxxxvii, note 1)
	£3 Sterling	20 Merks Scots	(Apostolic Camera, lxxxvii, note 1)
1488	£5 Sterling	20 Merks Scots	(Apostolic Camera, lxxxvii, note 1)
1501	£1 Sterling	£3 10s Scots	(ER, xi, 331*)
1503	£11 Sterling	50 Merks Scots	(PRO Transcripts 31/9/31, f.77)
	£4 Sterling	20 Merks Scots	(PRO Transcripts 31/9/31, f.79)
1506	£5 Sterling	20 Merks Scots	(PRO Transcripts 31/9/31, f.111)
1507	£6 Sterling	£20 Scots	(PRO Transcripts 31/9/31, f.169)
1504-1507	£4 Sterling	£14 Scots	(TA, iii, 414)
1512	£1 Sterling	£4 4s Scots	(TA, iv, 305)
1513	£1 Sterling	£4 Scots	(TA, iv, 527)
1518	£250 Sterling	£1000 Scots	(PRO Transcripts, 31/9/31, f.336)
1521	£8 Sterling	40 Merks Scots	(PRO Transcripts, 31/9/31, f.369)
1524	£10 Sterling	£40 Scots	(PRO Transcripts, 31/9/32, f.19)
	£240 Sterling	£1000 Scots	(PRO Transcripts, 31/9/32, f.25)
1526	£13 Sterling	80 Merks Scots	(PRO Transcripts, 31/9/32, f.93)
	£16 Sterling	100 Merks Scots	(PRO Transcripts, 31/9/32, f.103)
	£6 10s Sterling	40 Merks Scots	(PRO Transcripts, 31/9/32, f.104)
	£36 Sterling	£140 Scots	(PRO Transcripts, 31/9/32, f.110)
1527	£9 11s Sterling	£40 Scots	(PRO Transcripts, 31/9/32, f.119)
	£6 Sterling	40 Merks Scots	(PRO Transcripts, 31/9/32, f.122)
1529	£6 Sterling	40 Merks Scots	(PRO Transcripts, 31/9/32, f.123)
1530	£6 Sterling	£30 Scots	(PRO Transcripts, 31/9/32, f.145)
	£14 Sterling	100 Merks Scots	(PRO Transcripts, 31/9/32, f.166)
1531	£3 Sterling	20 Merks Scots	(PRO Transcripts, 31/9/32, f.190)

1532	£5 Sterling	£20 Scots	(PRO Transcripts, 31/9/32, f.212)
	£265 Sterling	£1060 Scots	(R.K. Hannay, 'The Foundation of the College of Justice', SHR 1918, 36.)
1534	£26 Sterling	£160 Scots	(SRO, RH 2/6, vol. iii, ff.281-6)
1564	3s 4d Sterling	£1 Scots	(R.K. Hannay, op.cit. 36)
1571	£1 Sterling	£5 10s Scots £5 6s Scots	(Bannatyne Misc., iii, 131)
1576	£1 Sterling	£6 Scots	(RPC, ii, 656)
1582	£1 Sterling	£7 6s 8d Scots	(Hopetoun MSS, 1, p. 105)
1594	£1 Sterling	£10 Scots	(SRO, E 30/14)
1616-1621	£4000 Sterling	£48000 Scots	(Thomson, Coldingham, app. xlvii.
	£300 Sterling	£3600 Scots	(HMC, xii, (1891) app. pt. 8. from 432; original in SRO GD 267/31/97)

Testoon

| 1590 | English Testoon | 9s 8d | (CP, i, xcii) Minted from 1488 at 12d.[19] Not minted after 1553.[20] |

C. Relative Values of Scottish and English Money

The English value is held constant at 1 and the Scots value varies.

Year		Source
c.1150-c.1350	1:1	(CP, i, lxxii, ER, ii, xcv)
1355	1:1 plus	(Foedera, iii, pt. 1, 297) Scots money only accepted as bullion in England.
1357	1:1	(APS, i, 492)
1358	1:1	(Knighton, Chronicle, i, 101)
1365	1:1 plus	(APS, xii, 13) Only sterling to pay ransom. (ER, ii, xcviii)
1366	1:1	(APS, i, 497)
1367	1:1 plus	(Foedera, iii, pt. 2, 838)
1373	1:1 1/3	Penny
1374	1:1 1/3	Penny
1385	1:1 3/20	Noble
1387	1:1 1/3	Penny
1390	1:2	Penny. See note on this exchange rate.
1393	1:1 plus	(Statutes, 17 Rich 2, c.1) No Scots money in England.
1393	1:1 7/16c.	Noble
1398	1:2	Penny
1422	1:1 1/2	Noble
1424	1:1 plus	(APS, ii, 6, c. 24) Act to make Scots equal English coinage - not implemented.
ante1430	1:2	Noble
1430	1:2 3/8 c.	Noble
1434	1:2 1/4	Noble

Year	Relative Value	Source
1434	1:2 7/10	Noble
1452	1:3 3/10	Noble
1452	1:3	Penny
1466	1:2 1/2	Rose Noble, Groat
1467	1:3 1/2	Rose Noble
1468	1:2 4/5	Rose Noble (Old Edward Noble)
1475	1:3 1/2	Rose Noble, Angel
1483	1:5	Sterling, probably referring to time of black money.
1486	1:3	Sterling
1485-1487	1:3 1/3	Sterling
1487	1:4 2/5	Sterling
	1:2 6/7	Sterling
	1:4 1/3	Sterling
1488	1:3 3/5	Angel
	1:2 2/3	Sterling
1492	1:4 1/2 c.	Angel
1501	1:3 1/2 c.	Sterling
1503	1:3	Sterling
	1:3 1/3	Sterling
1502-1506	1:4 3/4	Angel
1506	1:3 1/2	Groat
1506	1:2 2/3	Sterling
1507	1:3 1/3	Sterling
1507	1:3 1/2 c.	Angel
1512	1:4	Groat
1512	1:4 1/5	Sterling
1513	1:4	Sterling
1512-1516	1:4 1/5	Angel
1518	1:4	Sterling
1521	1:3 1/3	Sterling
1521	1:4 1/5	Angel
1524	1:4	Sterling
	1:4 1/6	Sterling
1524	1:4 1/2	Angel
1526	1:4 c.	Sterling
1527	1:4 c.	Sterling
1527	1:4 4/9	Sterling
1529	1:4 4/9	Sterling
1530	1:5	Sterling
1531	1:4 4/9	Sterling
1532	1:4	Sterling
1532	1:4 3/11	Angel
1532	1:4 1/2	Sterling
1534	1:6 1/6 c.	Sterling
1534	1:4 1/8	Angel
1536-1538	1:4	Angel
1539	1:4 2/5 c.	Angel

Year	Relative Value	Source
1544	1:4 1/4	Angel
1540-1544	1:4 1/2 c.	Angel
1555	1:3 4/5	Angel
1561	1:4	Angel
1564	1:6	Sterling
1566	1:5 1/2	Angel
1569	1:5 3/5	Angel
1576	1:6	Sterling
1582	1:7 3/5	Angel
1582	1:7 1/3	Sterling
1590	1:10 2/5	Angel
1594	1:10	Sterling
1597	1:10 c.	Angel
1616-1621	1:12	Sterling

D.   French Exchange Rates

Blanc Couronne

1523	Great Bank of France	6d	(SRO, ADC, xxxv, f.12b) The blanc couronne minted in 1515 had a currency value of 12d in France.[21]

Crown or Ecu

1385	Scutum	3s 11d	(APS, i, 554) The écu couronne from 1380 was worth 22s 6d.[22] The écu d'or from 1351 was worth 25s.[23]
1398	French Crown	4s 2d	(APS, i, 572) The écu couronne was the only crown minted at this time.
1417	Gold Crown	8s 11 3/4d 10s	(F. McGurk, 'The Papal Letters of Benedict XIII concerning Scotland 1394-1418', Glasgow University Thesis, 570 no. 1117; 571 no. 1121; 573, no. 1129.)
1422	4 Gold Crowns	£1 Scots	(CSSR, i, 301)
1451	Crown	6s 8d	(APS, ii, 39-41, c. 8)
1451	Dalphynis Crown	6s 8d	(ibid.) One type of écu couronne had a dolphin on the obverse.[24]
1456	Crown	11s	(APS, ii, 46, c.7)
1456	Dalphyn	11s	(ibid.)
1458	Crown	10s	(ER, vi, 352)
1467	Crown	12s 6d	(APS, ii, 88, c.1) The currency value of the écu neuf or the écu couronne minted in Louis XI's reign was 25s or 27s 6d before 1474 and 30s 3d thereafter.[25]
1468	Crown	11s	(APS, ii, 92, c.1)
1473	Crown	17s	(TA, i, 64, 84)
1475	Crown	13s 4d	(APS, ii, 112, c.9) This could be the new 30s 3d crown.

1482	Crown	14s	(ADA, 112*) This is taken to be the new 30s 3d crown.
1488	Crown	14s	(APS, ii, 212)
1488	Crown	15s	(TA, i, 97)
1491-1497	Crown	14s	(TA, i, 199,242,297,347). The écu couronne was not minted after 1483.[26]
1501-1508	Crown	14s	(TA, ii, 79,106,427; iii, 207,398; iv, 39)

Crown of Weight or Ecu Soleil

1504	60 Crowns	£50 8s	(TA, ii, 427) The écu couronne could also be a crown of weight. All references to exchange rates of crowns of weight have been placed in this section at present for two reasons: 1) the écu soleil and the écu couronne varied only slightly in weight and fineness;[27] and 2) since there are references to 'crowns' without qualification which must be the écu couronne it seems reasonable that the term 'crown of weight' refers to a different coin. First minted in 1475 the écu soleil was worth 36s 3d in 1494.[28]
1507	Crown of Weight	16s 6d	(TA, iii, 279)
		17s 6d	(ibid.)
		18s	(ibid.)
1512	Crown of Weight	18s	(TA, iv, 235; ER, xiii, 433)
1515-1516	Crown of Weight	18s	(ER, xiv, 106, 163)
1523	Crown of the Sun	20s	(ADCP, 181) The écu soleil had been minted at the value of 40s tournois since 1519.[29]
1526	Crown of the Sun	18s	(Hopetoun MSS, p. 95)
1536	Crown of the Sun	20s	(TA, vii, 155)
1538	Crown of the Sun	22s	(TA, vii, 3)
1537-1539	Crown of the Sun	22s	(TA, vi, 467; vii, 2,45,62; vii, 51)
1540	Crown of Weight	£1 2s	(TA, vii, 290)
1544-1545	Crown of the Sun	22s	(TA, viii, 253, 365; Hopetoun MSS, p.95
1552	Crown of the Sun	25s	(TA, x, 62,84) The crown of the sun was not minted after 1547-1548.[30] The sun device was retained on the obverse of the current écu whose value was 45s tournois.[31]
1555	Crown of the Sun	23s	(Hopetoun MSS, p.98)
1561	Crown of the Sun	26s 3d	(Hopetoun MSS, p.101) The value of the écu d'or minted in 1561 was £2 10s.[32]
1567	Crown of the Sun	33s	(TA, xii, 49,75,76)
1580	Crown of the Sun	43s	(CP, i, xciv). The value of the écu d'or minted in 1575 was £3.[33]
1582	Crown of the Sun	50s	(CP, i, xciv)
1591	Crown of the Sun	56s	(APS, iii, 526)
1597	French Crown	£3 5s 10 3/4d	(Hopetoun MSS, p. xciv)

Karolus

1523	Carolus	5d	(SRO, ADC MSS, xxxv, f.126) The Karolus minted only in 1488 was worth 10d.[34]
1545	Carolus	5d	(RPC, i, 2)
1551	Carolus	5d	(RPC, i, 118)

Liart

| 1551 | Lyart | 1½d | (RPC, i, 118) This coin had a currency value of 3d and was minted from 1467 onwards.[35] |

Livre Tournois

1501	Livre Tournois	9s	(TA, ii, 110)
1504	Livre Tournois	10s	(TA, ii, 448)
1505-1506	Livre Tournois	9s 6d	(TA, iii, 29, 55)
1507-1512	Livre Tournois	10s	(TA, iii, 298; iv, 294)
1532-1534	Livre Tournois	10s 6d	(TA, vi, 43, 232)
1538	Livre Tournois	9s	(TA, vi, 414)
1545	Livre Tournois	10s	(RPC, i, 10)

Mouton

| 1385 | Mouton | 4s 2d | (APS, i, 554) The Mouton d'or was worth 20s tournois.[36] |

Quart d'Ecu

| 1597 | Quart de Lewis de France | 15s 1^1/4 | (Hopetoun MSS, p. xcv) This is most probably the quart d'ecu worth 15s. |

Royal

| 1451 | Rial of France | 6s 8d | (APS, ii, 39-41, c. 8) This is the royal d'or minted in 1359 with a face value of 25s tournois.[37] |

Salut

1451	Salute	6s 8d	(APS, ii, 39-41, c.8) This coin was minted at a value of 25s tournois from 1421 to 1423.[38]
1456	Salut	6s 8d	(APS, ii, 46, c.7)
1467	Salut	13s 4d	(APS, ii, 88, c.1)
1468	Salut	13s 4d	(APS, ii, 92, c.1)
1475	Salut	15s 6d	(APS, ii, 112, c.9)
1488	Salut	16s	(TA, i, 97)

Sous

1545	Sous	6d	(RPC, i, 2) The sous or blanc couronne was worth 12d.[39]
1551	Half Sous	3d	(RPC, i, 118)
1551	Sous	6d	(RPC, i, 188)

Testoon

1545	Testoon	5s 6d	(RPC, i, 2) The face value of the testoon in 1545 was 11s.[40]

E. Relative Values of French and Scottish Money

The Scots value is held constant at 1 and the French value varies.

Year	Relative Value	Source
1385	1:5 5/6	Crown
1385	1:4 1/4	Mouton
1398	1:4 3/4c.	Crown
1417	1:2 7/9	Crown
	1:2 1/2	Crown
1422	1:4 1/2	Crown
1456	1:2 3/11	Crown
1458	1:2 1/2	Crown
1467	1:2	Crown
1468	1:2 3/11	Crown
1473	1:1 1/2	Crown
1475	1:2 1/4	Crown
1482	1:1 5/7c.	Crown
1488	1:1 6/7	Crown
1491-1497	1:1 5/7c.	Crown
1501	1:2 2/9	Livre
1504	1:2	Livre
1505-1506	1:2 1/9	Livre
1507	1:2 1/4	Crown of Weight
1507-1512	1:2	Livre
1512	1:2c.	Crown of Weight
1515-1516	1:2c.	Crown of Weight
1523	112	Karolus
1526	1:2 2/9	Crown of the Sun
1532-1534	1:1 10/11	Livre
1536	1:2	Crown of the Sun
1537-1539	1:1 9/11	Crown of the Sun
1538	1:2 2/9	Livre
1540	1:1 9/11	Crown of Weight
1544-1545	1:1 9/11	Crown of the Sun
1545	1:2	Livre
1545	1:2	Testoon
1545	1:2	Sous

Year	Relative Value	Source
1551	1:2	Sous and Half Sous
1552	1:1 4/5	Crown of the Sun
1555	1:1 11/12	Crown of the Sun
1561	1:2	Crown of the Sun
1567	1:1 1/2	Crown of the Sun
1580	1:1 3/7	Crown of the Sun
1582	1:1 1/5	Crown of the Sun
1591	1:1c.	Crown of the Sun
1597	1:10/11	French Crown
1597	1:1	Quart d' Ecu

F. Other Exchange Rates

1) Flemish

Crown

1597	Flemish Crown	£3 5s 10$\frac{3}{4}$d	(Hopetoun MSS, p. xciv)

Ducat

1504	Flemish Ducat	7s great 21s Scots	(TA, ii, 243)
1507	Flemish Ducat	6s 8d great 20s Scots	(TA, iii, 278)
1508	Large Ducat	6s 8d great 20s Scots	(TA, iv, 28)
	Flemish Ducat	6s 8d great 20s Scots	(TA, iv, 140)

Pound Great

1428	£1 Great	£2 Scots	(ER, iv, 436)
1437	£100 Great	£234 15s 9d Scots	(ER, v, 22)
1456	£10 Great	£25 Scots	(ER, vi, 116)
1457	£1 Great	£3 Scots	(ER, vi, 311)
1469	£1 Great	£2 15s Scots	(ER, viii, 658,659,662,665)
1473	£30 Great	£66 13s 4d Scots	(TA, i, 48)
1480	£1 Great	£3 Scots	(ADC, 68)
1481	£33 Great	£100 Scots	(ER, ix, 153)
1483	£1 Great	£3 6s 8d Scots	(ADC, p. ccxii)
1484	£1 Great	£3 13s 4d Scots	(ADA, 134*)
1490	£1 Great	£3 6s 8d Scots	(ADC, 196)
1495	£1 Great	£3 Scots	(ER, x, 535)
1497	£1 Great	£3 10s Scots	(Halyburton Ledger, 105)
		£4 18s Scots	(ibid.,)
1505	£1 Great	£3 Scots	(TA, iii, 85,89,159)
1506	£100 Great	£266 13s 4d Scots	(TA, iii, 55)
1507	£1 Great	£2 13s 4d Scots	(TA, iii, 278)
1512	£1 Great	£3 Scots	(TA, iv, 300)
1525	£1 Great	£3 15s Scots	(ADCP, 228)

Noble

1393-1398	Flemish Noble	9s 4d	(APS, i, 569, 572)
1451	Flemsih Noble	12s 8d	(APS, ii, 40, c.8)
1597	Geintis Noble	£7 14s 10½d	(Hopetoun MSS, p. xcv)

Rider

1451	Rider of Flanders	6s 8d	(APS, ii, 40, c.8)
1456	Rider of Flanders	11s	(APS, ii, 46, c.7)
1468	Rider of Flanders	11s	(APS, ii, 91, c.1)
1475	Rider of Flanders	15s 6d	(APS, ii, 112, c.9)
1488	Rider of Flanders	15s	(TA, i, 167)

Scutum

| 1385 | Scutum Flandrie | 3s 11½d | (APS, i, 554) |
| 1398 | Scutum Brabancie | 3s | (APS, i, 572) |

2) Hungarian (?)

Ducat

| 1597 | Ungaris Ducat | £3 9s 10$^{2/3}$d | (Hopetoun MSS, p. xcv) |

4) Netherlands

Lion

1464	Lew	13s 4d	(APS, ii, 30, c.52) This is the Leeuw or Lion of the Burgundian Netherlands. From 1474 to 1485 its value varied from 6s to 7s 6d great.[41]
1467	Lew	15s 6d	(APS, ii, 88, c.1)
1475	Lew	17s 6d	(APS, ii, 112, c.9)

5) Papal

1296	160 Merks Sterling	800 Florins	(Hoberg, Dunblane, 47)
1297	100 Merks Sterling	500 Florins	(Hoberg, Brechin, 23)
1297	120 Merks Sterling	600 Florins	(Hoberg, Ross, 102)
1299	250 Merks Sterling	1250 Florins	(Hoberg, Moray, 82)
1301	100 Merks Sterling	500 Florins	(Hoberg, Dunblane, 47)
1308	60 Merks of Silver	300 Florins	(Hoberg, Dunblane, 47)
1318	500 Merks of Silver	2500 Florins	(Hoberg, Glasgow, 59)
1323	500 Merks of Silver	2500 Florins	(Hoberg, Glasgow, 59)
1337	500 Merks of Silver	2500 Florins	(Hoberg, Glasgow, 59)
1339	500 Merks of Silver	2500 Florins	(Hoberg, Glasgow, 59)
1367	500 Merks Sterling	2500 Florins	(Hoberg, Glasgow, 59)
1391	500 Merks Sterling	2500 Florins	(Hoberg, Glasgow, 59)

These equivalents were used by the Papal Camera in calculating what was due from Scottish bishoprics for the payment of common services.

ante 1393	Florin de la Chambre 3s 11d.c.		(Favier, 36) This and all other equivalents taken from Favier have been worked out by using the Table of Relative Values of French and Scottish money. They are, therefore, only approximations.
post 1393	Florin de la Chambre 4s 2½d.c.		(Favier, 36)
1378-1409	Florin de la Chambre Romain 4s 2½d.c.		(Favier, 36)
1461	2½ Ducats of Gold of the Camera	£1 Scots	(CA, ii, 52)
1524	600 Ducats of Gold of the Camera	£1000 Scots	(PRO, Transcipts, 31/9/32, f.25)
1526	100 Ducats of Gold of the Camera	£200 Scots	(PRO, Transcripts, 31/9/32, f.106-7)

7) Rhenish

Guelder

1456	Rhenish Guelder	8s	(APS, ii, 46, c.7)

8) Spanish

Ducat

1508	Spanish Ducat	20s	(TA, iv, 48)
1545	Double Ducat	48s	(RPC, i, 10; TA, viii, 415)

Florin

1378-1409	Florin of Aragon	2s 10d.c.	(Favier, 36) These exchange rates from Favier have been worked out by using table E above. They are, therefore, only approximations.
1378-1409	Florin of Barcelona	6s 7d.c.	(Favier, 36)

Pistol

1581	Pistolettes of Spain	42s	(CP, i, p. xcv)
1591	Pistolet of Spain	55s	(APS, iii, 526)

9) Ducats

The following exchange rates of ducats are listed although it has not been possible to identify their country of origin.

1488	Ducat	16s	(TA, i, 167)
1497	Ducat	15s 6d	(TA, i, 358,379,384)
1503	Ducat	15s 6d	(TA, ii, 384)
1503	Heavy Ducat	£7	(TA, ii, 243)

1507	Ducat of Weight	15s 6d	(TA, iii, 364)
1507	Ducat of Weight	18s 6d	(TA, iv, 72)
1511	Ducat	19s	(TA, iv, 317)
1511-1512	Crossed Ducat	19s	(TA, iv, 196, 321)
1512	Double Ducat	36s	(TA, iv, 353)
1512-1513	Ducat of Weight	19s	(TA, iv, 336,341,349,397,403)
1516	Light Ducat	15s 6d	(TA, v, 73)
1524	Ducat of Weight	20s	(APS, xii, 41) Increased from 19s
1537	Crossed Ducat	20s	(TA, vi, 301)
1540	Double Ducat	44s	(SHS M, x, 32, 39)
1543	Crossed Ducat	24s	(TA, viii, 240)
1544	Single Ducat	23s	(TA, viii, 291)
1558	Double Ducat	56s	(TA, x, 359)

NOTES

1. The Tables given in this paper were compiled from information submitted to the Scottish Medievalists' Conference as part of an Economic History Project. The contributors in alphabetical order were Rev. M. Dilworth, Mr J. Galbraith, Dr A. R. Murray, Mrs J. Murray, Mr J. J. Robertson, Mr W. W. Scott and Dr D. E. R. Watt. The compiler is indebted to Mrs J. Murray for the helpful advice and comments which he received from her at this symposium but stresses that any remaining errors and inaccuracies are his responsibility alone. Further contributions to these lists would be gratefully received.

2. SGR, 17.

3. SGR, 30.

4. Cambridge Economic History, ii, 593.

5. S. E. Rigold, 'The trail of the Easterlings', BNJ VI, (1949-51), 31-55.

6. CP, i, lxxvi, for Pinkerton, Essay on Medals, (London 1808), i, 444.

7. Brooke, 183.

8. Ibid.

9. BD, ii, 79.

10. Brooke, 156.

11. Brooke, 184.

12. Brooke, 186.

13. Brooke, 189.

14. Brooke, 116.

15. Brooke, 135.

16. Brooke, 156.

17. Brooke, 149.

18. Brooke, 168.

19. Brooke, 169.

20. Brooke, 187.

21. BD, ii, 315.

22. BD, ii, 270.

23. BD, ii, 255.

24. BD, ii, 273.

25. BD, ii, 288.

26. BD, ii, 298, 303.

27. BD, ii, 298.

28. BD, ii, 299, 303.

29. BD, ii, 314.

30. BD, ii, 314, 323.

31. BD, ii, 323.

32. BD, ii, 328.

33. BD, ii, 332.

34. BD, ii, 303.

35. BD, ii, 299, 326, 328.

36. BD, ii, 271.

37. BD, ii, 256.

38. BD, ii, 284.

39. BD, ii, 314.

40. BD, ii, 314.

41. P. Grierson, 'Coinage in the Cely Papers', Miscellanea Mediaevalia in Memoriam Jan Frederick Neirmayer, (Groningen, 1967), 380-404.

ABBREVIATIONS AND BIBLIOGRAPHY

SHS   Scottish History Society

SRO   Scottish Record Office

PRO   Public Record Office

ADA   The Acts of the Lords Auditors of Causes and Complaints, ed, T. Thomson, (Edinburgh, 1839)

ADC   The Acts of the Lords of Council in Civil Causes, ed, T. Thomson and others (Edinburgh, 1839 and 1918-)

ADCP   Acts of the Lords of Council in Public Affairs 1501-1554: Selections from Acta Dominorum Concilü, ed, R. K. Hannay, (Edinburgh, 1932)

AL   Liber S Thome de Aberbrothoc, (Bannatyne Club, 1848-56)

Apostolic Camera   The Apostolic Camera and Scottish Benefices, ed, A. I. Cameron, (1934)

APS   The Acts of the Parliaments of Scotland, ed, T. Thomson and C. Innes,   (Edinburgh, 1814-75)

AR   Registrum Ephiscopatus Aberdonensis, (Spalding and Maitland Clubs, 1845)

Bannatyne Misc.   The Bannatyne Miscellany, (Bannatyne Club, 1827-55)

BD   A. Blanchet and A. Dieudonné, Manuel de Numismatique Francaise, (Paris, 1916)

Brooke   G. C. Brooke, English Coins, (London, 1950)

CA   Charters of the Abbey of Coupar Angus, ed, D. E. Easson, (SHS, 1947)

CP   R. W. Cochran-Patrick, Records of the Coinage of Scotland, (Edinburgh, 1876)

CSSR   Calendar of Scottish Supplications to Rome 1418-22, ed, E. R. Lindsay and A. I. Cameron, (SHS, 1934)

ER   The Exchequer Rolls of Scotland, ed, J. Stuart and others, (Edinburgh 1878-1908)

FA   W. Fraser, The Annandale Family Book, (Edinburgh, 1894)

Favier   J. Favier, Les Finances Pontificales a L' Epoque de Grand Schisme d' Occident 1378-1409, (Paris, 1966)

FC   W. Fraser, The Book of Carlaverock, (Edinburgh, 1873)

FD   W. Fraser, The Douglas Book, (Edinburgh, 1885)

FK   W. Fraser, The Stirlings of Keir, (Edinburgh, 1858)

FM   W. Fraser, The Melvilles Earls of Melville and the Leslies Earls of Leven, (Edinburgh, 1890)

Foedera   Foedera, Conventiones, Litterae et Cuiuscunque Generis Acta Publica, ed, T. Rymer, Record Commission edition, (London, 1816-69)

GR   Registrum Episcopatus Glasguensis,   (Bannatyne and Maitland Clubs, 1843)

Halyburton Ledger   Ledger of Andrew Halyburton 1492-1503, ed, C. Innes, (Edinburgh, 1867)

HMC   Historical Manuscripts Commission

Hoberg   H. Hoberg, Taxae pro Communibus Servitiis, Studi e Testi, 144, (1949)

Hopetoun MSS   Printed in CP, i

Knighton, Chronicle   H. Knighton, Chronicon Henrici Knighton, (Rolls Series, 92; London 1889-95)

Lindsay,   View of the Coinage of Scotland   J. Lindsay, A View of the Coinage of Scotland, (Cork, 1845)

PR   Registrum de Panmure, ed, J. Stuart, (Edinburgh, 1874)

Prot. Bk. Rbt. Lauder   Protocol Book of Robert Lauder, in SRO, Burgh Records of North Berwick B. 56

Prot. Bk. Ros   Protocol Book of Gavin Ros 1512-32, (Scottish Record Society, 1908)

RK   A Genealogical Deduction of the Family of Rose of Kilravock, H. Rose and L. Shaw, (Spalding Club, 1848)

RP   Registrum Monasterii de Passelet, (Maitland Club, 1832; New Club, 1877)

RPC   The Register of the Privy Council of Scotland, ed, J. H. Burton and others, (Edinburgh, 1877-)

SGR   Regustrum Cartarum Ecclesie Sancti Egidii de Edinburgh (Bannatyne Club, 1859)

SHS M   The Miscellany of the Scottish History Society, (SHS, 1893-)

TA   Accounts of the Lord High Treasurer of Scotland, ed, T. Dickson and Sir J. Balfour Paul, (Edinburgh, 1877-1916)

Thomson, Coldingham   A. Thomson, Coldingham Parish and Priory, (Galashiels, 1908)

WCC   Charter Chest of the Earldom of Wigtown, (Scottish Record Society, 1910)

YW   Calendar of Writs preserved at Yester House 1166-1503, ed, C. C. H. Harvey and J. Macleod, (Scottish Record Society, 1930)

THE ORGANISATION AND WORK OF
THE SCOTTISH MINT 1358-1603

Joan E. L. Murray

This paper is primarily concerned with the mint organisation and the work of the mint itself, i.e. mainly the fabrication of coins in accordance with specified standards of weight and fineness, impressed with the required design and inscription which served to identify the issuing authority and the currency value. It will hardly touch on subjects like decisions about these standards, currency values and arrangements for the supply of bullion, which were the responsibility of higher authority, although mint officials might be called on for advice. It is however natural to include some consideration of the exchange of bullion for new coin, although in principle this was a distinct function from that of the mint; and likewise, for the sixteenth century, the conditions when there was a tack of the cunyie house, i.e. in English terms, the mint was farmed.

Until 1358 there is very little evidence about Scottish mints other than that which can be deduced from the coins, but from that date the source documents show a structure like that long established elsewhere in Europe. There is also an absence of Scottish documentary evidence for the beginning of the fifteenth century, but the extent of agreement between the late-fourteenth century organisation and that after 1424 leaves very little doubt that the same would apply in the intervening years, at least in principle. Similarly, early-seventeenth century evidence for Edinburgh and the fuller archives of other countries provide a useful background for interpreting the Scottish records of our period, in spite of some obvious differences, such as in the scale of operation. The officials known for the mint, as established in Edinburgh on David II's return from captivity, were warden, moneyer, assayer and die sinker, of whom the first three had charters of their office under the Great Seal. In broad terms, the moneyer was the contractor for making the coins while the warden's function was more administrative, safeguarding the interests of the king and his subjects.[1]

As the warden was the principal mint official until about 1500 his duties should be considered first, and those of his differently titled successors in the highest office. As laid down in 1393[2] and several times later in less detail, the warden was responsible for the issued coins keeping the standards of weight and fineness, i.e. not differing from these by more than the authorised remedy or tolerance. He had custody of the uncoined bullion, of the dies when not in use, and of the coined money. Every week he was to select pieces of that week's work, of each metal, for the internal assay and the trial of the pyx. The latter, at the exchequer, was the last check on the fineness before the responsible officials obtained their acquittance for the period covered. The first Scottish record of such a trial is for 1438, covering two years, but the period could be much longer.

The warden's fees were paid out of the king's profit (the Scottish records do not use the term seigniorage), and they appeared on the expenses side of the mint accounts when these were rendered at the exchequer: the 1358 rate of one penny for each 12 ounces of coin - at that time one mint pound - was maintained up to 1450.[3] In 1488 the warden was to have a yearly fee of £10, 'cum omnibus aliis proficuis'.[4] The warden also had certain judicial powers over the other mint officials and servants, who were not subject to the local court, as part of their privileges granted by David II and confirmed by James VI. From some time in James IV's reign and up to 1555, the term mint-master appears to have been applied to the same office as the early warden's. Thus Maister David Scot, a royal chaplain, could be referred to as 'maister of the cunyeis' in 1511 but also as custos monete in 1513, and even as magister conetator in 1516 (but referring to the last four years of James IV's reign).[5] In 1519, for a special coinage of unicorns, the treasurer or his clerk was to be 'maister of the said cunye, to se that it held the wecht and fynes, and keip the irnis', which were certainly duties of the early wardens.[6] In 1527 Adam Boyd was appointed 'warden principale and kepar of the kingis cunye irnis',[7] and thereafter there are frequent records of warden and counterwarden, both with duties similar to the early warden but clearly in a subordinate potition. By this time the coiner is regularly referred to as master coiner, and it may be difficult to distinguish his office from that of mint-master except by comparison of several records. Thus we find Robert Barton in 1529 as 'master of the cunye' as well as treasurer, comptroller and great custumar,[8] sandwiched between references to James Acheson as goldsmith and master coiner in 1526 but as magister monete in 1531;[9] Acheson was clearly always the contractor or master worker (an English term). By this time, if we have evidence that the mint-master was paid a fixed sum yearly then we can take it that he was the principal official, not the master worker, since the latter was not salaried but continued to receive so much for the work, according to the bullion coined.

In 1555 the new title of general was introduced for the principal official, the first holder of this office being David Forrest, who was magister cone in the treasurer's account in October 1555.[10] He was a prominent protestant, who was prepared to assist in a coinage for the Lords of the Congregation in 1559 and fled to England in November of that year.[11] His absence was stated to be 'in greit hurt and prejudice of oure soveranis profit of thair cunye', and he was replaced.[12] A letter under the Privy Seal in 1561 giving this office to Herbert Maxwell details his duties.[13] In connection with the exchange - an office then held by the master coiner - he was to keep a register of the 'spaces [types of coin], werk, wecht, fynes and price', the names of the sellers and date of receipt, and also to be present at the payment. For the coinage itself, the general (like the warden and counterwarden) was to keep a register of the weight, fineness and quantity. He was also to see that the pieces for assay were put in the box, of which he kept one of the four keys - the other key-holders were not mint officials, normally. Some supervision of the quality of the striking was also involved: he was to 'tak tent diligentlie' that the coins were 'weill wrocht and cunyeit, havand the ring about', which made it harder for clipping to pass unnoticed. Seventeenth-century evidence shows that it was now the general who exercised jurisdiction in the Warden Court.[14] Besides a yearly fee the general was remunerated by the right to a limited coinage of his own bullion free of any profit to the king: in 1560, two stones of silver and a pound of gold, but later three stones of silver.[15]

David Forrest seems to have performed his duties in person, but presumably the more routine ones could be delegated, since even the counterwarden in 1570 was given power to appoint deputies and substitutes.[16] The warden in 1358 apparently had a deputy, since the mint accounts show that John Goldsmith was associated with Adam Tor in the receipt of one fee, and he also had a half-penny per pound of metal coined as his fee pro clava, which must be connected with the warden's duties.[17] Two charters are listed as giving John Goldsmith the offices of 'probationis auri et argenti' and of 'examinatorum monete' respectively:[18] although the English index gives the latter, too, as assaying, the term can hardly have had that meaning in the 1527 charter to the Hochstetters, which states that two Scots 'erunt examinatores monete pondusque et probitatem considerabunt'.[19]

In this period in Scotland, monetarius probably always meant a master coiner, in the sense of one who engaged and paid his own workmen, although in general 'the class of persons' covered by the term moneyer ' is difficult to define'.[20] In France in 1266, for example, the moneyers were those workmen who actually struck the coins, but there is no evidence of this usage in Scotland, where we find strikers or printers in the vernacular records. During the period, there was little change in the coining processes of melting, forging, working and printing. Perhaps the best Scottish documentary evidence about the forging and printing is the list of worklooms to be supplied to Richard Wardlaw, as the first contractor for coining bawbees, in 1538.[21] The molten metal was cast into lingots, hammered into sheets, cut up with shears, and the pieces were presumably held in the rounding tongs for further cutting to weight and shape. In 1597, James Acheson claimed to have devised a new form of working, which would give greater accuracy in weight and shape; and when a copper coinage was ordered the following month this was to be wrought and forged in a mill 'and be the said miln maid reddy to the prenting', the latter clause presumably implying the use of a stamp to cut out the coin blanks.[22] The master coiner's account rendered in 1604 includes the expense of repairing a house for the copper mill,[23] but it is uncertain whether the same method was adopted at this time for the gold and silver. The coin blanks were next blanched to remove oxidation. The impression was applied by hammering, with the blank between the fixed pile die and the trussel. Cases of the master coiner contracting out the melting and forging are known for the second half of the sixteenth century.[24]

The metal was assayed after melting, and again after coining. The coiner - master of the money in 1451 - was answerable until each batch (technically journey) had passed this second assay,[25] and the whole batch was rejected if the fineness differed from the standard by more than the remedy,[26] which for the silver was two grains above or below, whenever known in this period. Exceptionally, in 1691 the master coiner was given permission for the issue of a journey which was finer than the standard by more than the remedy, himself paying the difference due to fewer coins than proper having been struck from that quantity of fine silver.[27] 'The Compt of the Coynyehous' available from 1582 includes accounts of the profit or loss on the remedies of weight and fineness,[28] but these are not mentioned in the fifteenth century accounts; and in

1577 the coiner was to 'tak the lois upoun his awin chargeis'.[29] For the bigger coins, certainly, the weights were tested individually by the warden or counter-warden, and those outside the remedy were cut and returned to be melted.[30] For the small billon and copper coins, the remedy of weight was presumably always applied only as the number in a given weight. In 1583, the remedy was eight of the eightpenny groats (of billon) or sixteen fourpenny ones, in every eight ounces.[31] In the register of the lions (hardheads) for four months of 1558, a maximum of 16 pieces light or heavy in the pound is recorded, but applying to each journey overall, of several stone.[32]

It is difficult to tell whether there was any subordination among the coiners named up to 1451. In David II's reign, James Mulekyn of Florence was 'monetarius noster infra regnum' in his charter, but he and another Florentine, Bonage (Bonagio), were both simply monetarius in 1364, and the latter, who was monetarius noster in 1393, was surely more than a striker.[33] The 1367 document ordering a reduced weight standard was addressed to a single warden and moneyer, and also uses the term magister monetarius, (unlike the other fourteenth century ones), when stating how much he should receive for the fabrication, for himself and his workmen.[34] In 1451, five king's coiners were named whose pennies were still to be current.[35] Of these, Robert Gray and Alexander Tod (for Stirling) rendered individual accounts at the exchequer, while John Dalrymple junior did so in 1448 as Robert Gray's deputy. In 1450, Gray and John Dalrymple senior rendered a joint account, while in 1447 Gray disclaimed any responsibility for John Dalrymples's coinage:[36] as the latter was the king's merchant, it is possible that this was a case of bullion belonging to the king, accounted for only by weight with the king getting stock and profit, whereas the normal accounts were of the royal profit. The remaining man was John Spethy, presumably the same as the king's goldsmith John Spedy in 1426,[37] and possibly no longer active at the mint in the period for which we have accounts. As in the case of Bonage, it seems safe to assume that all these were more than strikers; perhaps some were subcontractors, responsible to Gray. It appears, however, that goldsmiths might undertake the lowly work of striking, since the advice of the three estates in 1451 included that 'the prentaris and strikaris be na goldsmythis and utheris may be gottyn'.[38]

There is little documentary evidence about mints other than Edinburgh. Under Robert II there was certainly a separate warden for Perth, which was nearly as active as Edinburgh, and also for Dundee, coining on a small scale later in the reign;[39] but, as also for Aberdeen under David II, some obverse dies were exchanged between mints and all the dies had punches in common with Edinburgh ones.[40] In Robert III's reign there may have been die-sinkers working independently at different mints. Later the provincial mints may have had more the status of branch mints, not only because of die exchanges but because of the movement of coiners. Alexander Tod, who rendered accounts for Stirling in 1443 and 1444, was presumably the same as the later Edinburgh coiner; and the Gilbert Fish whose coins were known to the common people in 1493 as Berwick groats was presumably the goldsmith of that name recorded in Edinburgh in James III and James IV's reigns.[41]

The foreign expert coiners - James Mulekyn and Bonage from Florence in the fourteenth century, Colin Caignart from Flanders at the end of James IV's reign,[42] and John Missarvy from England briefly under Mary[43] - were presumably occupied solely at the mint or on goldsmith work for the king, but most of the recorded Scottish coiners before James IV probably did not have specialised qualifications. What was required in 1488 was a trusted man 'of lawte and knawlage to be maister of his monye' (in this case distinguished from warden),[44] and the same monetary background that a merchant would need in foreign trade might be adequate, rather than a goldsmith's technical knowledge. Certainly Robert Gray, who was also at times master of works at Edinburgh castle and of the navy, and custumar, appears to have been in a very different position from the master coiners of the second half of the sixteenth century and later, of whom several had previously been assayer or sinker. But this is not a clear-cut distinction by date: John Spethy has already been mentioned, and there was also John Laundale who rendered an account as coiner in 1453, but afterwards disappears from the records, who was probably the same as the king's goldsmith active in 1428 and 1429.[45]

One point should be made about the interpretation of the coinage accounts in the Exchequer Rolls for much of the period 1433 to 1476. There is some ambiguity in the phrase used for the weight for the billon coins, so many pounds and ounces argenti fabricati in denariis et obulis or in minuta pecunia. This could be taken to refer to the fine silver used in this way, but I believe that the correct interpretation is the metal as coined at about one half silver. Certainly in the late sixteenth century accounts the royal profit on the billon coinage is regularly quoted according to the weight 'past the irnis', i.e. as coined. In the period to August 1587, for example, 566 stones passed the irons in eight-penny and fourpenny groats at three deniers fine, i.e. three twelfths silver, and the king's profit on these was at the rate of £17 2s. 9d. per stone.[46] From 1459 to 1476 the rates charged were one penny per ounce for the small money and twopence per ounce for the silver coined in groats, and it is much easier to believe that this represents about the same profit in each case on the fine silver content, rather than a reduced charge when the same quantity of silver was used on the alloyed coins. This applies particularly to years when the bulk of the output was in pennies and halfpennies, as in the 1466 account, with nearly 122 lbs. as against less than 11 lbs. coined in groats. The payments to the warden and die-sinker, at one penny per twelve ounces fabricated, whether gold or silver, tend to support the same interpretation, since the smaller coins presumably meant as much work for these officials, in relation to the weight coined, as the fine silver and gold ones. There were some factors to offset their greater number to the ounce. For the die sinker, each die for pennies and halfpennies would involve less work and might be used to strike more coins. The warden probably checked their weight in bulk only, but they would be more trouble to count. In England, there were often complaints about the shortage of halfpennies and farthings, and the master worker was sometimes allowed a higher rate for the extra labour of making them (of fine silver); but it appears unlikely that this Scottish coiner was paid any more, at this period, since the Hopetoun manuscript records for 1556 to 1558 the same coining charge of £8 per stone both for billon pennies at 42 to the ounce and for testoons at 5 to the ounce.[47] The sizing of the coin blanks for the small money was obviously not done as accurately as for the fine silver or the gold.

Melting the coinage metal was a particularly important part of the coiner's responsibilities, in that it included bringing it to the correct fineness, other than by refining. The Scottish standard for the fine silver coins at the end of the sixteenth century was 11 deniers, a little below the sterling standard, although earlier they were to be as fine as in England. Burnt silver, as required from the merchants according to their exports of staple goods, was clearly refined, but not necessarily 'utter fine' - an English statute in 1487 laid down a minimum standard for refined silver of rather above 23/24ths.[48] This could be melted with a suitable quantity of baser silver to bring it to the required coinage standard. Some less fine silver was certainly acceptable: in 1490 the coiner was to pay 'the veray avale' for Scottish silver work which was not as fine as Paris silver or the new work of Bruges.[49] Surprisingly, in 1385 the Scottish moneyer was to accept new blanks of France, then six deniers fine, and give pound for pound of Scottish money, except the loss of six blanks in each pound for the working.[50] As this is believed to be before any Scottish billon coinage, the pound for pound phrase may refer to the fine silver content. It must have been hard for the mint to deal with any substantial quantity of bullion at six deniers fine, at that date, when a large proportion of the other bullion was probably other foreign money, particularly English - if one can judge by the English concern, and the disappearance of English coin from the Scottish hoards deposited late in Robert II's reign. In France, at least, the mint buying price was not always in proportion to the precious metal content, when it was bought in ingots ready alloyed for the billon coinages. This leads me to surmise that availability of base bullion on the continent at a cheaper rate than fine silver may have been a contributory reason for debasing the pennies and halfpennies in the new coinage of 1393, although I accept that there was also an advantage in the larger size of coin produced in this way: the Act of Parliament made it quite clear that the intrinsic value of the alloyed coins was on a par with the fine silver, on this occasion.[51]

It is abundantly clear from the late-sixteenth century records that the mint was not equipped to refine bullion on any substantial scale, although of course some of the processes were familiar. Assaying was a small-scale refining process, followed by comparing the original weight with that of the pure metal. Gold could be purified of the alloying silver by cementation, mentioned in James IV's reign, in connection with coining gold ryals.[52] However the normal custom was to mix finer and baser bullion in suitable proportions. In the words of a post-1603 document, 'the withdrawing of the redundant and substituting of the deficient metall because <u>chargeable</u> is not usuall'.[53] Thus in 1564 the queen was advised to eliminate the nuisance of the base lions or hardheads (also called lyarts in this document) by accepting them at the mint with 1 2/3 ounces of fine silver to each mark weight of hardheads, for a coinage 3 deniers fine.[54] In 1591 the half-merks and fortypenny pieces of 8 deniers fine were to be taken in at virtually the same price for the silver content as the finer silver, but only if accompanied by five times their weight of silver at 11 deniers, thus allowing a new coinage of half-merks at $10\frac{1}{2}$ deniers without refining.[55] For the baser old coins, when the plan was to bring them all to $10\frac{1}{2}$ deniers, the first agreement for refining (made in 1591 with Francis Napier, the assayer) contained a clause that the king would forgo his profit on the coinage of the silver thus refined,[56] although the currency values of most of these billon coins were by then below their intrinsic values, because of inflation since they were struck, together with devaluation of the hardheads and Mary placks.

160

There were earlier cases of refining, or at least the intention of doing this. When the James III placks were called in, in 1486 - at 2d. instead of the 3d. at which they were current immediately before the king was to 'ger put the samyne to the fire and of the substance that may be fynit of the samin to gar mak ane new penny of fyne silvir'.[57] And according to the Hopetoun manuscript 'Anent Cunyie', when Queen Elizabeth called in the base English coin in 1560 'a greit pairt was brocht in this realme affynit be ...... and dyvers personis and brocht to the Cunyehouse'.[58]

In Scotland as in England the king tried to maintain a monopoly of exchanging bullion, in old coin or otherwise, for coin, although not of exchanging in the sense of giving silver or white money for gold, or vice versa. In fact in 1541 'all maner of personis havand quhite money' were enjoined to 'reddely change all maner of gold' without charge.[59] Obviously it was when old and foreign coins were being taken as bullion for the mint that the exchanger was particularly important, although money coined out of bullion in ingots or household plate, etc, also was issued by exchange. In Scotland the warden or the coiner normally held the office of exchanger too, while in David II's reign the moneyer James Mulekyn seems to have been deputy to the warden in this office.[60] In 1427, three Edinburgh burgesses separately received acquittances which included all profits of the king's exchange and the new money made when he held that office.[61] One of these was Robert Gray, the coiner for many years. The others were William Cameron, brother to the bishop of Glasgow, and Robert Lauder, from whom the king purchased the tenement at the east gate of St. Giles kirkyard, which was then the mint.[62] At the beginning of the post-1424 coinage it may have been the policy to withdraw at least the light groats of the previous reign, but the Bonage groats - presumably the heavier front-face Robert groats, since another moneyer is recorded in about 1397[63] - were still officially current in 1467. In 1456, of the money named in Alexander Sutherland's testament, £80 was in Bonage groats and £300 in sixpenny groats,[64] i.e. of the fleur-de-lis, as coined for James I and James II up to 1451. It seems likely that the exchange was no longer active enough after 1427 to require more than one responsible man. A policy of conserving in circulation th the old Scottish money and likewise certain foreign coins was clearly laid down in 1475,[65] and also in 1456, when Parliament enacted that the coiners should not 'cunye' this money (which must here mean use it as bullion), under pain of death.[66] It is thus not surprising that no exchangers are recorded for a considerable period.

In 1486, when the placks were called in, it was the two coiners, Tod and Livingstone, who were to receive them up to the end of May and find surety that they would make payment for them by the end of September.[67] In 1488, however, Parliament asked the king to appoint separate men as warden and as wislar and changer, to have their accustomed fees as in old times.[68] In 1496, it was the master of money and coiners under him who were to pay the merchants for their bullion.[69] In the big recoinages in James VI's reign we again have records of other exchangers to supplement the master coiner. In 1592, Alexander Hunter was named as the king's exchanger, in association with the master, while all others were prohibited from making exchange of gold, silver or alloyed money.[70] In 1602, there were four 'exchangeris and dependeris on the hous', at a monthly wage.[71]

161

Delays in paying for the bullion, such as that in 1486, must have been particularly unpopular, and the need to raise a capital sum to sustain the exchange was recognised. In 1598 the currency of all foreign money was prohibited and it was to be brought to the mint at specified prices, 'yit in respect of the present skarsitie of his Majesties awin cunyie' it was necessary to delay this, so that the king and council could 'procure ane sufficient suirtie to all inbringers of gold and silver to the cunyie-house, that they sall receive immediatelie after the deliverie of the samin without delay the just valour and price theirof'.[72] This was more than four months after a six-year tack of the mint to Thomas Foulis and others had been signed,[73] so it is interesting to note the continuing responsibility of the royal administration for the exchange. The early-seventeenth century accounts of the master coiner include in his allowed expenses the interest on money borrowed to supply the exchange.

The first recorded tack of the cunye house was in 1547. The tacksmen had authority to buy all sorts of coin as well as uncoined gold and silver, and they doubtless did this vigorously in order to get sufficient profits to cover the sum guaranteed to the Treasurer. The coinage standards were unchanged, and it is interesting that, although the tacksmen apparently had a free hand over the striking of bawbees, the major billon coinage then, this was not the case with the baser placks, pennies and halfpennies, which were only to be coined as thought expedient by the governor and council.[74] During a tack the salaried officials carried on with their normal duties, if they were willing to, and in practice the master coiner did so too, by agreement with the tacksmen, and in any case without prejudice to his rights when the tack expired. The conditions of the 1594 tack empowered the tacksmen to appoint controllers at their own expense, 'for comptrolling of the saidis wardane and assayair in thair officeis, that nowther his maiestie the saidis taxmen the subiectis be preiugeit';[75] and the contract between the tacksmen and Thomas Acheson (here called their master coiner) included a clause that a register of the weight and fineness should be kept, 'the maister cunyeouris hand writ in our comptrolleris buik' and vice versa. Acheson undertook to coin twenty-four stone weight of silver and two of gold weekly, and to deliver it within eight days of receipt of the bullion from the exchangers and refiners.[76]

One tack, that in 1581, was certainly considered prejudicial to the country and was soon rescinded. This was partly because the conditions of that new coinage, of sixteen-shilling pieces and their fractions, set too high a price on the silver; but it was also alleged that the tacksmen used the best old money as bullion, contrary to their contract.[77] The intention of parliament was certainly that the alloyed money, except the countermarked placks and hardheads, should be refined for this new coinage, as well as using the fine silver. In 1602, there was a complaint about the current tacksmen by the general, Archibald Napier of Merchiston. He 'put in a bill' at the convention of the estates, saying that the tacksmen had been getting a high profit 'and so would have shown the King to be abused' by the tack, 'but the credit of the Treasurer, Comptroller and other partners bare it down' and he got no support.[78] The general may have been prejudiced, after his controversy with Thomas Foulis, one of the present partners, over the refining ten years before, when his son's contract had been cancelled because Foulis made an offer to arrange for this to be done at a profit to the king, using English experts.[79] The tack to Foulis in 1598 was

162

stated to be in payment of the king's debts to him, but it is not clear why a tack was entered into, rather than just making repayment a charge on the royal profits, at a fixed rate; possibly it was only because he would 'do his utter and exact deligence' for getting in the bullion that these profits would be high enough for him to recover his debts and still pay the king the yearly duty of £5000 for the mint. [80]

In 1601, the conditions for the tack stated that the prices at which the tacks-men might buy were not laid down;[81] but even when prices were fixed, when there was no tack, it might not be possible to observe them. Thus in 1533 the treasurer and comptroller were allowed to pay more than the currency value for gold coin, to use as bullion;[82] and in 1584 the purchase of silver by individuals who had precepts for a free coinage had so driven up the price in Scotland that the master coiner had to be authorised to raise his buying price. [83]

The full complement of mint officials, whose fees appear in the master coiner's accounts at the end of the sixteenth century, were general, warden, counterwarden, assayer sinker, and (from 1590) a grinder and temperer of the irons. At busy times they received extraordinary wages in addition, which might be at the same rate per month, as in 1587, double, as in 1582 to 1586, or even higher. [84] In this century their gifts of office were usually under the Privy Seal only, but exceptionally John Acheson had a charter under the Great Seal after being deprived of his office as master coiner in 1560, on the death of Mary of Guise. [85] Occasionally past officials were paid pensions out of the royal profit, and even a forger had such a pension in 1590 to 1593, although he had presumably been employed by the master coiner, not the king. [86]

The die sinker's work is of course of particular interest to the numismatist. Although the emphasis on the weight and fineness of the coins was very important, to ensure their intrinsic value, concern for their artistic quality was not lacking. Some of the credit here may be attributed to the sovereigns, whose interest in the mint was not solely as a source of revenue. A prestige element could be expected in their attitude, particularly to the true portrait pieces and to the gold, which was appropiate for royal gifts to ambassadors, for example. There is a fair amount of scattered evidence of the use of foreign engravers. John of Cologne, inpressor, who was paid twenty merks de mandato regis in the 1358 mint account, was presumably engraver and sinker, although that Latin term could certainly be used for a printer or striker. [87] In 1451, irons for the new coinage were to be 'gravin within the cunye place', [88]and the use of the term sinker at most other times does not imply that the official at the Scottish mint was not an engraver, himself capable of making the punches used for making the dies. In the late sixteenth century accounts, there were payments to Thomas Foulis for the first dies of new coinages, at the rate of £40 per denomination extra to his normal fees as sinker, and he was also paid for dies for the portrait coins in 1582, while James Gray was still the sinker. [89]

In James III's reign, the formula MONETA NOVA on the medal sent to the shrine of St. John the Baptist at Amiens has been taken to be an indication of continental workmanship. [90] In James IV's, there is a record of 'cunyie Irnis and the punschionis of the samyne brocht hame', which must mean from abroad. [91] For Mary's reign, there are several relevant records in the French archives. In 1553, the Cour des Monnaies gave permission to John Acheson, as die-sinker of the mint of Scotland, to make dies with the queen's portrait.[92] The other cases involve French engravers. In 1558, Guillaume Martin engraved effigies of Francis and Mary, for coins bearing their devices - perhaps those used for the Scottish ducats of that date as well as for the French marriage medal or pattern coin with the same obverse design of facing busts under one crown; and in February 1561 Mary obtained permission for Anthoine Brucher to engrave dies and puncheions for new Scottish money.[93] For Mary and Darnley, too, there is in the Ashmolean Museum a design by Etienne de Laune with their facing busts, but not very closely resembling the 1565 coin with that obverse type. As other evidence of royal interest, there are records showing that James IV, V and VI visited the mint. In 1506, the treasurer gave twenty French crowns 'to the King himself, quhilk wes set on the syment riall and part cunyeit in riales thareof'.[94] French crowns were already finer than the normal Scottish gold coins at that time, and the refining as well as an apparently quite unknown type indicate that the ryals were pieces de plaisir. James V's visit is indicated by payment of drinksilver to the cunye house in March 1539 (old dating);[95] it is tempting to associate this with the new coinage of ducats dated 1539, either the normal portrait type or the unique piece carrying symbols of the Order of the Thistle. James VI was accustomed to visit his mint before 1597, and was urged in that year to 'tak occasion to visite your awin work ... and be better sein in the knawledge thairof'.[96] He also presided at the the trial of the pyx in England, in 1611 and at other times. It was of course Charles I who was responsible for the appointment of a later foreign engraver, Nicholas Briot, as master coiner in Scotland, and the Scots accepted him as engraver for the king's portrait on the coins before they would agree to having him as master.

There was undoubtedly some Scottish use of mint control marks - a term intended to denote marks which were meaningful to the initiated but not necessarily to the general public and which did not affect the denomination, as recognised by the major features of the type, together with size. It is not appropriate to go into numismatic details here, like the reasons for concluding that any particular mark falls into this category, but various purposes of such marks may be mentioned. In 1366, a notable sign was to be used when there was a return to the English weight standard;[97] in 1490, 'a signe and takin maid in the prenting hafand difference fra the first cunye' was probably because of the change of coiner;[98] and when a unified coinage was being discussed in 1604, 'some small secret poynt ... that the one Mynt may not bear the default of the other if any happen to be found'.[99] Otherwise, some control marks can be identified by study of the coins themselves, the most convincing cases being those of a coiner's initial, sometimes added to a die which is also known with-.out it. This must have served to identify the responsible man, either because of a change of coiner or to distinguish an individual rather than a joint responsibility. There are two cases of the latter in James III's reign, when Thomas Tod and Alexander Livingstone were in office, and earlier than 1488 when parliament complained that with two 'maisteris of the money ... it can nocht be understandin clerely quhilk of thame has faleyeit quhether ane or baith'.[100] It would also be particularly important to distinguish any issues which were struck to a different standard. French records give many details of minor differences used during a period of debasement when the essential type and currency value were unaltered; and a possible Scottish case may be mentioned, a distinctive plack which was probably struck after James V ordained in 1533, the coinage of 120 stones of alloyed money at two deniers fine, in placks or otherwise.[101]

There is no evidence that the coiners were actually culpable in 1488, nor their predecessors in 1473, when the provision that they should be 'punyst as efferis gif thare be falt fundin' (in the fineness of the placks) was perhaps a routine formula rather than an expression of real suspicion.[102] One case is known of a mint employee being brought to trial, in 1516, 'for art and part in the forgery of placks and pence ... in the cunyie house ... by stealth' at the end of James IV's reign, but he was found innocent:[103] possibly the coins, if indeed not up to the standard, could be proved to be from a different workshop, since there were two master workers in 1509, apparently separately responsible, and the man accused, Alexander Atkinson, was then a servant of one of these, Richard Wardlaw.[104] It is naturally impossible to say that the mint officials were always blameless, but the known irregularities in this period were at times of civil strife, as in 1559 and in 1572, when the assayer joined the Marians in Edinburgh castle and took part in a coinage there.

NOTES

1. The following abbreviations are used:-

ADCP — Acts of the Lords of Council in Public Affairs, 1501-1554.
APS — Acts of the Parliaments of Scotland.
Cal S P Scot — Calendar of State Papers relating to Scotland and Mary, Queen of Scots.
ER — The Exchequer Rolls of Scotland.
RMS — Registrum magni Sigilli Regum Scotorum.
RPC — Register of the Privy Council of Scotland.
RSS — Registrum Secreti Sigilli Regum Scotorum.
SRO — Scottish Record Office.

RCS — R. W. Cochran - Patrick, Records of the Coinage of Scotland, 1874. (Vol. I unless otherwise stated). Where the RCS record is also printed in one of the above sources, both references are given, separated by a semi-colon, but the spelling of RCS has been used in quotations. In particular, y rather than z has been used throughout for consonantal y.

Compt — Thomas Acheson's Compt of the Coynyehous, 1582 onwards (SRO E. 101/2).

2. APS I, 207; RCS, 13-14.

3. ER I, 615; RCS, 4.

4. RMS XII, No. 36; RCS, 53.

5. TA IV, 250 for 1511: TA IV, 391; RCS, 53: Protocol Book of John Foular (Scottish Record Soc., 1944) II, No. 26 (Original in SRO).

6. ADCP, 140; RCS, 62.

7. RSS I, No. 3858.

8. RSS I, No. 4104.

9. APS II, 310; RCS, 55: TA V, 406; RCS, 58.

10. RCS 98: TA X, 261; RCS, 82. The fuller title, 'master general of the king's mint', occurs in 1575, in Calendar of Writs preserved at Yester House (Scottish Record Soc., 1930), No. 783.

11. John Knox, History of the Reformation (ed. Dickinson, 1949) I, 258: Cal. S P Scot I, 265.

12. RSS V, No. 733. Forrest was restored to office by January 1562, and apparently also held it de facto for the second half of 1560 or longer.

13. RSS V, No. 815.

14. RCS II, 130.

15. RSS V, No. 733: Compt, passim; RCS II, 314.

16. RSS VI, No. 874.

17. ER I, 615; RCS, 4.

18. RMS I, 592, Nos. 1175, 41 and 595, Nos. 1220, 40.

19. ADCP, 268; RCS, 65.

20. P. Grierson, Numismatics (Oxford, 1975), 99.

21. ADCP, 473.

22. RCS, 268; SRO E. 105/12. A Lauderdale Mint Paper dated 1603 mentions James Acheson's 'pane and travell tane in mending and repairing of the tua mylnis and the cuttar thairof quhilk wrocht the lait pennie and tua pennies peces of copper' — SRO list of these microfilmed papers.

23. Compt, 35 v.

24. RCS, 89: RPC II, 598-601; RCS, 142-144.

25. APS II, 40; RCS, 20.

26. RCS II, 106.

27. RPC (Third Series) XVI, 71; RCS II, 234.

28. In March 1555, David Forrest was to account for these remedies — RPC XIV, 13. It was presumably because the master coiner at that time (John Missarvy) was a foreigner that this became the responsibility of the mint-master (probably not yet made the general). Similarly it was the warden who rendered the mint accounts in 1358 to 1364, not the Florentine moneyer, Mulekyn; and likewise in 1513, when the Fleming, Caignart, was probably the master coiner (see note 42).

29. RPC II, 600; RCS, 144.

30. RCS II, 106. In 1604, a maximum tolerance was specified for every 12 ounces, as well as the remedies of weight for the individual pieces, which for gold and silver alike were 2 grains on the larger pieces and one on the smaller ones.

31. RCS, 159.

32. SRO E. 102/1.

33. RMS I, No. 101: ER II, 159; RCS, 5: APS I, 569; RCS 12.

34. APS I, 502; RCS 1-2.

35. APS II, 40; RCS, 20.

36. ER V, 279.

37. ER IV, 414.

38. APS II, 41; RCS, 21.

39. ER II, 430, 457: ER III, 680.

40. There is a full study of the use of provincial mints and the die-links between mints, in I. Stewart, "Scottish Mints", Mints, Dies and Currency (ed. R. A. G. Carson), 1971.

41. APS II, 233; RCS, 49: TA I 28, 321.

42. RSS I, No. 2009: TA IV, 275. These have the spellings Canyart, Cunyeart. Caignart has been chosen here because he can probably be identified with the Nicolas Caignart who bid unsuccessfully in 1504 for the farm of Antwerp mint, a reference for which I am much indebted to Dr. P. Spufford — A. de Witte, Histoire Monétaire des Comtes de Louvain, Ducs de Brabant II (Antwerp 1896), 121.

43. TA X, 261, 278, 296; RCS, 82, 98.

44. APS II, 182; RCS, 42.

45. ER V, 556; RCS, 28: ER IV, 442, 503.

46. Compt, f. 14, 15. As there was no coinage of fine silver in this period, the 3 stone weight of silver a year coined for the general was on this occasion represented by 12 stone weight a year past the irons in these alloyed coins.

47. RCS, 99.

48. R. Ruding, Annals of the Coinage (1840) I, 294. The refined silver 'might bear twelve pennyweights of alloy in a pound weight, and yet be as good as sterling' or better.

49. APS II, 221; RCS, 48.

50. APS I, 554; RCS, 8.

51. APS I, 569; RCS, 12.

52. TA III, 334. Other gold refined by setting 'on the cimont riall' was delivered to Quinta Essencia the alchemist, or used for gilding.

53. RCS, p. lxx. I have made the obvious emendation, chargeable instead of changeable. Also in 1577, '... or taking alsmekill fyne gold abuif the ordinar fynnes as to alloy it that is within the fynnes' — RPC II, 600; RCS, 144.

54. RCS, 92.

55. APS III, 526; RCS, 118.

56. RCS, 254. The silver which Napier refined was to be returned to him as coin, 'stock and haill proffeit thairoff free of all chairges' except the master coiner's fee.

57. APS II, 174; RCS, 41.

58. RCS, 100. The edge of this Hopetoun manuscript is missing at the gap.

59. APS II, 373; RCS, 57.

60. RMS I, 591, Nos. 1169, 35 and 594, Nos. 1204, 24.

61. RMS II, Nos. 96-98.

62. RMS II, No. 207.

63. RMS I, 634, Nos. 1758, 12.

64. "The Testament of Alexander Suthyrland of Dunbeath", Miscellany of the Bannatyne Club III (Edinburgh, 1855), 93, 99.

65. APS II, 112; RCS, 38.

66. APS II, 46; RCS, 22. E. Burns misunderstood the meaning of 'cunye' in this context.

67. APS II, 174; RCS, 41. The APS editorial dating of this Act is 1486; it was presumably before 27 April 1486, the date of an instrument recording Livingstone's acceptance of £15 in placks, for payment to the owner according to a royal proclamation — Protocol Book of James Young (Scottish Record Soc., 1952), No. 58.

68. APS II, 182; RCS, 42.

69. APS II, 238; RCS, 50.

70. RPC IV, 715; RCS, 177.

71. Scroll account of Thomas Acheson, 20th June 1602 to 1st December 1602 — Heriot's Hospital document, No. 22 in Inventory.

72. RCS, 194.

73. RCS, 269.

74. RSS III, No. 2181.

75. RPC V, 122; RCS, 184.

76. Heriot's Hospital documents, Nos. 16, 17 in Inventory.

77. APS III, 215; RCS, 113; RCS, 105, 106.

78. Cal S P Scot XIII, 939.

79. RPC IV, 731; RCS, 179: RCS, 256-264.

80. RPC V, 470; RCS, 191.

81. RPC VI, 315; RCS, 201.

82. RSS II, No. 1526. This was for a coinage of gold crowns at a reduced fineness.

83. RCS, 162.

84. Compt, passim.

85. RCS, 101. James VI confirmed this gift in 1578 — RSS VII, No. 1608.

86. Compt, 23 v. and f. 27.

87. ER I, 615; RCS, 3. In 1578, the master coiner had power 'fusores, excussores et impressores eligendi' — RSS VII, No. 1608.

88. APS II, 40; RCS, 20. 'Irons' was the normal term for dies.

89. RCS, 248.

90. I. Stewart, "Some Scottish Ceremonial Coins", PSAS XCVIII (1964-1966), 260.

91. TA II, 222.

92. PSAS IX (1873), 506-7; E. Burns, Coinage of Scotland II, 269. Patterns were to be struck at the Paris mint, but Burns' assertion that the 1553 Scottish testoons were made in Paris, by the mill and screw, has been discredited in J. K. R. Murray, "The Scottish Coinage of 1553", BNJ XXXVII (1968), 98-109.

93. F. Mazerolle, Les Médailleurs Francais (Paris, 1902) I, 43, 55. More-There is however no evidence here of a French engraver for the portrait gold coins introduced in 1555. Queen Mary employed Nicolas Emery to make dies in 1555, but these were for jettons (as also in 1553 and 1558) not for Scottish coins.

94. TA III, 334.

95. A. L. Murray, "Accounts of the King's Pursemaster, 1539-1540", Misc. of Scottish History Soc., X (Edinburgh, 1965), 30.

96. RCS, 269; SRO E. 105/12.

97. APS I, 497; RCS, 1.

98. APS II, 221; RCS, 48.

99. RCS, 274. A difference in the crown was agreed, but in fact the mints were also distinguished by initial mark, the Scottish mint using a thistle.

100. APS II, 182; RCS, 42.

101. RSS II, No. 1512. The coin is described in I. H. Stewart, The Scottish Coinage (1967), 203, and fig. 301.

102. APS II, 105; RCS, 36.

103. Protocol Book of John Foular (Scottish Record Soc., 1944) II, No. 26.

104. RSS I, Nos. 1830, 1831.

DEBASEMENT: THE SCOTTISH EXPERIENCE IN THE FIFTEENTH AND SIXTEENTH CENTURIES[1]

C. E. Challis

I

Although in theory currency debasement may be defined relatively easily, it is in practice often impossible to delineate in any fine detail in the context of fifteenth- and sixteenth-century Scotland: partly because it is sometimes hard to pierce the veil cast over Scottish monetary affairs by the paucity of extant documentary material; partly because the appearance of Scottish coin of poor quality was not necessarily accompanied by handsome fiscal returns — the usual concomitant of significantly reduced coinage standards; and partly because debasement took place within an overall context of currency depreciation. Because this latter phenomenon was distinct from debasement proper, yet all too often is confused by modern commentators with it, it is perhaps worth reminding ourselves at the outset of this discussion of where the distinction lay.

Currency depreciation is linked with the supply of and demand for gold and silver. If demand for the precious metals consistently outstrips supply, prices will increase and cause full-bodied coins of gold and silver to become undervalued and liable to be melted down, clipped, or circulated at unofficially high rates. In such circumstances a government has no alternative but to adjust its currency, usually either by reducing a coin's weight or by increasing its face value, to ensure the circulation of a pound tale which is correctly tarriffed according to market prices and therefore immune from speculation. Naturally, if the size of the adjustment is significant, so that the face value of the coin issued from the mint at the new, enhanced values is much greater than that of the old coin surrendered, the adjustment will result in a useful fiscal return. But, even if this is so, we should be clear that such a return will be purely coincidental to the main aim, the protection of the circulating medium; of limited duration, lasting in effect only so long as any old coin continues to trickle back for reminting; and incapable of repetition until some indeterminate future date, when market forces will once again cause bullion prices to rise to such a point that currency becomes significantly undervalued.

The implication of all this for the Scottish currency in the fifteenth and sixteenth centuries is obvious enough. In the first place, since international bullion prices did rise throughout this period Scottish currency was bound to depreciate irrespective of any governmental tampering with the coinage for fiscal purposes. Secondly, since the rise in prices was relatively leisurely, the rate of depreciation would also have been fairly slow; the distance between adjustments in the coinage being measured in decades rather than in

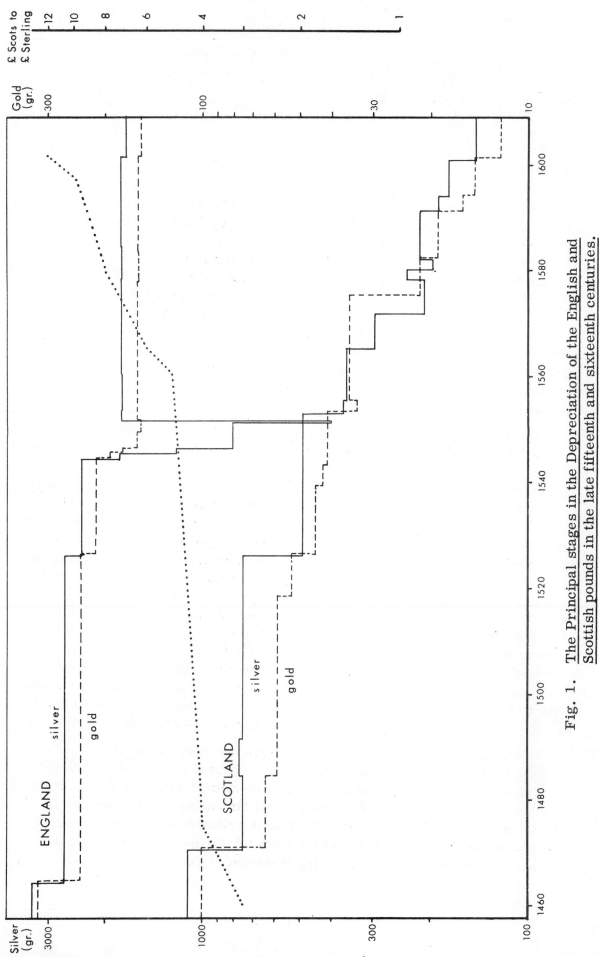

£ Scots to
£ Sterling

Gold
(gr.)

Silver
(gr.)

ENGLAND

silver

gold

SCOTLAND

silver

gold

Fig. 1. The Principal stages in the Depreciation of the English and
Scottish pounds in the late fifteenth and sixteenth centuries.

single years. And, thirdly, since Scotland was bound up in an international trend, one would have expected the depreciation of her currency to have marched roughly in step with that of her neighbours, more particularly perhaps with that of England, which answered the international movements in bullion prices by adjustments to her coinage in 1464, 1526, 1551, and 1601.[2]

Figure 1 sets out the broad trend and extent of the depreciation of the Scottish pound in the fifteenth and sixteenth centuries, and in comparing that depreciation with that of the pound sterling shows quite clearly that the full extent of the fall is not to be accounted for purely in terms of the normal currency depreciation already described. Overall, the metallic content of the Scottish pound fell from 99 grains of fine gold or 1100 gr of fine silver in 1456 to no more than 12.2 gr of fine gold or 146.6 gr of fine silver by the time James VI succeeded Elizabeth I, a drop of roughly 87 per cent. In comparison, over the same period of time, the pound sterling, whether measured in terms of gold or of silver, had sunk by only a fraction over 51 per cent. It was precisely because the Scottish pound had fallen in value much faster than the general trend demanded that it consistently depreciated in terms of the pound sterling. In 1456, when the Scottish pound had contained roughly one-third of the gold in the English pound, the two currencies had been exchangeable at the rate of three to one, but by the early seventeenth century, when the Scottish pound was no more than one-twelfth to one-thirteenth of its southern counterpart, the rate had settled at twelve to one. The explanation of why the depreciation of the Scottish and English currencies diverged so markedly is obviously bound up with debasement. Both countries experienced the phenomenon but whereas in England it was a short, violent acquaintance-ship, confined essentially to the years 1542 to 1551, in Scotland it stretched over a longer while and was to linger until the very end of the period now under consideration.

To outward appearances debasement and currency depreciation may often appear to be very much alike, for the mechanism by which debasement is achieved may be similar to that used in alterations to allow for currency depreciation; namely, a reduction in the weight of coins or an increase in their face value. And the result of both operations may be similar in that both lead to the circulation of a pound tale of lower intrinsic value. But the similarity is no more than superficial. Debasement is a fiscal device which enhances the face value of coin so far above its intrinsic value that a substantial revenue is produced, even though the whole operation may involve considerable administrative costs and increases in the mint price. Thus, whereas an adjustment to take account of currency depreciation seeks to redress imbalance, by bringing undervalued currency in to line with current market prices, and is by this very act an essentially honest manipulation, debasement, by creating coin whose face value is far in excess of what current market prices demand, produces imbalance and is unquestionably a dishonest operation.

A further difference between currency depreciation and debasement is that, whereas, as we have seen, the former is linked to international movements over which individual countries have no immediate control, the latter is purely particular. Any government can decide on a debasement policy at any time, quite irrespective of what is happening in neighbouring countries, and is itself solely in control of the timing and structure of each and every stage of that debasement. In view of this we should be in no doubt that the debasement of the Scottish currency, which is the subject of this paper, was an arbitrary act, engineered by the Scottish government purely for its own ends. The following discussion will seek to show the various stages through which this debasement went and to assess how far it is possible to calculate the fiscal return.

II

Obviously enough, the calculation of the precise fiscal yield of the Scottish debasement depends upon the availability of a fairly comprehensive and detailed set of accounts; yet, as anyone who has any acquaintance with the records of this period will know, this is not a prerequisite which can be satisfied. Few records now survive and of those which do there are all too many which are infuriatingly enigmatic.[3] Perhaps the most important single deficiency arises from the fact that there is no uniform set of accounts for the master-coiner of the principal mint at Edinburgh, let alone for those who operated elsewhere. And in attempting to indicate the implications of this deficiency it will be convenient to divide the two centuries under review into four fairly distinct phases: the first half of the fifteenth century, 1450 to 1487, 1488 to 1578, and 1578 to 1603.

1400-1450

For much of this period there are no accounts whatsoever but in 1433 those of the master-coiner of Edinburgh begin and then run continuously, save for the period 12 July 1435 to 13 September 1436, until 1450. Two accounts also cover production at Stirling between 1442 and 1444.[4] Table 1 summarizes the information in the Edinburgh series, though it is fair to say that in reality the picture was not always as neat and tidy as its figures suggest. To begin with there is more than a hint that the accounts do not necessarily list all revenue arising on coin struck at Edinburgh. In his account for 1444-7 the master-coiner says quite explicitly that 1 lb 1 oz of gold and 26 lb 5 oz of silver are not charged in his account on the grounds that John Dalrymple is responsible for them, and one wonders how common such an alternative accounting system was.[5] As far as the discharge of the accounts is concerned, there are certainly inconsistencies and omissions. The fees of the chief royal officials — the warden and the engraver — are invariably charged up, but payments for making the coins, buying equipment, making assays, and so on, never at all.

But despite these deficiencies we should not be too eager to reject the evidence of the master-coiner's accounts. Unless there is good evidence, which as a matter of fact we do not seem to have, that the master-coiner consistently and substantially understated mint revenue, there seems to be no particular warrant for being unduly perplexed about an odd inconsistency on the charge of his accounts. And by the same token, although it would be

Table 1. The accounts of Robert Gray, master-coiner at Edinburgh, 1433-50

1.1 Coin produced

	Coin produced					
Date	Gold		Silver (groats)		Billon (1d and $\frac{1}{2}$d)	
	lb	oz	lb	oz	lb	oz
16 May 1433- 4 Jun 1434	22	14*	114	$7\frac{1}{2}$	-	
4 Jun 1434-12 Jul 1435	31	$2\frac{1}{2}$	143	$7\frac{1}{2}$**	50	1
13 Sep 1436-18 Jul 1438	37	$14\frac{1}{2}$	236	15	80	0
18 Jul 1438-23 Jun 1440	10	11	160	0	35	0
23 June 1440- 2 Sep 1441	1	8	26	11	16	8
2 Sep 1441-17 Jul 1442	1	14	29	8	10	0
17 Jul 1442-19 Jul 1443	5	6	27	8	40	0
19 Jul 1443-23 Jun 1444	1	5	12	8	-	
18 Sep 1444-18 Jul 1447	7	0	92	4	-	
18 Jul 1447- 7 Sep 1448	4	$5\frac{1}{2}$	78	$6\frac{1}{2}$	-	
7 Sep 1448-21 July 1450	1	14	54	2	-	
Totals	125	$14\frac{1}{2}$	975	$13\frac{1}{2}$	231	9

1.2 Seignorage

	Seignorage per lb					
Date	Gold		Silver (groats)		Billon (1d and $\frac{1}{2}$d)	
	lb	oz	lb	oz	lb	oz
16 May 1433- 4 Jun 1434	16	0	8	0		
4 Jun 1434-12 Jul 1435	16	0	8	0	5	0
13 Sep 1436-18 Jul 1438	16	0	5	4	5	0
18 Jul 1438-23 Jun 1440	16	0	5	4	5	0
23 Jun 1440- 2 Sep 1441	16	0	5	4	5	0
2 Sep 1441-17 Jul 1442	16	0	5	4	5	0
17 Jul 1442-19 Jul 1443	16	0	5	4	5	0
19 Jul 1443-23 Jun 1444	16	0	5	4		
18 Sep 1444-18 Jul 1447	16	0	5	4		
18 Jul 1447- 7 Sep 1448	16	0	5	4		
7 Sep 1448-21 Jul 1450	16	0	5	4		

1.3 Profits

Date	Income			Expenditure			Profit		
	£	s.	d.	£	s.	d.	£	s.	d.
16 May 1433– 4 Jun 1434	73	16	9	1	10	5	72	6	4
4 Jun 1434–12 Jul 1435	94	16	7	9	3	4	85	13	3
13 Sep 1436–18 Jul 1438	113	10	2	16	8	4	97	1	10
18 Jul 1438–23 Jun 1440	59	19	4	6	19	$0\frac{1}{2}$	53	0	$3\frac{1}{2}$
23 Jun 1440– 2 Sep 1441	12	8	10	4	4	7	8	4	3
2 Sep 1441–17 Jul 1442	11	17	4	3	1	6	8	15	10
17 Jul 1442–19 Jul 1443	15	2	0	3	3	9	11	18	3
19 Jul 1443–23 Jun 1444	4	7	8	1	9	8	2	18	0
18 Sep 1444–18 Jul 1447	30	4	0	3	8	0	26	16	0
18 Jul 1447– 7 Sep 1448	24	7	8	3	11	8	20	16	0
7 Sep 1448–21 Jul 1450	15	18	8	7	5	8	8	13	0
Totals	456	9	0	60	5	$11\frac{1}{2}$	396	3	$0\frac{1}{2}$

Notes

*   In the account this figure is given as 306 oz which, normally speaking, would represent 19 lb 2 oz. However, given the allowances claimed by the warden and engraver [1d per 12 oz coined money], it is plain that in this case 300 represents three long hundreds of 120 each. The total sum is, therefore, 366 oz, or 22 lb 14 oz.

**   Here again use of the long hundred is implied by the allowances claimed; hence the figure in the accounts, 123 lb $7\frac{1}{2}$ oz, has been increased by 20.

Source: ER, 1406-36, 577-8, 625-7; ER, 1437-54, 65-7, 89-91, 102-3, 118-19, 127-8, 151, 278-9, 303, 388.

Table 2. Income accounted for by the master-coiner at Edinburgh, 1452-87

2.1 Coin produced

	Coin produced					
Date	Gold		Silver (groats)		Billon (1d and $\frac{1}{2}$d)	
	lb	oz	lb	oz	lb	oz
17 May 1452-19 Jun 1453			338	12		
15 Nov 1456-26 Jul 1457	0	$10\frac{3}{4}$	197	$4\frac{3}{4}$*		
18 Aug 1458-20 Jul 1459	0	4	273	11	204	12
20 Jul 1459-14 June 1464	12	$2\frac{1}{2}$	385	14	94	$8\frac{1}{2}$
14 Jun 1464- 3 Jul 1465	4	$6\frac{3}{4}$	69	13	66	$12\frac{1}{2}$
3 Jul 1465-18 Jun 1466	1	1	10	$14\frac{3}{4}$	121	$13\frac{1}{2}$
18 Jun 1466-22 Jun 1468	3	$10\frac{3}{4}$	93	$0\frac{1}{2}$	53	15**
12 Mar 1473-27 Jul 1476	13	5	273	0	140	8
7 Oct 1486-18 Aug 1487	8	1	181	0		
Totals	43	$9\frac{3}{4}$	1823	6	682	$5\frac{1}{2}$

2.2 Seignorage and Income

	Seignorage per lb						Income		
Date	Gold		Silver (groats)		Billon (1d and $\frac{1}{2}$d)				
	s.	d.	s.	d.	s.	d.	£	s.	d.
17 May 1452-19 Jun 1453			2	8			45	3	4
15 Nov 1456-26 Jul 1457	omitted		omitted				omitted		
18 Aug 1458-20 Jul 1459	omitted		omitted		omitted		50	1	0
20 Jul 1459-14 Jun 1464	16	0	2	8	1	4	67	9	$6\frac{1}{2}$
14 Jun 1464- 3 Jul 1465	16	0	2	8	1	4	16	9	$11\frac{1}{2}$
3 Jul 1465-18 June 1466	16	0	2	8	1	4	10	8	$5\frac{1}{2}$
18 Jun 1466-22 Jun 1468	omitted		omitted		omitted		669	8	$10\frac{1}{2}$
12 Mar 1473-27 Jul 1476	16	0	2	8	1	4	56	8	4
7 Oct 1486-18 Aug 1487	16	0	2	8			30	11	8
Total							946	1	2

Notes: * According to the account, this total is for groats and pence, in which case, if literally interpreted, it may include billon coins. However, 'pence' may simply be shorthand for 'pence of twopence' i.e. half-groats, a common fifteenth-century usage, in which case the whole amount ought to be designated silver, as it is here. Be that as it may, the accountant has certainly used the long hundred of 120 in declaring the amount of coin produced.

** In these years there was some coinage of copper money but the quantity is omitted from the accounts. However, the fiscal yield, £650, is included under 'Income'.

Source: ER, 1437-54, 556; 1455-60, 311, 502-3; 1460-9, 291-2, 368-9, 429, 580-1; 1470-9, 392; 1480-7, 548-9.

illuminating to have details of the master-coiner's working expenses, we should not lament their absence too vehemently. If they were included on the discharge we should also have to list them on the charge of the master-coiner's account, otherwise we could not strike a balance for each operation. By omitting all reference to the master-coiner's fees and expenses the accounts as they stand automatically adjust both sides of the reckoning, and provided this was done with some consistency there is no reason to suppose that the net income which can be established from the accounts stands in substantial need of adjustment.

The conclusion to be drawn from Table 1 seems obvious enough. Output of silver and gold, particularly of gold, was low, with the result that the Crown's revenue from the mint was also extremely low, averaging a mere £25 per annum over the period as a whole. Bearing in mind that the 1430s and 1440s are customarily associated with the issuing of debased coin, such a conclusion may, at first sight, seem somewhat paradoxical. But in reality this is hardly so. To be sure, these years did see the production of billon pence and halfpence yet there can be no doubt that, in the first place, with the one exception of the year 1442-3, production of billon was always outmatched by that of normal silver; and, secondly, the rate of seignorage was always lower on billon than on coin of gold and silver at the usual standards. In effect, the issuing of billon in these years seems to have been no more linked with fiscal policies than the normal production of gold and silver. Indeed, if it could be assumed that the government minted small quantities of low grade coin simply to satisfy the needs of everyday small-scale commodity transactions, the whole phenomenon of a billon coinage at this time might be explained without so much as mentioning debasement.

1450-1487

In the second accounting phase which I have suggested, 1450-87, the master-coiner's reckonings are still to be met but are of much less value; partly because the series as a whole becomes increasingly fragmented, before dying out completely towards the end of 1487, and partly also because the structure of the accounts deteriorates. While the charge remains fairly straightforward, in that it still records the output of gold and silver and the revenue to which it gave rise, the discharge is usually either completely missing or sadly incomplete in the sense that often it consists simply of a statement as to which person or royal official mint revenue has been paid. In effect the careful itemization of mint expenses, such as fees and rent, now disappears and we must assume either that the total charge on the account has become a net figure, or that the running expenses of the mint have been covered in some other way.

Problematical though the last few master-coiner's accounts of the fifteenth century may be, they do at least enable us to distinguish two quite distinct patterns of mint activity. In the first place, it seems clear that from about 1450 the rate of mint production became heavier in silver and billon, lighter in gold, and that the overall return to the Crown on this coin was slightly downwards. This decline in revenue was obviously linked with the seignorage rates, which, though remaining unaltered on gold at 16s 0d per lb, as in the immediately preceding period, fell on the coinage of groats from 5s 4d to

2s 8d, and on small money from 5s 0d to 1s 4d. Secondly, in marked contrast to this general experience, there was a brief period of fiscal exploitation in 1466-7, when black, or copper, money was produced at a profit of £650.

This distinction between the general and the particular, the ordinary and the extraordinary, highlights the dilemma posed by the failure of evidence delineated in Table 2; for, clearly, the significance of mint output in the periods for which seemingly we now have no accounts — principally the 1470s and the 1480s — will vary according to whether we see that output as part of the ordinary or the extraordinary patterns. In hazarding our guess we must obviously recognize that there was a further issue of copper coins, perhaps in the early 1470s — which would almost certainly have had fiscal implications — and two issues of billon coins, the first between about 1471 and 1473 and the second in the early 1480s — which may have had fiscal implications.[6] But such recognition must be qualified by the fact that at present we have no means of knowing either the extent of the fiscal yield in each case, or whether these issues did in practice form part of a coherent and important fiscal policy.

1488-1578

Between 1488 and 1578 we have no master-coiner's accounts to guide us and we must rely instead almost exclusively on those of the king's treasurer. In 1488 he was charged with £457 17s 6d coming from the coinage of 52 lb 6½ oz of broken silver vessels and from that point onwards the proceeds of the coinage appear with some regularity on the charge of his account.[7] For our present purposes this accounting procedure is certainly disadvantageous, because by no means all of the treasurer's accounts survive and by no means all of those that do include the profits on the coinage. Moreover, since the treasurer was concerned to record the sums with which he was charged, rather than the details of how these sums had been created in the first place, it is often the case that even when his accounts do survive and do mention the coinage they contain relatively few details. This being so, it need hardly be said that, in summarizing the rather bald statements in the treasurer's accounts, Table 3 produces figures which must be treated with the utmost caution.

Of all the columns given there the last is the least complicated, because the totals it contains represent no more than the simple round sums, in marks or pounds, agreed on by the Crown and its contractors by way of farm. Obviously, these figures do not give us any idea either of the overall size of production or of the total fiscal yield, but they do indicate the Crown's net share.[8] The figures in Column 2 are less straightforward. Here, it would seem, is the 'ordinary' revenue of the mint, arising on the coinage of bullion taken there, for the most part, by the Crown's subjects and others. Usually, these sums are said to be net but in practice we may question if this was in fact the case, simply because, from time to time, we can detect some items of mint expenditure on the treasurer's discharge and deduce from this that, in theory at least, he was supposed to receive allowances corresponding to the difference between gross and net revenue. Thus, a sum recorded in the treasurer's accounts as net should be regarded as net only in the sense that

Table 3. Income accounted for by the treasurer, 1488-1574

(1) Date	(2) Coinage of gold and silver £ s. d.			(3) Conversion of plate, coin etc. £ s. d.			(4) Farm £ s. d.		
4 Jun 1488–24 Feb 1492				457	17	6			
1 Feb 1497–Jul 1498	20	0	0						
10 Feb 1505–4 Aug 1506				1,915	12	0½			
6 Aug 1506–6 Sep 1507	1,711	15	8	486	0	10½			
6 Sep 1507–8 Aug 1508	2,488	3	9						
25 Aug 1511–14 Aug 1512	6,095	1	3½	738	10	0			
29 Oct 1512–8 Aug 1513	346	0	0						
17 Aug 1525–1 Aug 1526	210	0	7½						
25 Jun 1526–18 Aug 1526	30	0	0						
15 Oct 1526–29 Aug 1527	385	8	6½						
1 Aug 1529–1 Sep 1530	606	10	3						
2 Oct 1530–6 Sep 1531	509	0	8						
6 Sep 1531–22 Aug 1532	643	6	8						
22 Aug 1532–26 Sep 1533	441	8	0						
26 Sep 1533–2 Oct 1534	436	1	4						
30 July 1535–10 Feb 1536	284	14	0						
10 Feb 1536–12 Sep 1536	491	10	0						
24 Aug 1536–4 Jun 1537	492	17	6						
15 Feb 1538–18 Apr 1538	150	12	9						
20 May 1538–18 Aug 1539	2,330	18	4[2]						
18 Aug 1539–2 Sep 1540	1,421	6	4	825	1	6			
2 Sep 1540–7 Sep 1541	4,785	9	6	402	8	10			
7 Sep 1541–16 Aug 1542	3,536	19	6	503	10	10			
13 Aug 1543–7 Aug 1546	5,433	19	3½						
7 Aug 1546–31 Mar 1547	405	14	8	358	5	6½			
1 Apr 1547–31 Mar 1548							1,200	0	0
1 Apr 1548–31 Mar 1550							2,400	0	0
1 Apr 1550–16 Sep 1550	1,400	0	0	1,383	12	2½	866	13	4
1 Nov 1551–30 Nov 1552							2,333	6	8
1 Mar 1553–1 Mar 1554							2,333	6	8
15 Jan 1555–24 Oct 1555	1,257	19	10						
1 Dec 1559–11 Jun 1560	15,083	18	11½						
1 Jun 1561–20 Feb 1562	1,512	15	7						
20 Feb 1562–1 Jan 1563	547	15	4						
10 Jan 1566–10 Jan 1568							6,666	13	4
9 Feb 1568–9 Feb 1569							3,333	6	8
9 Feb 1569–9 Feb 1570							3,333	6	8
9 Feb 1570–9 Feb 1571							3,333	6	8
9 Feb 1571–9 Feb 1572							3,333	6	8
9 Feb 1572–9 Feb 1573							3,333	6	8
9 Feb 1573–7 Mar 1573							232	2	5¼
7 Mar 1573–1 Jun 1574	45,055	2	11¼						
1 Jun 1574–1 May 1576	17,739	16	6¼						

Source: TA, 1473-98, 168, 312-14; 1506-7, 31, 245; 1507-13, 12-13, 171-2, 360, 391; ER, 1523-9, 295; TA, 1513-31, 273, 294, 355-6, 406; TA, 1531-8, 16, 72, 178, 244, 274, 296, 378; 1538-41, 85, 249, 386-7; 1541-6, 20, 219-21; 1546-51, 19-20, 1551-9, 14, 138, 261-2; 1559-66, 4, 53, 150, 239-40; 1566-74, 110, 198, 394; 1574-00, 106.

Notes

1. Wherever possible the dates given here indicate the actual period of production, but in those cases where the account omits this information the period covered by the account itself is given.

2. This sum includes £76 which still remained in the hands of Richard Wardlaw at the time of accounting.

it was the clear sum with which he himself was charged; generally speaking, it is not in fact a true reflection of mint revenue.[9] A further hazard in interpreting these net figures is this: since the accounts do not give either the rate of seignorage or the amount of gold and silver coined we have (unless the actual contract survives) no means of gauging the exact extent to which the Crown was in fact exploiting the coinage. The treasurer's figure may represent a relatively small output at a very high rate of seignorage or, equally, the exact opposite, but he gives no clue as to where the truth actually lies.

The figures in Column 3 represent 'extraordinary' income in the sense that they were profits generated by the coinage of bullion sent to the mint by the Crown. Sometimes this bullion took the form of foreign coin, or of bullion bought in the market place, or, more occasionally, of freshly mined gold; but, more often than not, the Crown dealt in chains of gold and pieces of plate. But by no means all the figures mentioned by the treasurer under this head are included here, because quite clearly some of them are no more than the monetary equivalent of the original plate or ornament. Perhaps this can be seen most clearly of all in the reckonings for 1543-6 in which the sums accounted for in respect of the silver items are calculated at rates which are quite specifically said to be exclusive of the margin of profit.[10] But we may infer that such a practice also obtained on other occasions — 1497-8, 1507-8, 1511-12, 1541-2, 1546-7 and 1573-4 — and here again we must obviously make adjustments to the treasurer's figures to allow for this.[11] In one instance, 1543-6, this procedure has certainly resulted in some understatement of the Crown's 'extraordinary' income from the coinage, for here the profits on the gold items coined were calculated by contemporaries together with the capital value and in attempting to exclude the latter from the present calculations the former has, regrettably, also been sacrificed.

All these difficulties which beset the interpretation of the figures in the treasurer's accounts mean that for the better part of a century we are on very unsure ground in trying to set a firm figure on the fiscal return from the coinage. Unless we can be sure that the totals mentioned by the treasurer are actually net profits we have no clear way of calculating what the overall size of those revenues was. What we need is a yardstick against which to measure the treasurer's accounts and it is in providing this that much of the importance of the last accounting phase, 1578-1603, lies.

1578-1603

In this last twenty-five years we are fortunate in that the master-coiner's accounts once again survive in encouraging numbers. The series is not complete from 1578, because normal mint operations, and their accounting procedures, are interrupted by periods of mint farming.[12] The immediate joy of encountering a series, albeit an incomplete series, of accounts is tempered in some degree by the rather enigmatic structure of these accounts, and it might be helpful to examine one of these in detail to indicate just where the problems lie. The example taken here (Table 4) is for 1582-3; incidentally, the only one of the master-coiner's accounts of the later sixteenth century printed by Cochran-Patrick.[13]

The first Charge, or Charge by Weight, is perfectly straightforward, being no more than a statement of the total amount of coin produced. As for the Discharge it is important to note, firstly, that all the items relate to gross profits, and, secondly, that on certain of them — numbers 1 to 5 — the master-coiner intended to make no formal account by tale. The profit on item 5 he had paid to the general of the mint as part of his fee; that on item 4 to Katherine Young; that on item 3 to the Conservator of Flanders; that on item 2 to those who provided 20 st. of fine silver as a "float" for the recoinage of the 16s piece and its fractions, and that on item 1 he wanted for himself, to cover his costs on the same recoinage. His appropriation of this last sum was fully justifiable, for the Act setting out the terms of the recoinage had specifically provided for him and William Naper to deliver both stock and profit in full recompense of their expenses sustained by the coinage "to such as shall be appointed in their names to receive the same".[14]

With all these sums already accounted for, Acheson was left with a little over 418 st. for which he had to make account by tale: consequently, this sum became the Charge of the next part of his account. The Discharge then listed all his out payments: to the principal officers of the mint for their fees, to a whole miscellany of royal creditors, and for general mint expenses. Obviously one would not expect the payments of which he had discharged himself in the "weight" part of the account to be listed here, but one would expect that he would have listed his own outgoings — for melting, striking and so on. Clearly, this is a cost which ought to be taken into account, but, equally clearly, it was one which was thought at the time to lie outside the context of the formal account. It can, I suggest, be supplied in the following way. Assume that the face value of 1 lb of coin (FV) is equal to the sum of its intrinsic value (IV), the king's profit (KP), and the coining charge (CC). Let FV equal £32, as the weight and value of the coins tell us was the case, IV equal £29. 6 (i.e., 16 oz of silver at 37s per oz), and KP equal £1.9, as the account suggests (i.e., £12,719 19s divided by 418 st 6 lb 12 oz 20 dwt.). The coining charge must in fact be 50p., a figure which can incidentally also be substantiated by empirical enquiry.[15]

Table 4.1   Account of Thomas Acheson, master-coiner, 1582-3

	st.	lb.	oz.	dwt.
CHARGE in weight				
Coined in pieces of 10s, 20s, 30s and 40s	607	7	0	0

	st.	lb.	oz.	dwt.
DISCHARGE in weight				
(1) coined in pieces of 10s etc. from 16s pieces, surrendered according to the Act	150	0	3	3
(2) to the provost and his partners for their costs	21	13	8	0
(3) to the Conservitor of Flanders	10	14	8	3
(4) to Katherine Young	3	0	0	0
(5) to the general of the mint, for his fee	3	4	5	19
(6) total upon which the accountant is charged by tale	418	6	12	20
	607	7	0	0

	£	s.	d.
CHARGE by tale			
418 st. 6 lb. 12 oz. 20 dwt. 'converted into money'	12,719	19	0
In remedies of weight and fineness	125	17	11
	12,845	16	11

	£	s.	d.
DISCHARGE by tale			
Paid by precept to various persons	7,513	6	8
To the officers of the mint for extraordinary wages in converting the 16s pieces	160	0	0
Payments to royal officials, etc.	9,428	13	5
Mint fees (general, warden, counter-warden, assayer, sinker) 1581-2	126	13	4
Mint fees (general, warden, counter-warden, assayer, sinker) 1582-3	316	13	4
Sundry payments outside the mint	60	0	0
Repairs to mint and other expenses of the same	323	0	1
	17,928	6	10
Owing to Acheson	5,082	9	11

Table 4.2   Account of Thomas Acheson, master-coiner, 1582-3

	£
Face value of the money coined in 10s pieces, etc.,	
607 st. 7 lb. at £32/lb.	311,008
Remedies in weight and fineness	125.89
	311,133.89
Cost of silver put in the coins of 10s etc.,	
607 st. 7 lb. at 37s. per oz	287,682.40
Master-coiner's charge for producing coin, at 50 p per st.	4,859.50
Cost of converting 16s pieces (1)	4,560.35
Cost of supplying the 'float' for the recoinage (2)	664.05
Paid to the general of the mint as part of his fee (5)	99.39
Extra wages for the mint officials during the recoinage	160.00
Mint officials fees. 1581-2	126.66
Mint officials fees. 1582-3	316.66
Repairs and other mint expenses	323.00
	298,792.01
Net profit	12,341.88

Source: SRO. E 101/2

If we now re-draft Acheson's reckonings we can establish a clear net
profit (Table 4.2).   On the charge we have the full face value of the coin produced, calculated at the standard rate, plus additional sums arising from the
coin being less than standard in weight and fineness. Against this we can set
the cost of silver, his own charges, the fees of the king's officials in the
mint, and general mint expenses. Also, we should include the cost of con-
verting 16s pieces, providing a "float" for that operation, and paying part of
the general's fees;   all these are clearly identifiable costs of running the mint.
Deducting this total (£298,792) from £311,133 we arrive at a net profit of
£12,341.

The significance of this type of calculation needs no emphasising, for it
enables us to clear our minds on two very important questions. Firstly, does
the net profit which can be established from the master-coiner's account
coincide with that which is recorded by the treasurer for the same operation,
and thus encourage us to accept the treasurer's total for periods for which
the master-coiner's accounts do not survive? And, secondly, can the master-
coiner's accounts fill some of the gaps which exist in the treasurer's accounts
and thus help to round out our general understanding of the fiscal return?

The answer to these questions is both negative and positive. On the positive side we can list an encouraging number of occasions for which the accounts of the master-coiner survive yet for which those of the treasurer contain no information: 1579-80, 1583-87 and 1588-92. On one occasion the two sources, which are incomplete in themselves, can be used to complement one another and give some idea of total operations. This is in respect of the stamping operations of 1578-80 which entailed withdrawing existing coin and re-issuing it at an enhanced value. The master-coiner's account deals with operations between December 1578 and June 1580, but can tell us nothing of the opening months of stamping - September, October and November 1578. In contrast, the treasurer's account covers operations from the start down to the end of February 1580. By using this account until early 1580 and then adding on details of the last few months of operations from the master-coiner's accounts we can establish gross profits for the entire recoinage.[16]

On the negative side we must record that whereas in some instances there is a close correspondence between the profits listed by the treasurer and those which can be established from the accounts of the master-coiner there are also those in which a great disparity exists. The account we have just been examining in some detail, that for 1582-3, is an example of close correspondence, for the treasurer gives a total of £12,845 as against the real figure of £12,341 - an overstatement by a mere 4 per cent.[17] The similarity is closer still for operations in October and November 1601: the respective figures being £25,233 and £25,713, an understatement by the treasurer of under 2 per cent.[18] As examples of great disparity we may cite the account periods December 1602 to August 1604, and August 1587 to August 1588. In the first instance the treasurer understates mint profits by some £5,711, or about 35 per cent, and in the second he errs in the same direction by some 46 per cent.[19]

At the very end, then, our road does indeed run into sand: the treasurer's accounts may be useful, or equally they may not, and more often than not we do not have the means to judge which is the case. Consequently, most of the figures which stretch invitingly before us for much of our third accounting period, 1488-1578, and on into the last, 1578-1603, lose some of their value. Of course these figures are useful when all else fails, to give us some very rough orders of magnitude, but it would be unwise to press them further, unless there is very clear supporting evidence from elsewhere.

Discouraging though these conclusions about the figures contained in the treasurer's accounts may be, they do not, fortunately, preclude some calculation of the fiscal yield of the coinage in the last twenty-odd years of the sixteenth century. As already explained, the master-coiner's accounts run in a fairly continuous sequence from the late seventies through to the end of the century and beyond, and from these a fairly clear picture emerges (Table 5.4). Certainly there are gaps - 14 December 1580 to 7 April 1582, 1 February 1594 to 28 September 1601, and 29 November 1601 to 10 December 1602 - but each one can be satisfactorily explained. Each one, in fact, results from the operation of a 'tack' or farm.

The first of these, between the Crown and certain Edinburgh burgesses, including Thomas Acheson, later master-coiner, was supposed to run for three years and bring in 100,000 marks to the depleted royal treasury.[20] Yet after only six months the whole project collapsed. The pretext for this, according to the government, was that the new silver money was so 'hurtful and pre-judical' to the country that it was necessary 'to have the same reduced to a lower price without loss of his highness's subjects or yet to the tacksmen',[21] but it seems just as plausible to suggest that the farm was abandoned because the level of production at that time simply could not generate the income promised. The king was desperate for money. In June he had assigned on the mint farm £40,000 owing to the treasurer, £4,838 13s 4d. owing to the town of Edinburgh and £5,120 to various individuals.[22] Clearly if there was no hope of these sums being paid then there was no alternative but to abandon the farm. Late in 1581 and on into the first half of 1582 the mint grappled with the problem of recoining the sixteen-shilling piece, and as it did so it once again slipped back under the Crown's control.[23]

It was not until 26 January 1594 that the mint was again farmed out, once more to the town of Edinburgh. The contract was intended to run for two years and three months and produce 110,000 marks, payable in weekly instalments of 1000 marks.[24] As far as can be judged from the receiver-general's accounts, which record the appropriate weekly payments for the early months of 1596, it was entirely successful.[25] Upon the expiry of this agreement, at the end of April 1596, the mint seems to have lain idle for a little over two years,[26] so it was not until the summer of 1598 that a new farm was granted, this time to Thomas Foullis and Robert Jowsie for six years. Foullis and Jowsie were owed large sums of money by the Crown and it was to allow them to recoup that they were granted the whole profit of the mint in return for an annual payment of £5,000.[27] At first, the farmers enjoyed their grant undisturbed, as can be seen by the payment of the farm into the treasurer's coffers,[28] but in 1601 came substantial alterations. To begin with the king had still not paid off sums totalling £41,000 left owing to the treasurer on earlier accounts, so in September the mint revenues were duly assigned for this purpose.[29] Then, almost immediately, the whole arrangement was scrapped in favour of a one year farm which was to run from 1 December 1601 and produce £45,899 9s 6d. Most of this sum was to be for debt reduction purposes but a little, £5,000, was to go to Foullis and Jowsie, who were still thought to be enjoying their grant, as compensation for the intrusion.[30]

Combining the sums which were won through the operation of the mint farm with those realized from the direct management of the mint we arrive at a total fiscal yield from the coinage, between 1579 and 1604, of approximately £293,000 (Table 6).

III

If the calculation of the fiscal yield of the Scottish coinage in the fifteenth and sixteenth centuries was the primary objective of this paper, it is, nevertheless, perhaps worth touching in conclusion on some of the wider issues upon which these calculations have a bearing.

Table 5. Profits on the Coinage, 1579-1604, according to the accounts of the master-coiner[1]

5.1 Gold

(1) Date	(2) Fineness c. gr.	(3) Coin produced Weight st. lb. oz.			(4) Gross profit/st. £ s. d.			(5) Gross profit £ s. d.		
1 Apr 1580- 1 Sep 1580	21 0		6	0	384	0	0	144	0	0
1 Sep 1580-15 Oct 1580	21 0	1	10	9	384	0	0	637	10	0
15 Oct 1580-14 Dec 1580	21 0	1	4	4	384	0	0	486	0	0
1 May 1583-21 Apr 1586	21 6	6	11	10	220	0	0	1,479	16	10½
21 Apr 1586- 7 Aug 1587	21 6	3	13	5	220	0	0	843	1	0
7 Aug 1587-7 Aug 1588	21 6		6	9	220	0	0	90	4	8
7 Aug 1588-1 Sep 1590	23 7	29	3	0	610	2	8	17,808	5	4
	23 7	11	9	6	354	2	8	4,102	8	4½
1 Sep 1590-1 Nov 1592	23 7	2	5	10	354	2	8	832	14	11
	22 0	3	6	14	490	13	4	1,682	16	8
1 Nov 1592-1 Feb 1594	23 7		5	6	354	2	8[2]	118	19	4
	22 0	11	5	4½	490	13	4	5,559	5	8
28 Sep 1601-29 Nov 1601	22 0	29	5	3½	682	13	4	20,020	15	0
10 Dec 1602-23 Aug 1604	22 0	13	12	10½	682	13	4	9,502	7	0[3]
Totals		115	9	11½				63,308	4	10

5.2 Silver

(1) Date	(2) Fineness d. gr.	(3) Coin produced Weight st. lb. oz.			(4) Gross profit/st. £ s. d.			(5) Gross profit £ s. d.		
15 Dec 1579-1 Mar 1580	11 0	21	10	0	40	5	4	870	15	4
1 Mar 1580-31 Mar 1580	11 0	10	8	0	40	5	4	422	16	0
1 Apr 1580-1 Sep 1580	11 0	34	1	0	40	5	4	1,371	11	8
1 Sep 1580-15 Oct 1580	8 0	25	2	0	68	16	0	1,728	12	0
15 Oct 1580-14 Dec 1580	8 0	26	11	0	68	16	0	1,836	2	0
7 Apr 1582-1 May 1583	11 0	607	7	0	30	8	0	18,591	19	11[3]
1 May 1583-21 Apr 1586	11 0	303	7	0	22	2	6	6,713	11	1
21 Apr 1586-7 Aug 1587	11 0	18	2	0	22	2	6	401	0	3½
7 Aug 1587-7 Aug 1588	11 0	3	8	0	22	2	6	77	8	9
7 Aug 1588-1 Sep 1590	11 0		14	10	22	2	6	20	4	6
1 Sep 1590-1 Nov 1592	10 12	232	9	8	34	14	8	8,078	15	1
1 Nov 1592-1 Feb 1594	10 12	54	8	8	34	14	8	1,894	1	0
28 Sep 1601-29 Nov 1601	11 0	153	15	7¼	51	10	0	7,929	5	0
10 Dec 1602-23 Aug 1604	11 0	214	11	6¼	51	0	0	11,050	4	4[3]
Totals		1,707	3	7½				60,986	6	11½

5.3 Billon

(1)	(2)		(3)			(4)			(5)		
	Fineness		Coin produced Weight			Gross profit/st.			Gross profit		
Date	d.	gr.	st.	lb.	oz.	£	s.	d.	£	s.	d.
1 May 1583-21 Apr 1586	3	0	1,925	1	0	17	2	9	32,991	14	0
21 Apr 1586-7 Aug 1587	3	0	565	15	0	17	2	9	9,699	0	0
7 Aug 1587-7 Aug 1588	3	0	140	0	0	17	2	9	2,399	5	0
7 Aug 1588-1 Sep 1590	3	0	77	15	0	17	2	9	1,335	14	0
	0	12	1,198	5	0	8	15	4	10,505	4	1½
1 Nov 1592-1 Feb 1594	0	1	26	11	0	20	0	0	533	15	0
Totals			3,933	15	0				57,464	12	1½

5.4 Net Profits

(1)	(6)			(7)			(8)		
	Gross profit			Expenses			Net profit		
Date	£	s.	d.	£	s.	d.	£	s.	d.
15 Dec 1579- 1 Mar 1580	870	15	4	38	6	8	832	8	8
1 Mar 1580-31 Mar 1580	422	16	0	150	8	4	272	7	8
1 Apr 1580-1 Sep 1580	1,515	11	8	206	6	8	1,309	5	0
1 Sep 1580-15 Oct 1580	2,366	2	0	236	19	4	2,129	2	8
15 Oct 1580-14 Dec 1580	2,322	2	0	182	13	4	2,139	8	8
7 Apr 1582-1 May 1583	18,591	19	11	6,250	2	6	12,341	17	5
1 May 1583-21 Apr 1586	41,185	1	11½	5,311	13	7	35,873	8	4½
21 Apr 1586-7 Aug 1587	10,943	1	3½	2,207	8	4	8,735	12	11½
7 Aug 1587-7 Aug 1588	2,566	18	5	703	13	4	1,863	5	1
7 Aug 1588-1 Sep 1590	33,771	16	4	2,885	0	0	30,886	16	4
1 Sep 1590-1 Nov 1592	10,594	6	8	2,327	0	0	8,267	6	8
1 Nov 1592-1 Feb 1594	8,106	1	0	1,101	0	8	7,005	0	4
28 Sep 1601-29 Nov 1601	27,950	0	0	2,236	6	0	25,713	14	0
10 Dec 1602-23 Aug 1604	20,552	11	4	4,174	19	2	16,377	12	2
Totals	181,759	3	11	28,011	17	11	153,747	6	0

Source: SRO. E22/20; E101/2.

Notes

1. With the single exception of the account of 28 September 1601-29 November 1601, there is no mention in the master-coiner's reckonings of his own allowance, or coining charges. Thus the figures which he gives for the Crown's 'free profit', and which are listed here as 'gross profit per st.' (column 4), represent the profit margin after his own costs have been deducted and before those for which the Crown was responsible have been taken into account. The gross profit (column 5) is the product of columns 3 and 4 and the separate totals arrived at for the production of gold, silver and billon in any given accounting period (column 1) are summed in column 6. The expenses chargeable to the Crown — such as the fees of the principal mint officials, the cost of repairs, rent, equipment, and

so on — are totalled in column 7, and the net profit (column 8) is arrived at by deducting these figures from those in column 6.

2. No profit margin is given in the account for this particular issue but it is assumed here to have been similar to that in the immediately preceding period.

3. In each of these cases the total gross profit is larger than the product of columns 3 and 4 because the master-coiner has accounted additionally for the remedies at the assay and shear: 1582-3, silver £125 17s 11d; 1602-4, gold, £87 15s 0d; 1602-4, silver, £99 18s 4d.

Table 6. Total profits on the coinage, 1579-1604

Date	From the master-coiner			From the Mint Farm		
	£	s.	d.	£	s.	d.
15 Dec 1579–14 Dec 1580	6,682	12	8			
15 Dec 1580–6 Apr 1582				[10,000	0	0]
7 Apr 1582–1 Feb 1594	104,973	7	2			
1 Feb 1594–30 Apr 1596				73,333	6	8
1 May 1596–1 Aug 1598		no output				
2 Aug 1598–27 Sep 1601				15,000	0	0
28 Sep 1601–29 Nov 1601	25,713	14	0			
30 Nov 1601–9 Dec 1602				40,899	9	6
10 Dec 1602–23 May 1604	16,377	12	2			
Totals	153,747	6	0	139,232	16	2

Source: Table 5.4; above p. 188ff. The figure given in square brackets for 1580-2 is purely an estimate.

First of all, since debasement is by definition a fiscal device, the justification for which is usually rooted in a shortfall in government revenue, it seems useful to compare the figures given in the tables above with what is known of total government revenue in these years. Such a comparison cannot in fact be as neat and tidy as one might wish, for the problems noted in the course of this essay in respect of the financial accounts are but a microcosm of those attaching to a study of the wider whole. Yet the figures which do emerge are highly illuminating. Take, for a start, the revenues from crown land which can be fairly reliably gauged from the comptroller's accounts. In the second half of the fifteenth century the net return from this source rose from just under £2,000 to just over £5,000 per annum.[31] In absolute terms these are not large figures nor, of course, do they in any way represent total government revenue but even these figures from just one source tower above any which surviving evidence links with the proceeds of the mint. Even in the mint's best fiscal year, 1446-7, when the black money was made, it was still clearly outstripped by land in the ratio of one to three. In the early sixteenth century the point is made more plainly still. The Crown's approximate net ordinary revenue in 1507-8 was £29,055, in 1523-6 £13,115 and in 1539-40 £45,956 but to these sums the mint contributed no more than £2,488, £210 and £2,246.[32] In effect, in the fifteenth and early sixteenth centuries, say roughly to the end of the third decade, the coinage was hardly of overwhelming fiscal importance. The Scottish kings certainly flirted with debasement at this time and had their returns, which were of some importance in odd, exceptional years; but it has yet to be conclusively shown that when they built up their nest-eggs, as both James III and James V undoubtedly did,[33] it was from the coinage that they gathered the greatest share.

From about 1540 the whole fiscal importance of the coinage changed. At first, this change was scarcely dramatic, though the return from the mint did climb consistently into four figures and occasionally, as in 1559-60, hiccupped into five. But then, seemingly from as early as 1573, the mint became firmly harnessed to the government's fiscal policy. The Crown and its advisers broke with tradition, and saw nothing wrong in doing so. "The coinage is one of the special points belonging to the Crown [ran an Act of parliament of 1599] and the profit that may be had by the same is appropriated by all princes within their realms and dominions to their own particular uses. And it has been seen by experience that princes upon necessity of wars and other weighty affairs have at all times raised and heightened the prices of the coinage."[34] This is hardly the place to rehearse in detail the exact nature of the "weighty affairs" which did drive the Scottish Crown to adopt its debasement policy but it certainly is not out of keeping to emphasise that it was precisely this policy which effected the catastrophic decline in the Scottish pound. In contrast to England which restored her currency in 1551 and, apart from the odd, small depreciation between 1553 and 1560, between 1578 and 1582, and again after 1601, kept her currency restored into the seventeenth century, Scotland allowed or, more correctly, forced her pound to depreciate. The rot set in during the reign of Mary but it was in that of her son, James VI, that most damage was done.

Turning from the level of the fiscal yield to the manner in which it was achieved, it is worth noting that Scotland pursued a course which often differed markedly from that of her southern neighbour in the middle of the sixteenth century. As we have seen, debasement can be achieved in a variety of ways, depending on the precise formula employed in juggling with the face value of a coin, its weight and fineness. In England during the great debasement of the 1540s the pattern preferred (with the odd, notable, exception, as, for example, the 3 oz. issue of 1551) was some reduction in weight allied with a fairly substantial decrease in fineness. Thus whereas before the debasement English silver had been produced at 11 oz 2 dwt. fine and 45s per lb., the majority of debased silver was at 48s per lb and of 9, 6, and 4 oz fine (or the equivalent of 4 oz fine, as were the issues of 6 and 8 oz from 1549 to 1551).[35] The experience of gold was very similar. In Scotland, in contrast, the pattern preferred when debasement really got under way was somewhat different. To be sure, there were coins struck at standards below the traditional one of 11d fine: testoons at 9d in 1555, nobles or half-mark pieces at 8d between 1571 and 1577 and again in 1580, balance half-marks at $10\frac{1}{2}$d in the early 1590s, and a wide variety of villainous billon pieces - placks, bawbees, and hardheads - at various times throughout the sixteenth century. And it is equally true that some gold was produced below the traditional standard of 22 c., as were the gold écus of Mary and the Lions of 1582-8 - both $21\frac{1}{2}$ c. fine.[36] But when all this has been said, a case still exists for arguing that a large proportion of the profits of the Scottish debasement came from simply enhancing the face value of coins of reasonably sound fineness. In October and November 1601, for example, all the substantial net profit of the mint - £25,713 - came from the coinage of £6 and £3 pieces at 22 c., and the mark and its fractions at 11d. And between December 1602 and August 1604, when net profits of £16,377 were realized, the case was similar.[37] The Scottish experience shows in fact that the assumption which it is so easy to make about debasement - that profits come _only_ through the issuing of coin of poor fineness - simply will not do. Potentially the degree of fineness is always a good indicator but, as Table 5 shows, in reality it needs always to be seen in the wider context of the level of production, the rate of seignorage, and the overall cost of production.

By way of conclusion it is perhaps appropriate to touch upon another consideration of some importance; namely, the mechanism by which bullion reached the Scottish mint during the debasement period, for here again there was a considerable difference between the Scottish and the English experience. It will be recalled that in England three essentially distinct devices were used: raising the mint price of gold and silver, forcing coin back to the mint by banning its circulation, and contracting with special suppliers. The second device enjoyed a limited vogue, affecting only the testoon which was withdrawn in 1548-9, while the third was of particular importance only after the effectiveness of the mint price began to wane and the conversion of testoons was virtually complete. In practice it was in fact the mint price which was of principal importance for much of the English debasement and it is hardly surprising, therefore, that between 1544 and 1551 we can chronicle a substantial rise in respect of both gold and silver, especially silver.[38] In Scotland the emphasis was rather different. Certainly there were increases in the mint price; for example, gold rose from £252 to £432 per troy lb between 1580 and 1601.[39] And there was also some government contracting, as in the late 1560s when the merchants permitted to export 26,000 st of lead were bound to render to the queen the equivalent of 1300 oz of fine silver, reckoned at 30s per oz.[40] But these were by no means the dominant factor. Over and over again, the Scottish mint was supplied by existing currency being banned and reissued from the mint in worse form. Between 1578 and 1580 the process was simply one of re-stamping. The coins involved in the fraud were all silver - the 30s piece, the 20s piece, the 10s piece and the testoon - and the ostensible pretext for their withdrawal was the difficulty of retaining silver in Scotland following rises in foreign currencies. That there was probably some genuine concern over an adverse flow of silver need not be doubted, for on 31 May 1577 the Privy Council had tried to ensure that the laws against transporting were put in force. Yet the overriding fiscal motive behind the enhancement can readily be seen from the announcement made on 29 July 1578. All the coins in question were to be surrendered to the mint before 1 March following. Such as were false were to be broken and redelivered to their owners, but the rest were to be received at enhanced rates: the thirty-shilling piece for 32s 6d, the twenty-shilling piece for 21s 8d, the ten-shilling piece for 10s 10d, and the testoon for 6s 6d. Each piece was then to be counter-marked before being reissued at even higher rates: the thirty-shilling piece at 36s 9d and the rest of the coins in proportion. Thus the king might expect a gross profit equivalent to about 14 per cent of the original face value. Not surprisingly, such a transparent fraud did not readily commend itself to the Scottish people, who not only felt some reluctance in bringing their coins to the mint in the first place, but also cavilled at receiving them back at the enhanced values. The government, however, was not to be deterred; and, partly by lengthening the days during which the old coin might be surrendered - first to 1 May 1579, then to 1 August, and finally to 20 October 1579 - and partly by threatening all who possessed unstamped coin after the appointed day with outright confiscation, managed to achieve some measure of success. The total gross profit was just short of £46,000.[41]

The method preferred in the 1580s and 1590s was the actual reminting of coin. In December 1583 it was decided to withdraw all 12d pieces, bawbees, placks, 3d groats and half-placks before the following July and recoin them into 8d groats and their halves at 3d fine.[42] In 1591 all silver, with the exception of penny and twopenny placks, was to be recoined at $10\frac{1}{2}$d fine, and also all gold, save the thistle noble, was to be reissued at 22 c.[43] Similar steps were taken for the seventh and eighth coinages of James VI between 1594 and 1604.[44] In 1597 all foreign coin was demonetized for the same purpose.[45]

The explanation of why the Scottish government had to rely on such a cumbersome mechanism - and it must be stressed that it was relatively cumbersome, involving as it undoubtedly did endless delays and by no means any certainty that all the prohibited coin would in fact be surrendered - is obviously bound up with the reactions of the Scottish people to the entire fiscal policy. These reactions and the economic consequences to which they led are in many ways the most interesting side of the Scottish debasement, but to enter into any reasonable discussion of them would take us well beyond the bounds of an introductory essay.

NOTES

1. I should like to thank Mrs. J. E. L. Murray for her helpful comments on this paper and also Dr. A. L. Murray, not least for his assistance at the Scottish Record Office and for allowing me to consult his unpublished thesis 'The Exchequer and Crown Revenue of Scotland, 1437-1542' (Edinburgh, 1961).

2. Currency depreciation in England during the late fifteenth and sixteenth centuries is discussed in C. E. Challis, The Tudor Coinage (Manchester, 1978), chapter 5.1. For the general european phenomenon see C. M. Cipolla, 'Currency Depreciation in Medieval Europe', Economic History Review, 2nd ser. xv (1962-3), 413-21.

3. R. W. Cochran-Patrick did a magnificent job in bringing together the great bulk of the surviving documentary material on the Scottish coinage in one manageable collection - The Records of the Coinage of Scotland from the earliest period to the Union (Edinburgh, 1876). Occasionally, however, certain documents eluded him; more commonly, he did not transcribe documents, particularly the accounts, in full; and invariably left dates in old style. His important work must, therefore, be used with caution and wherever possible I have at least gone back to the printed calendars of documents, if not always to the original manuscripts. The principal abbreviations I have adopted in citing documents are as follows:

APS The Acts of the Parliaments of Scotland

CP The Records of the Coinage of Scotland from the earliest period to the Union (Edinburgh, 1876)

ER The Exchequer Rolls of Scotland (Edinburgh, 1878-1903)

RPCS The Register of the Privy Council of Scotland

RSS Registrum Secreti Sigilli Regum Scotorum (Edinburgh, 1908-1966)

SRO Scottish Record Office, Edinburgh

TA The Accounts of the Lord High Treasurer of Scotland (Edinburgh, 1877-1970)

4. ER, 1437-54, 131, 157

5. These weights and all those which follow in this article are reckoned according to contemporary usage which was as follows:

24 grains (gr.)	= 1 pennyweight (dwt.)			
576 gr.	= 24 dwt.	= 1 ounce (oz.)		
9,216 gr.	= 384 dwt.	= 16 oz.	= 1 pound (lb.)	
147,456 gr.	= 6,144 dwt.	= 256 oz.	= 16 lb.	= 1 stone (st.)

Unless otherwise stated, all sums of money are expressed in terms of the Scottish pound.

6. For these issues see I. H. Stewart, The Scottish Coinage (1955), passim.

7. The exception to this general rule came in 1525-6 when the profits of the mint were paid to the comptroller. Murrary, op.cit. p. 250; Acts of the Lords of Council in Public Affairs, ed. R. K. Hannay (1932), pp. 239-40; ER, 1523-9, 295.

8. The full details of the farm begun in 1547, which, in the first instance, was to run for a year at a rent of 1800 marks, are set out in RSS, 1542-8, no. 2181. The initial agreement seems subsequently to have been extended to the end of March 1550, and then to have been superseded by another at the higher annual return of £2,333 6s 8d.

The farm which began in 1566 was initially for two years but was then renewed for ten. The arrangement [? revised] as set out in an agreement of 23 January 1571, for three years beginning on 1 February following, was that the farmer should pay the Crown 5000 marks annually and half the 'free profit'. Since this man, Robert Richardson, the king's treasurer, had already paid £9,000 "in the common service and affairs of this realm", however, he was in practice allowed to pocket the whole profit of the mint during the three-year term. RSS, 1567-74, no. 1090.

9. An obvious exception here is the revenue recorded in column 2 for 1573-4 and 1574-6. In these years the profits of the mint were assigned to the Regent and the sums recorded in the treasurer's account are the net sums which the former received.

10. Thus, for example, in accounting for £3,957, 0s 10d received on the coinage of certain silver vessels the treasurer was simply recording the receipt of the capital value of 18 st. 15 lb. $9\frac{3}{4}$ oz. valued at 16s $3\frac{1}{2}$d per oz. The profit on the coinage of this sum must have been included in the treasurer's overall figure of £5,433 19s $3\frac{1}{2}$d., given here in column 2.

11. The sums excluded are as follows:

1497-8 £727 13s., being the face value of the gold unicorns listed;
1507-8 £42, being the value of the gold chain coined;
1511-12 £1,089 5s. 4d., being the value of 23 links of a gold chain;
1541-2 £394 5s. 2d., being the value of plate sold to the mint;
1543-6 £12,715 4s. 3d., being the value of gold and silver plate surrendered to the mint [see the qualification in the text on this sum];
1546-7 £211 7s., being the value of the silver — 25 lb. $10\frac{3}{4}$ oz. 10s. $3\frac{1}{2}$d. per oz. — the rest of the total given in the account, £569 12. $6\frac{1}{2}$d., is assumed to be profit;
1573-4 £2,271 9s., being the value of 1037 oz. 2 dwt. of silver sent to the mint by the exporters of lead.

12. See below, pp. 185ff.

13. CP, ii, 313-17.

14. APS, iii, 216.

15. In the agreement struck in 1577 between the Regent and John Acheson the latter was allowed 5s. per mark weight of 8 oz. RPCS, 1569-78, 599.

16. See below, p. 192.

17. Table 4.2; SRO. E22/20; E22/3 fo. 23r.

18. Table 5.4; CP, i, 250.

19. Table 5.4; CP, i, 249.

20. RPCS, 1578-85, 390-1.

21. APS, iii, 215.

22. RPCS, 1578-85, 390-1, 393-4.

23. APS, iii, 215-16; RPCS, 1578-85, 462-4, 468, 481, 498-500. Although Thomas Acheson took over from Robert Acheson in February 1582 he did not begin his formal account until 7 April following.

24. RPCS, 1592-9, 119-24.

25. ER, 1595-1600, 139.

26. SRO, E101/2 fo. 30v; RPCS, 1592-5, 404, 411.

27. RPCS, 1592-3, 463, 470-1; CP, i, 269-71.

28. CP, i, 250.

29. RPCS, 1599-1604, 287.

30. Ibid., pp. 292, 314.

31. Murray, op. cit. p. 197.

32. Ibid., Appendix pp. 120-1; above, Table 3.

33. R. Nicholson, Scotland: the later middle ages (Edinburgh, 1974), p. 531; G. Donaldson, Scotland: James V to James VII (Edinburgh and London, 1965), p. 57.

34. APS, iv, 181.

35. Challis, op. cit., chapter 2.3. Here quantities are expressed in sterling and the troy lb. of 12 oz.

36. Stewart, op. cit. appendix II.

37. Above, Table 5.4.

38. Challis, op. cit. chapter 3.3.

39. RPCS, 1578-85, 283-4; 1599-1604, 314-16.

40. TA, 1566-74, 110. For bullion flowing to the mint in the early seventeenth century as a result of mercantile activity, see SRO. E101/2 fos. 33-6.

41.   SRO. E22/3 and 20; <u>APS</u>, iii, 108; <u>RPCS</u>, <u>1578-85</u>, 17-18, 32-3, 100, 158-9, 196.

42.   <u>RPCS</u>, <u>1578-85</u>, 623-4; <u>APS</u>, iii, 310-11.

43.   <u>APS</u>, iii, 526-7.

44.   <u>RPCS</u>, <u>1599-1604</u>, 314-16; <u>APS</u>, iv, 49-50, 85-6; <u>RPCS</u>, <u>1592-9</u>, 151.

45.   <u>APS</u>, iv, 121-2. See also <u>RPCS</u>, <u>1599-1604</u>, 27-8.

THE SYMPOSIASTS

Miss M. M. ARCHIBALD, Assistant Keeper, Department of Coins and Medals, British Museum, London WC1B 3DG.

Professor G. W. S. BARROW, Professor of Scottish History, University of St. Andrews, St. Andrews KY16 9AJ.

N. Q. BOGDAN, Esq., Director, Perth High Street Archaeological Excavation, Department of Medieval History, University of St. Andrews, St. Andrews KY16 9AJ.

John D. BRAND, Esq., 5 Ridley Road, Rochester, Kent MB1 1UL.

Dr. C. E. CHALLIS, Lecturer in Modern History, University of Leeds, Leeds LS2 9JT.

Professor A. A. M. DUNCAN, Professor of Scottish History, University of Glasgow, 9 University Gardens, Glasgow G12 8QH.

Dr. J. M. GILBERT, Co-ordinator of the Economic History Project of the Scottish Medievalists' Conference, 182 Beech Avenue, Langlee, Galashiels, TD1 2LG.

N. M. HOLMES, Esq., Huntly House Museum, Canongate, Edinburgh EH8 8DD.

Dr. C. M. KRAAY, Keeper, Heberden Coin Room, Ashmolean Museum, Oxford.

N. J. MAYHEW, Esq., Assistant Keeper, Heberden Coin Room, Ashmolean Museum, Oxford.

Dr. D. M. METCALF, Assistant Keeper, Heberden Coin Room, Ashmolean Museum, Oxford.

Dr. A. L. MURRAY, Scottish Record Office, P.O. Box 36, Edinburgh EH1 3YY.

Mrs. J. E. L. MURRAY, M.B.E., 13 Homecroft Drive, Uckington, Cheltenham GL51 9SN.

Col. J. K. R. MURRAY, 13 Homecroft Drive, Uckington, Cheltenham GL51 9SN.

Professor Ranald G. NICHOLSON, Professor of History, University of Guelph, Ontario, Canada N1G 2W1.

S. E. RIGOLD, Esq., Inspector of Ancient Monuments for England, Department of the Environment, 23 Savile Row, London W1X 2AA.

Dr. Grant G. SIMPSON, Lecturer in the Department of History, University of Aberdeen, AB9 2UB.

R. B. K. STEVENSON, Esq., Keeper of the National Museum of Antiquities of Scotland, Queen Street, Edinburgh EH2 1JD.

Ian STEWART, Esq., M.P., House of Commons, London SW1A 0AA.

D. R. WALKER, Esq., General Editor, <u>British Archaeological Reports</u>, 122 Banbury Road, Oxford OX2 7BP.

A. B. WEBSTER, Esq., Lecturer in the Dept. of History, Keynes College, The University, Canterbury, Kent CT2 7NP.

P. WOODHEAD, Esq., 65 Aldsworth Avenue, Goring-by-Sea, Worthing, Sussex BN12 4XG.

British Archaeological Reports

122 Banbury Road, Oxford OX2 7BP, England

List of Titles

Information on new B.A.R. publications is sent regularly on request from the above address.

BAR Supplementary Series

B.A.R. -S1, 1975, "The Lewis Collection of Engraved Gemstones in Corpus Christi College, Cambridge", by Martin Henig. ISBN 0 904531 33 3. 153 pp., 29 plates. Price £2.90 post free.

B.A.R. -S2, 1975, "Defended Sites of the Late La Tène in Central and Western Europe", by John Collis. ISBN 0 904531 34 1. 267 pp., 100 figs. Price £5.50 post free.

B.A.R. -S3, 1976, "Le Périple d'Hannon/The Periplus of Hanno", by Jacques Ramin. ISBN 0 904531 35 X. 125 pp., 4 maps. Bilingual volume, full texts in French and English. Price £2.40 post free.

B.A.R. -S4, 1976, "Coins of the Ancient Thracians", by Yordanka Youroukova: translated from the Bulgarian by V. Athanassov. ISBN 0 904531 36 8. 153 pp., 28 plates. Price £2.80 post free.

B.A.R. -S5, 1976, "The Metrology of the Roman Silver Coinage, Part I: from Augustus to Domitian", by D. R. Walker. ISBN 0 904531 37 6. 159 pp., 17 figs. Price £2.50 post free.

B.A.R. -S6, 1976, "Portraits and other Heads on Roman Historical Relief up to the Age of Septimius Severus", by Anthony Bonanno. ISBN 0 904531 38 4. 304 pp., 76 pages of plates. Price £5.90 post free.

B.A.R. -S7, 1976, "Prolegomena to the Study of the Second Jewish Revolt (A.D. 132-135)", by Shimon Applebaum. ISBN 0 904531 39 2. 100 pp., 2 maps. Price £1.95 post free.

B.A.R. -S8, 1976, "Dacian Trade with the Hellenistic and Roman World", by Ioan Glodariu, revised by the author, translated from the Romanian by Nubar Hampartumian. ISBN 0 904531 40 6. 337 pp., 62 plates and figs., 4 tables. Price £6.80 post free.

B.A.R. -S9, 1976, "Greek and Roman Coins from Aphrodisias", by David J. MacDonald. ISBN 0 904531 41 4. 53 pp., 3 plates. Price £1.25 post free.

B.A.R. -S10, 1976, "The Roman Cemetery at Gerulata Rusovce, Czechoslovakia", by Ľudmila Kraskovská, revised by the author, translated from the Slovak by Hana Schuck. ISBN 0 904531 42 2. 114 pp., 85 figs., 6 plates. Price £2.50 post free.

B.A.R. -S11, 1976, "Oppida: the Beginnings of Urbanisation in Barbarian Europe", ed. Barry Cunliffe and Trevor Rowley. Contributions by J. Collis, C. C. Haselgrove, Éva F. Petres, J. Břeň, D. Nash, B. Cunliffe, J. May, W. Rodwell. ISBN 0 904531 46 5. 367 pp., 121 figs., 2 plates. Price £6.75 post free.

B.A.R. -S12, 1976, "The Dal Pozzo Copies of the Palestrina Mosaic", by Helen Whitehouse. ISBN 0 905431 48 1. 98 pp., 43 pp. of figures and plates. Price £1.90 post free.

B.A.R. -S13, 1976, "Prehistoric Art in Bulgaria from the Fifth to the Second Millennium B.C.", by Anna Raduncheva: translated from the Russian by Caroline M. Schuck. ISBN 0 904531 59 7. 113 pp., 30 pp. of plates. Price £2.70 post free.

B.A.R. -S14, 1976, "L'Art pariétal de la Grotte de Gargas/Palaeolithic Art in the Grotte de Gargas", by Cl. Barrière avec la collaboration du Ali Sahly et des élèves de l'Institut d'Art Préhistorique de Toulouse. Translated from the French by W. A. Drapkin. Mémoires de l'Institut d'Art Préhistorique de Toulouse no. III. ISBN 0 904531 47 3. Parts i and ii: 409 pp., 144 figs., 93 plates. Bilingual volume, full texts in French and English. Price (Parts i and ii together) £8.50 post free.

B.A.R. -S15, 1976, "Aspects of the Notitia Dignitatum: papers presented to a Conference in Oxford, December 13 to 15, 1974", ed. R. Goodburn and P. Bartholomew. Contributions by J. C. Mann, J. J. G. Alexander, J. P. Wild, M. M. Roxan, J. S. Johnson, M. W. C. Hassall, A. L. F. Rivet, R. M. Price, J. F. Matthews, R. S. O. Tomlin and C. E. Stevens. ISBN 0 904531 58 9. 224 pp., 28 plates, 1 colour plate. Price £4.20 post free.

B.A.R. -S16, 1976, "The Archaeology and History of the Carpi from the Second to the Fourth Century A.D.", by Gh. Bichir, revised by the author, translated from the Romanian by Nubar Hampartumian. ISBN 0 904531 55 4. Part i, Text, 211 pp., 23 figs. and plates. Part ii, Illustrations, 191 pp., 188 figs. and plates. Price (Parts i and ii together) £8.90 post free.

B.A.R. -S17, 1976, "The Thraco-Roman Villa Rustica near Chatalka, Stara Zagora, Bulgaria", by Dimitur Nikolov, translated from the Bulgarian by Michael Holman. ISBN 0 904531 60 0. 169 pp., 118 figs. and plates. Price £3.60 post free.

B.A.R.-S18, 1977, "Roman Lamps from Ulpia Traiana Sarmizegetusa", by Dorin Alicu and Emil Nemeş, Introduction by Hadrian Daicoviciu; translated from the Romanian by Nubar Hampartumian. ISBN 0 904531 62 7. 209 pp., 51 plates, 38 figs. Price £4.50 post free.

B.A.R.-S19, 1977, "Archaeology and Anthropology: Areas of Mutual Interest", ed. Matthew Spriggs. Contributions by R. W. Chapman, Roy F. Ellen, Roland Fletcher, John Gledhill, L. M. Groube, Colin Haselgrove, Ian Hodder, Sir Edmund Leach, M. J. Rowlands and Matthew Spriggs. ISBN 0 904531 63 5. 176 pp., 11 figs. Price £3.30 post free.

B.A.R.-S20, 1977, "Monte Irsi, Southern Italy: The Canadian Excavations in the Iron Age and Roman Sites, 1971-1972", ed. Alastair Small. Contributions by Graeme Barker, R. J. Buck, Gisèle Deschênes, H. Hjelmqvist, Marie-Odile Jentel, Jeremy Rossiter, Alastair Small and Edith Mary Wightman. ISBN 0 904531 66 X. 296 pp., 38 plates, 42 figs. Price £5.50 post free.

B.A.R.-S21, 1977, "Typologie et Préhistoire de L'Asturien du Portugal/The Asturian in Portugal. Typology and Chronology", by Jean Maury: translated from the French by Elisabeth Weeks. ISBN 0 904531 67 8. 105 pp., 46 figs., 10 plates. Price £2.10 post free.

B.A.R.-S22, 1977, "The Metrology of the Roman Silver Coinage, Part ii: from Nerva to Commodus", by D. R. Walker. ISBN 0 904531 68 6. 120 pp., 12 figs. Price £2.30 post free.

B.A.R.-S23, 1977, "The Aes Coinage of Emporion", by Leandre Villaronga; translated from the Spanish by Elisabeth Weeks. ISBN 0 904531 70 8. 99 pp., 15 plates. Price £2.20 post free.

B.A.R.-S24, 1977, "The Fifth-Century A.D. Treasure from Pietroasa, Romania, in the light of recent research", by Radu Harhoiu, translated from the Romanian by Nubar Hampartumian. ISBN 0 904531 72 4. 89 pp., 31 illustrations. Price £2.00 post free.

B.A.R.-S25, 1977, "The Merovingian Archaeology of South-West Gaul", by Edward James. ISBN 0 904531 71 6. Part i: Text, 318 pp., 90 plates, 49 figs. Part ii: Catalogues and Bibliography, 229 pp., 97 plates, 1 fig. Price (parts i and ii together) £10.00 post free.

B.A.R.-S26, 1977, "Beakers in Britain and Europe: Four Studies. Contributions to a Symposium organised by the Munro Lectureship Committee, Edinburgh University", ed. Roger Mercer. Papers by Lawrence Binfield, Humphrey Case, Richard Harrison and Stephen Shennan. ISBN 0 904531 83 X. 101 pp., 31 figs. Price £2.00 post free.

B.A.R.-S27, 1977, "Australia's Oldest Wreck: The historical background and archaeological analysis of the wreck of the English East India Company's ship Trial, lost off the coast of Western Australia in 1622", by Jeremy N. Green. ISBN 0 904531 77 5. 60 pp., 15 figs. Price £1.50 post free.

B.A.R.-S28, 1977, "Natural Environment and Human Settlement in Prehistoric Greece, based on original fieldwork", by John L. Bintliff. ISBN 0 904531 79 1. Part i, 369 pp., 27 figs. Part ii, 365 pp., 41 figs. Price (parts i and ii together) £13.50 post free.

B.A.R.-S29, 1977, "Sources and Techniques in Boat Archaeology: Papers based on those presented to a Symposium at Greenwich in September 1976, together with edited discussion", ed. Sean McGrail. Papers by Carl Olof Cederlund, Arne Emil Christensen, J. F. Coates, J. M. Coles, Ole Crumlin-Pedersen, J. de Jong, Angela Care Evans, Octavio Lixa Filgueiras, J. M. Graham, Basil Greenhill, C. W. Gregson, Olof Hasslöf, J. F. Levy, Sean McGrail, J. E. G. McKee, Peter Marsden, J. Roelfzema, Timothy Severin, David Sturdy, David M. Wilson and E. V. Wright. National Maritime Museum, Greenwich, Archaeological Series No. 1. ISBN 0 904531 82 1. 315 pp., 115 illustrations. Price £6.00 post free.

B.A.R.-S30, 1977, "Roman Pottery Studies in Britain and Beyond: papers presented to John Gillam, July 1977", ed. John Dore and Kevin Greene. Papers by John Dore, Kevin Greene, P. T. Bidwell, Joanna Bird, Eric Birley, David J. Breeze, Peter Carrington, G. B. Dannell, M. J. Darling, Alec Detsicas, Elisabeth Ettlinger, R. A. H. Farrar, M. G. Fulford, B. R. Hartley, Katharine F. Hartley, J. W. Hayes, Catherine Johns, D. P. S. Peacock, J. R. Perrin, Valery Rigby, George Rogers, Vivien G. Swan, Graham Webster, Peter V. Webster, D. F. Williams, Christopher J. Young. ISBN 0 904531 84 8. 333 pp., 52 figs., 3 plates. Price £6.30 post free.

B.A.R. -S31, 1977, "The Chronology of the Early Iron Age in Serbia," by Rastko Vasić. ISBN 0 904531 86 4. 151 pp., 56 figs. Price £3.00 post free.

B.A.R. -S32, 1977, "The Late Copper Age Coţofeni Culture of South-East Europe," by Petre Roman, translated from the Romanian by Nubar Hampartumian. ISBN 0 904531 85 6. 248 pp., 118 figs. Price £5.50 post free.

B.A.R. -S33, 1977, "Ancient Coinage," by A. N. Zograph, translated from the Russian by H. Bartlett Wells. ISBN 0 904531 87 2. Part i, "The General Problems of Ancient Numismatics," 157 pp., 17 figs. Part ii, "The Ancient Coins of the Northern Black Sea Coast," 309 pp., 50 plates. Price (parts i and ii together) £9.00 post free.

B.A.R. -S34, 1977, "The Animal Remains from Four Sites in the Kermanshah Valley, Iran: Asiab, Sarab, Dehsavar and Siahbid; the faunal evolution, environmental changes and development of animal husbandry, VIII-III millennia B.C." by S. Bökönyi. ISBN 0 904531 88 0. 132 pp., 36 figs. Price £2.60 post free.

B.A.R.-S35, 1977, "The Earlier Neolithic of Southern England and its Continental Background", by A. W. R. Whittle. ISBN 0 904531 95 3. 301 pp., 61 figs. Price £6.00 post free.

B.A.R.-S36, 1977, "The Loss of the Verenigde Oostindische Compagnie Jacht VERGULDE DRAECK, Western Australia 1656. An historical background and excavation report with an appendix on similar loss of the fluit LASTDRAGER", by Jeremy N. Green (Curator, Maritime Archaeology, Western Australian Museum), with contributions by Lous Zuiderbaan, Robert Sténuit, S. J. Wilson, Mike Owens. ISBN 0 904531 97 X. Parts i and ii, 507 pp., 115 illustrations. Price £10.00 post free.

B.A.R.-S37, 1977, "The Urban Saint in Early Byzantine Social History", by Julia Seiber. ISBN 0 86054 000 6. 117 pp., 1 map. Price £2.30 post free.

B.A.R. (British Series)

B.A.R. 3, 1974, "A Corpus of Early Bronze Age Dagger Pommels from Great Britain and Ireland", by Ron Hardaker. ISBN 0 904531 02 3. 65 pp., 7 figs., 2 plates. Price £0.80 post free.

B.A.R. 4, 1974, "Coins and the Archaeologist", ed. John Casey and Richard Reece. ISBN 0 904531 06 6. 271 pp., 44 figs., 5 plates. Price £3.50 post free.

B.A.R. 7, 1974, "A Corpus of Pagan Anglo-Saxon Spear-Types", by M. J. Swanton. ISBN 0 904531 04 X. 90 pp., 4 figs. Price £1.10 post free.

B.A.R. 9, 1974, "Grooved Ware Sites in Yorkshire and the North of England", by T. G. Manby. ISBN 0 904531 09 0. 133 pp., 43 figs., 2 plates. Price £2.00 post free.

B.A.R. 10, 1975, "Stamp and Roulette Decorated Pottery of the La Tène Period in Eastern England: a Study in Geometric Designs", by Sheila M. Elsdon. ISBN 0 904531 11 2. 115 pp., 19 figs., 5 plates. Price £2.30 post free.

B.A.R. 11, 1975, "Anglo-Saxon Garnet Inlaid Disc and Composite Brooches", by Richard Avent. ISBN 0 904531 21 X. Part i, Discussion, 126 pp., 30 figs., 6 maps, 8 tables, 4 colour plates; Part ii, Catalogue and Plates, 52 pp., 78 plates. Price (parts i and ii together) £5.80 post free.

B.A.R. 12, 1975, "Cirencester: the Development and Buildings of a Cotswold Town", by Richard Reece and Christopher Catling. ISBN 0 904531 12 0. 78 pp., frontispiece and 11 figs., 9 plates. Price £1.50 post free.

B.A.R. 13, 1975, "Settlement Types in Post-Roman Scotland", by Lloyd R. Laing. ISBN 0 904531 13 9. 46 pp., 25 figs. Price £1.00 post free.

B.A.R. 14, 1975, "Clay Pipes for the Archaeologist", by Adrian Oswald. ISBN 0 904531 14 7. 207 pp., 23 figs., 6 plates. Price £3.80 post free.

B.A.R. 15, 1975, "The 'Small Towns' of Roman Britain: Papers presented to a Conference, Oxford, 1975", ed. Warwick Rodwell and Trevor Rowley. ISBN 0 904531 17 1. 237 pp., 70 figs., 17 plates. Price £4.80 post free.

B.A.R. 16, 1975, "Bar Hill: A Roman Fort and its Finds", by Anne Robertson, Margaret Scott and Lawrence Keppie. ISBN 0 904531 18 X. 185 pp., 57 figs. Price £3.50 post free.

B.A.R. 17, 1975, "New Forest Roman Pottery: manufacture and distribution, with a corpus of the pottery types", by M. G. Fulford. ISBN 0 904531 19 8. 200 pp., 61 figs. Price £3.90 post free.

B.A.R. 18, 1975, "The Roman Milestones of Britain: their petrography and probable origins", by Jeffrey P. Sedgley. ISBN 0 904531 20 1. 56 pp., 5 figs. Price £1.00 post free.

B.A.R. 19, 1975, "Rams Hill: A Bronze Age Defended Enclosure and its Landscape", by Richard Bradley and Ann Ellison. ISBN 0 904531 22 8. 264 pp., 59 figs., 21 plates. Price £5.50 post free.

B.A.R. 20, 1975, "Later Prehistory from the Trent to the Tyne", by A. J. Challis and D. W. Harding. ISBN 0 904531 23 6. Part i, Discussion, 247 pp; Part ii, Catalogue and Illustrations. 178 pp., 100 figs., 10 plates. Price (parts i and ii together) £6.50 post free.

B.A.R. 21, 1975, "Roman Fort-Defences to A.D. 117, with special reference to Britain", by Michael J. Jones. ISBN 0 904531 24 4. 192 pp., 21 figs., 1 map, 6 plates. Price £3.90 post free.

B.A.R. 22, 1975, "Hanging-Bowls, Penannular Brooches and the Anglo-Saxon Connexion", by David Longley. ISBN 0 904531 25 2. 49 pp., 19 figs. Price £0.95 post free.

B.A.R. 23, 1976, "Bordesley Abbey, Redditch, Hereford-Worcestershire: First Report on Excavations 1969-1973", by Philip Rahtz and Susan Hirst. ISBN 0 904531 26 0. 295 pp., 41 figs. in text, 3 colour plates, 17 black and white plates; wallet with a further 20 figures. Price £5.90 post free.

B.A.R. 24, 1976, "A Corpus of Religious Material from the Civilian Areas of Roman Britain", by Miranda J. Green. ISBN 0 904531 27 9. 321 pp., 21 figs., frontispiece and 30 plates. Price £5.90 post free.

B.A.R. 25, 1976, "Neolithic Flint Axes from the Cotswold Hills", by Alan Tyler. ISBN 0 904531 28 7. 98 pp., 9 figs. Price £1.90 post free.

B.A.R. 26, 1976, "The Black Prince's Palace at Kennington, Surrey", by Graham J. Dawson. ISBN 0 904531 29 5. 213 pp., 20 figs. Price £3.90 post free.

B.A.R. 27, 1976, "Wawcott III: A Stratified Mesolithic Succession", by F. R. Froom. ISBN 0 904531 30 9. 209 pp., 85 figs. Price £3.90 post free.

B.A.R. 28, 1976, "Barrow Mead, Bath 1964: Excavation of a Mediaeval Peasant House", by Jayne Woodhouse. ISBN 0 905431 31 7. 73 pp., 15 figs., 4 plates. Price £1.30 post free.

B.A.R. 29, 1976, "Occupation Sites on a Chiltern Ridge: Excavations at Puddlehill and Sites near Dunstable, Bedfordshire. Part I: Neolithic, Bronze Age and Early Iron Age", by C. L. Matthews, Foreword and Summary by C. F. C. Hawkes. ISBN 0 904531 32 5. 209 pp., 123 figs., 9 plates. Price £3.90 post free.

B.A.R. 30, 1976, "Studies in the Archaeology and History of Cirencester: based on papers presented to a research seminar on the post-Roman development of Cirencester held at the Corinium Museum, November 1975", ed. Alan McWhirr. ISBN 0 904531 43 0. 200 pp., 39 figs., 6 plates. Price £3.90 post free.

B.A.R. 31, 1976, "The Production and Distribution of Metalwork in the Middle Bronze Age in Southern Britain", by M. J. Rowlands. ISBN 0 904531 44 9. Part i, Discussion, 218 pp., 28 figs. Part ii, Catalogue and Illustrations, 314 pp., 60 plates, 26 maps. Price (parts i and ii together) £7.50 post free.

B.A.R. 32, 1976, "Roman Military Stone-built Granaries in Britain", by Anne P. Gentry. ISBN 0 904531 45 7. 98 pp., 14 figs., 3 plates, 4 tables, 2 maps. Price £1.95 post free.

B.A.R. 33, 1976, "Settlement and Economy in the Third and Second Millennia B.C. Papers delivered at a Conference organised by the Department of Adult Education, University of Newcastle upon Tyne, January 1976", ed. Colin Burgess and Roger Miket. Contributions by John Barrett, C. Stephen Briggs, Colin Burgess, P. D. Catherall, D. V. Clarke, David Coombs, George Eogan, H. Stephen Green, Peter Hill, J. V. S. Megaw, Roger J. Mercer, Roger Miket, Francis Pryor, M. J. Rowlands, Stephen Shennan, Ian A. G. Shepherd, D. D. A. Simpson and J. B. Stevenson. ISBN 0 904531 52 X. 331 pp., 100 figs., 20 plates. Price £5.90 post free.

B.A.R. 34, 1977, "Bronze Age Spearheads from Berkshire, Buckinghamshire and Oxfordshire", by Margaret R. Ehrenberg. ISBN 0 904531 61 9. 95 pp., 1 plate, 28 figs. Price £1.90 post free.

B.A.R. 35, 1977, "The Medieval Moated Sites of South-Eastern Ireland: Counties Carlow, Kilkenny, Tipperary and Wexford" by Terence B. Barry. ISBN 0 904531 69 4. 247 pp., 10 plates, 33 figs., 24 tables. Price £4.70 post free.

B.A.R. 36, 1977, "Edwardian Monetary Affairs (1279-1344); A Symposium held in Oxford, August 1976", ed. N. J. Mayhew. Contributions by M. M. Archibald, J. F. Hadwin, T. H. Lloyd, M. Mate, N. J. Mayhew, D. M. Metcalf, N. J. Palmer, M. C. Prestwich, S. E. Rigold and D. R. Walker. ISBN 0 904531 64 3. 186 pp., 9 figs. Price £3.50 post free.

B.A.R. 37, 1977, "Studies in Celtic Survival", ed. Lloyd Laing. Contributions by L. A. S. Butler, Ms Margaret Faull, P. S. Gelling, Lloyd Laing, A. D. S. Macdonald, Alex Morrison, V. B. Proudfoot and C. A. R. Radford. ISBN 0 904531 65 1. 123 pp., 8 figs. Price £2.40 post free.

B.A.R. 38, 1977, "Roman Lead Coffins and Ossuaria in Britain", by Hugh Toller. ISBN 0 904531 73 2. 87 pp., 8 figs., 6 maps. Price £1.90 post free.

B.A.R. 39, 1977, "Bronze Boar Figurines in Iron Age and Roman Britain", by Jennifer Foster. ISBN 0 904531 74 0. 57 pp., 13 plates, 12 figs. Price £1.50 post free.

B.A.R. 40, 1977, "The Episode of Carausius and Allectus: the Literary and Numismatic Evidence", by Norman Shiel. ISBN 0 904531 78 3. 247 pp., 27 plates, 9 maps. Price £4.70 post free.

B.A.R. 41, 1977, "Roman Life and Art in Britain: A celebration in honour of the eightieth birthday of Jocelyn Toynbee," ed. Julian Munby and Martin Henig. Contributions by Martin Robertson, J. M. C. Toynbee, David Brown, Martin Henig, E. J. Phillips, T. F. C. Blagg, Joan Liversidge, D. J. Smith, David E. Johnston, John Casey, G. Lloyd-Morgan, Dom Perring, Martin Millett, Miranda Green, M. W. C. Hassall, Paul Arthur, Ralph Merrifield, Richard Reece, Julian Munby. ISBN 0 904531 91 0. Part i, 216 pp., 67 plates, 23 figs. Part ii, 244 pp., 34 plates, 22 figs. Price (parts i and ii together) £9.00 post free.

B.A.R. 42, 1977, "Pleshey Castle, Essex (XII-XVI Century): Excavations in the Bailey, 1959-1963," by Frances Williams. ISBN 0 904531 89 9. 250 pp., 19 plates, 46 figs. Price £5.00 post free.

B.A.R.43, 1977, "The Roman Pottery Industry of the Oxford Region", by Christopher J. Young. ISBN 0 86054 001 4. 391 pp., 84 figs., 14 tables. Price £8.00 post free.

B.A.R.44, 1977: "Gatcombe: The excavation and study of a Romano-British villa estate, 1967-1976", by Keith Branigan, with contributions from T. F. C. Blagg, Graeme Barker, L. F. Curtis, Robin Dennell, Keith Gardner, Hedley Hall, Dave Horwell, the late M. R. Hull, Dr. A. J. Parker, Juliet Rodgers, Dr. R. F. Tylecote, Andrew Tubb, Derek Webley, Cleo Witt and R. P. Wright. ISBN 0 904531 96 1. 257 pp., 20 plates, 38 figs. Price £5.00 post free.

B.A.R.45, 1977, "Coinage in Medieval Scotland (1100-1600). The Second Oxford Symposium on Coinage and Monetary History", ed. D. M. Metcalf. Contributions by D. M. Metcalf, S. E. Rigold, Ian Stewart, N. J. Mayhew, Ranald Nicholson, Mrs. Joan E. L. Murray, John M. Gilbert and C. E. Challis. ISBN 0 86054 002 2. 198 pp., 4 figs. Price £4.00 post free.